Dictionary of Mexican Rulers, 1325–1997

Dictionary of Mexican Rulers, 1325–1997

Juana Vázquez-Gómez

GREENWOOD PRESS
Westport, Connecticut • London

Library of Congress Cataloging-in-Publication Data

Vázquez Gómez, Juana.
    Dictionary of Mexican rulers, 1325-1997 : Juana Vázquez-Gómez.
      p.   cm.
    Includes bibliographical references (p.   ) and indexes.
    ISBN 0–313–30049–6 (alk. paper)
    1. Heads of state—Mexico—Biography—Dictionaries. 2. Spouses of
heads of state—Mexico—Biography—Dictionaries. 3. Mexico—
Biography—Dictionaries. 4. Mexico—History—Chronology.
I. Title.
F1205.V34   1997
972.002'02—dc21   97–9377

British Library Cataloguing in Publication Data is available.

Library of Congress Catalog Card Number: 97–9377
ISBN: 0–313–30049–6

First published in 1997

Greenwood Press, 88 Post Road West, Westport, CT 06881
An imprint of Greenwood Publishing Group, Inc.

Printed in the United States of America

∞™

The paper used in this book complies with the
Permanent Paper Standard issued by the National
Information Standards Organization (Z39.48–1984).

10 9 8 7 6 5 4 3 2

With all my love and gratitude to:

My aunts To and Nona, my mentors who made the first edition of the book possible.
My husband Sergio, for the many hours, months, and years he spent helping me finish this book.
My son Serge, who helped me with the translation.
My daughter Lorenza, who has always encouraged me in my ventures.
Juanis, Tete, and Franz.

CONTENTS

Preface   ix

Acknowledgments   xi

1.   The Aztecs, 1325–1524   1

2.   Encounter, Conquest, and the Colonial Period, 1502–1821   11

3.   From the War of Independence to the Díaz Dictatorship,
     1810–1910   55

4.   Revolution and Modern Mexico, 1910–1997   107

Glossary   143

Appendices
     A. Plans, Treaties, Conspiracies, and Constitutions since
         1799   147

     B. Names of Mexican Political Parties   155

     C. Acronyms   157

     D. Chronology   159

     E. Alphabetical Index of Rulers   167

Bibliography   175

Index   179

PREFACE

The purpose of this book is to provide concise information about the rulers of Mexico from 1325 to 1997. Addressed to the nonspecialist reader and the intermediate level student of Mexican history, the book is organized for easy consultation.

Presented in chronological order, there is data on 185 rulers: *tlatoanis, caciques*, captain generals, governors, viceroys, judges in residence, members of the *audiencia, oidores*, leaders, military and civil dictators, emperors, military chiefs, supreme commanders, regents and representatives of power, chiefs and leaders of the revolution, and presidents (appointed in name only, interim, and constitutionally elected).

The book is organized into four basic chapters that deal with four periods in history. It includes the names of those who governed the nation, regardless of how they reached power. Some did so through popular elections, but others seized power by force. Some governed only in name, and for some their mandates lasted for only a few minutes. Also mentioned are rebel leaders Emiliano Zapata and Pancho Villa because, even though they never reached the top of the political ladder, they did exercise considerable influence in Mexican politics for some time.

Each entry opens with specific information regarding the ruler's position and term, as well as biographical data regarding places of birth and death, followed by the name of a wife and parents, if known. General historic information follows regarding the ruler's life and position of power, as well as details of his triumphs and defeats. Any names and/or terms cited in the dictionary that are not followed by a parenthetical explanation can easily be found by consulting the various glossaries and appendix listings at the end of the book.

Historical research in Mexico can sometimes be difficult. Sources do not always coincide, especially regarding dates. To solve discrepancies, several criteria such as the number of coincidental versions, testimonies from witnesses, prestige of the publication consulted, and data from personal archives of relatives of the rulers were used.

It should be noted that whenever possible, the names of the wives of the rulers of Mexico are noted. Even though they may not have figured prominently at the side of their spouses, some did leave a mark in history, and some played key roles in the personal style of governing of their respective husbands. Research in this area proved to be an excruciating task. In Mexican history there is very little credit given to these women whose stature allowed them to marry men who later became presidents or rulers of Mexico. To find the names of some of the wives it was necessary to consult historical memoirs, history books, private archives, social reviews in magazines, and obituaries in newspapers, or to conduct interviews with relatives of the rulers. Needless to say, this is an area in desperate need of research.

ACKNOWLEDGMENTS

I would like to thank three special people whose personal effort made the English version of this book possible.

To David Fugate, my agent, the person who opened the doors for me in the U.S. publishing world. I will be forever grateful for everything you've done.

To Cynthia Harris, my editor, who believed in my book.

To my "unknown" historian/editor, for all his patience, witty commentaries, and enormous help.

1

THE AZTECS, 1325–1524

THE ORIGINS

The first inhabitants of Tenochtitlan, what is now Mexico City, were the Aztecs. They were not, however, the first inhabitants of the Valley of Mexico. The people of Ticoman, in the northern part of the valley, and Cuicuilco, in the southern tip, had lived there since the second century after Christ. Then came the magnificent civilization of Teotihuacan, which lasted for six centuries and left invaluable monuments such as the pyramids of the Sun and the Moon. Then came the Toltec culture whose dominant figure was their King-Priest Quetzalcoatl and whose influence spread across the valley until the barbarian tribes of the north, called Chichimecs, founded their empire in the same area.

Legend has it that the Aztecs were the last of the seven Nahuatlaca tribes who traveled south from the mythical Aztlan, the "country of the white heron," to the promised land in central Mexico.

Very little is known about the origin of the Aztecs and their pilgrimage. The most popular legend relates that while running away from Culhuacan, a city at the foot of the Cerro de la Estrella (Hill of the Star), this small and weak tribe, the Aztecs, found the place foretold by their god Huitzilopochtli: a vast valley where the air was pure and transparent, filled with lakes and forests, and surrounded by volcanoes. Here, on a small island that was part of an archipelago in Lake Texcoco, they found an eagle perched on a cactus devouring a serpent, the image from which the national emblem would later be formed.

There is no agreement on the meaning of the word *Tenochtitlan*. According to some interpretations it means "Tenoch's place," and it was named to honor the founder and *cacique* of the place. In other versions, it means "the place where cactus grows on stone." Between 1325 and 1519, the Aztecs built an impressive city with majestic temples and handsome canals, which served as streets at that time. The Aztec communities can best be described as a masterfully organized society whose artistic manifestations were considered treasures.

Whatever the case may be, the magnificence of the city has been documented in the chronicles of the Spanish conquistadors. Rising out of the water, surrounded by gardens, and crisscrossed by canals, the city boasted impressive temples carved in stone. There were also splendid palaces and superbly colored murals, tall pyramids, and broad public squares. The market was a lively spot: a place to buy and sell, but also a site to meet people and to celebrate with ceremonial dancing and singing.

THE PEOPLE

When the Aztecs arrived in the Central Valley around 1250, they found other tribes living there in the cities of Culhuacan, Tenayuca, Texcoco, Tlaxcala, Tacuba, and Azcapotzalco. At first (in 1276), the Aztecs lived in the forest of Chapultepec, on the edge of Lake Texcoco, and worked as mercenaries for the Tepanecs. Some years later (1325), they founded their city, Tenochtitlan. By 1428 they had forged a political arrangement with the kingdoms of Tenochtitlan, Texcoco, and Tacuba, known as the Triple Alliance. This alliance allowed each one of the tribes to keep its own *tlatoani*, or supreme ruler. He was also called *tlacatecuhtli* to signal his rank as chief of the armies. It was his prerogative to name a *tetecuhtin*, or governor, in cities and provinces dominated by the Triple Alliance.

The Aztecs considered their rulers to be the legal heirs of the Toltec sovereign Ce Acatl or Quetzalcoatl. Their rulers were called *tlatoanis* (chiefs of men), *caciques*, supreme priests, or emperors. Their mandate was for life; there is a controversy among historians on whether they inherited their mandate or were elected.

Aztec society was divided into four basic social classes: the *pipiltin*, or noblemen; the *macehualtin*, or common people; the *mayeques*, who were neither slaves nor free men and were mostly employed to work the land of the noblemen; and finally the *tlatlacotin*, who were slaves. Socially and politically, the Aztecs—also known as Mexicas—formed a theocratic and military society.

RELIGIOUS STRUCTURE

Mexica, or Aztec, life centered around religion, and political figures also served as supreme priests, therefore playing a dual role as public figures. The Mexicas' religion was polytheistic, but in the ritual, all the gods merged into one supreme God.

These people believed in ritual and human sacrifice, and by modern standards their ceremonies could be described as cruel and bloodthirsty. Perhaps they were, but their rituals and human sacrifices were inspired by their sacred religious writings.

The Mexica ecclesiastic structure was hierarchical. At the top of the hierarchy there were two high priests: Quetzalcoatl *Totec* Tlacamazqui (priest of our Lord Quetzalcoatl) and Quetzalcoatl *Tlaloc* Tlamacazqui (priest of the Rain God). They presided over the shrine of Huitzilopochtli (the God of War) and Tlaloc (the Rain God) at the Great Temple in Tenochtitlan. Inside the temple they performed their rituals, offerings, sacrifices, and other sacred acts.

The Mexicas believed that Quetzalcoatl (the Toltec prince) had organized and founded the priesthood. That is why the high priests carried his name. Below the high priests was the go-between Mexicatl Teohuatzin (the great military priest), who received the word of the high priest and took it to the masses. Last in the hierarchy were two men of great prestige: *Tlamacazqui* (the one who offers the sacrifice to the gods) and *Teohua* (he who takes care of God). These two men presided over the sacrificial ceremonies. At the lowest levels of the hierarchy there were a few priestesses.

The Mexica people were superstitious and believed in magic. They believed in the power of witches, magicians, clairvoyants, fortune tellers, and conjurers.

MILITARY STRUCTURE

The Mexicas were a mighty military tribe. They placed great importance on the rearing of strong and healthy warriors. Young men were sent to the *calmecac* (a school) where they learned to become either warriors or priests. The educational system at this school was quite strenuous and placed a special emphasis on praying and penance. Most young men were sent to battle with their mentors as a way of military training. This school also taught them the art of weapon fabrication. They made stone and bronze axes, obsidian-edged swords, arrows, and other battle gear, including shields.

The military operations of the Triple Alliance were entrusted to the Mexicas. Military operations had one main priority—to capture victims for the ritual sacrifice.

The commander in chief of military operations was the *tlatoani*. Under him were two great chiefs, *tlacatecatl* (chief of warriors) and *tlacochcalcatl* (chief of the house of spears). The job of the great chiefs was to give direction to the various warriors under their authority and to organize them under the legion of eagles or tigers. These were honorific titles given to warriors to distinguish the bravest, strongest, and most ferocious—qualities attributed to the animals from which they drew their names. There were also noblemen, military *caudillos*, strategists, leaders, communicators, and engineers in the army.

SOCIAL ORGANIZATION

Mexica society was partly an autocracy and partly a plutocracy. The townsfolk like the *macehualtin*, or the plebeians, had no representation. A caste-class system kept society divided according to profession. The people lived in *calpultin*, or neighborhoods. Land was allotted to them by the government. If the government believed that a certain family was not working its land enough, the land would be taken away. Property was inherited within the family; if there was no family member able to inherit it, then the land was given to the most needy neighbor.

Tenochtitlan's urban development grew beyond the city to include the barrios in neighboring lands on the shores of the lake. The Aztecs especially favored spreading into barrios inhabited by craftsmen whose craft was unknown in the Mexica culture. One example of this type of cultural conquest took place against the Amantecas from Amantla, near Azcapotzalco, a barrio formed by craftsmen who specialized in the art of decorating ornamental plumes. That was also the case with the *pochtecas* or *oztomecas*, from Pochtlan or Oxtoman, known and respected merchants who monopolized commerce in the region. They were also the bankers who loaned money for a profit. Mexica currency was the cacao bean.

Agriculture was at the center of life in Mexica society and the *macehualtin* cultivated corn, beans, cacao, maguey, chiles, cotton, and other staples. The *mayeques*, or serfs, plowed the earth for the landlords. When the landlord died, the crops, field, and the *mayeques* were inherited by his family. If a man fell into debt and died before paying it, his children became slaves. These slaves were called *tlatlacotin*. They could escape their enslavement by paying off their parent's debt, but this was unlikely. Slaves were also made of criminals and prisoners of war. These people formed the lowest class among the Mexicas.

The Aztecs were magnificent warriors. They were also talented poets, painters, architects, and artists with deep religious feelings. The mere fact that such a vast empire was created in such a short period of time has left those who study Mexican history in awe.

Rulers of Tenochtitlan, 1325–1524

*Population of Tenochtitlan 1450: Approximately 75,000
Inhabitants*

*By the beginnings of the 1500s, the valley had grown to
nearly 200,000 inhabitants*

TENOCH. "The Warrior Leader." *Position: Cacique* (Founder); *Term:*
1325.

Legend has it that Tenoch succeeded the god Huitzilopochtli as ruler of
the Aztecs once they finished their pilgrimage from the mythical Aztlan to
the valley and lake region that would later became Tenochtitlan.

Tenoch, who was a priest, ruled his people with courage and intelligence
in their first settlement on Chapultepec Hill. A few years later, he founded
the great Tenochtitlan in the heart of an island where they found the place
foretold by Huitzilopochtli. Very little is known about him except that he
had a very long life.

ACAMAPICHTLI (ACAMAPIC) (1350–1403). "The Lord of The Arrows." *Position: Tlatoani; Term:* 1377–1389.

Acamapichtli was the first ruler of the so-called "monarchic era" of the
Aztec Empire, which ends with the death of Cuauhtemoc in 1525, after the
arrival of the Spaniards. The Aztec rulers derived their dynasty from the
House of Culhuacan, and it was believed that Acamapichtli was the son of
a princess of Culhuacan, of Toltec origin.

He presided over the development of the island, extending it to the east.
Concerned with a possible attack from rival tribes, he was careful to preserve a good stretch of the lake between the city and the mainland. He was
a good warrior, but also a great politician who believed education was
better served when mixed with heavy doses of discipline. Under his guidance, Tenochtitlan became an island fortress inhabited by disciplined citizens who excelled in inventing new methods in the cultivation of their land,
and were also skillful in the fabrication of armaments.

The old king of Azcapotzalco, Tezozomoc, hired Acamapichtli to conquer lands for him, and the Mexicas prospered because of their military
skills. The Aztec armies of mercenaries conquered Xochimilco, Mixquic,
and Tlahuac for their employers.

HUITZILIHUITL. "The Hummingbird." *Position: Tlatoani; Term:* 1390–
1410.

Huitzilihuitl was the son of Acamapichtli. From his father he learned
that conquering lands brings power. Working as a mercenary for Tezozo-

moc, the master of the Tepanecs, he conquered Xaltocan, Cuautitlan, Chalco, and Texcoco, and the wealth from conquest trickled down to the Aztec people.

The god Huitzilopochtli became worshipped as the God of War, and practice refined the Aztec's military skills. From then on, the Mexica mentality had only one desire—conquest—because in the Aztec mythology the warrior was the favorite of the gods.

CHIMALPOPOCA (?–1428). "The Smoking Shield." *Position: Tlatoani; Term*: 1416–1428.

Chimalpopoca, who was the son of Acamapichtli and the brother of Huitzilihuitl, received his mandate in 1416. Concerned with urban development, Chimalpopoca ordered the construction of important public works, such as the aqueduct that ran from Chapultepec to Tenochtitlan, and supplied badly needed fresh water. He also ordered an ingenious engineering project for a road to Tacuba, which included folding wood bridges that were removed during the night.

Chimalpopoca was a compassionate, courageous, and loyal person who enjoyed family life. His considerable political skills allowed him to protect young Netzahualcoyotl from Tezozomoc, the powerful ruler of Azcapotzalco. Tezozomoc had killed Ixtlixochitl, the ruler of Texcoco, and Netzahualcoyotl's father took over his domains.

When Tezozomoc died, a family feud in the house of Azcapotzalco allowed Maxtla, the youngest of Tezozomoc's two sons, to seize power, killing his brother Tayautzin. Chimalpopoca took sides with the losing faction. Accused of being a traitor, he was imprisoned, caged, and exhibited in the public plaza. Chimalpopoca hanged himself. He is considered the first Mexica martyr.

ITZCOATL. "The Snake Armed with a Flint." *Position*: Ruler of Tenochtitlan during the Triple Alliance; *Term*: 1428–1440.

After the death of Chimalpopoca, the usurper Maxtla ordered that the ruler's position remain vacant. Defying the tyrant, the chiefs of the *calpultins* rebelled against Maxtla, and Itzcoatl became the chief of the Aztec tribe.

Itzcoatl was the son of Acamapichtli and a slave. He was also the half brother of the previous *tlatoani*. It was Itzcoatl who structured the Triple Alliance between his tribe and those of Tacuba and Texcoco. Itzcoatl was the first Aztec ruler to issue a public notice to the masses asking for their approval to eliminate Maxtla. Itzcoatl himself killed Maxtla in combat. Chimalpopoca's death was avenged, and Itzcoatl became the ruler.

Itzcoatl surrounded himself with wise counselors, including the architect Tlacaeletl, who was responsible for the Mexica's enormous military expansion. He also sought the advice of the artist, poet, and restored ruler of

Texcoco, Netzahualcoyotl. The Triple Alliance laid the foundation for what later became the Mexica Empire or confederation. Cuauhnahuac (today Cuernavaca), some 45 miles from Tenochtitlan, is considered his first military acquisition.

MOCTEZUMA ILHUICAMINA (MOCTECUHZOMA). "He Who Shoots at the Heavens." *Position*: Leader of the Triple Alliance; *Term*: 1440–1469.

Son of Huitzilihuitl, Moctezuma I, became the absolute leader of the Triple Alliance. His conquests went as far as Guatemala. He was also concerned with improving the urban infrastructure. He ordered the construction of many aqueducts to bring potable water to the capital city, as well as the creation of reservoirs to avoid city flooding. The inordinate number of natural catastrophes that plagued his tenure—earthquakes, droughts, snowstorms, and famine—dramatically increased the number of sacrifices that had to be made to the god Huitzilopochtli.

The Great Temple of Tenochtitlan (for the God of War) was built during his reign. He also began the so-called *Guerra Florida* (Floral Wars) to capture prisoners for the sacrifices. These Floral Wars were staged battles between Aztec warriors and soldiers from vassal tribes that were contemplating rebellion. The chieftains of the rebel tribes were invited to observe the sacrifice of the defeated behind a screen of roses, and later to eat their flesh at a banquet.

Moctezuma I is famous for having led the most disciplined and powerful armies ever seen in Tenochtitlan. During his rule, the City of Tenochtitlan was under the highest security, well protected by land and water.

AXAYACATL. "Water Face." *Position*: Emperor; *Term*: 1469–1483.

Axayacatl was the grandson of Itzcoatl. His nickname was given to him because of his strong tendency to sweat profusely. He was a ruler known for his deeds as an audacious warrior who continued the tradition of the *Guerra Florida* in order to maintain his supply of prisoners for human sacrifices. He fought against Tlatelolco, defeated it, and turned the kingdom into one more vassal of Tenochtitlan. Then he proceeded toward Michoacán, determined to conquer this central western region. The Aztecs, however, were defeated by the local Purepecha Indians.

In a battle against the Matlazincas (from the Highlands of Toluca), Axayacatl was injured and walked with a limp for the rest of his life. About this time, the Mexica Empire reached as far south as present-day El Salvador. He ordered the construction of the last phase of the god Huitzilopochtli's temple and the temple to Tlaloc (the Rain God), provider of the water for the lake on which the capital was built. He commissioned the carving of the great Aztec "Calendar," a huge stone that allowed the Aztecs to measure time with remarkable precision.

Throughout his rule he sought the advice of wise Toltecs. Axayacatl died at the age of thirty.

TIZOC (?–1486). "Pierced with Jades." *Position*: Emperor; *Term*: 1483–1486.

Tizoc was the brother of Axayacatl. Though sickly and perhaps even an invalid, Tizoc ruled for five years with furious energy. He beautified and expanded the capital city. He traveled to the Gulf coast, made vassals of the Huaxtec and Totonac tribes there, and founded Tuxpan on the coast in the present state of Veracruz. He also established an Aztec post in Yanhuitlán, Oaxaca.

Tizoc's deeds are celebrated on the famous cylindrical Tizoc Stone. It is believed that he was poisoned to death.

AHUIZOTL (?–1502). "Water Dog." *Position*: Emperor; *Term*: 1486–1502.

Ahuizotl was the elder brother of Axayacatl and Tizoc. He was a strong, ferocious, and bloodthirsty ruler. At the inauguration of the Great Temple in 1487, he ordered the sacrifice of many prisoners of war; an average of 1,000 victims a day were sacrificed over a period of twenty days. Each day blood ran like a river onto the pavement of the Great Plaza, and the stairs of the great pyramid were literally bathed in blood.

Ahuizotl is considered to be the mastermind of one of the world's worst holocausts. He conquered the Isthmus of Tehuantepec and invaded Chiapas. He also established control over the Maya Indians in the jungles of Petén. He attempted to conquer the Tarascans in Michoacán, but once again the Aztecs were defeated. For Ahuizotl, this was the biggest defeat of his career. He died during one of the cyclical floods that plagued the city of Tenochtitlan.

MOCTEZUMA XOCOYOTZIN (MOCTECUHZOMA) (1468–1520). "The Younger and Respectable Lord." *Position*: Emperor; *Term*: 1502–1520.

The son of Axayacatl, this emperor began his military career at a very early age. Moctezuma II was courageous, prudent, and deeply religious. Humble at times, he could often be seen sweeping the floor of the great *Teocali*, the House of God. He could also be arrogant and authoritarian with the common people. In time, he went through a psychological change and became more interested in the priesthood than in the military.

Luxury and abundance were characteristics of his rule. Proclaiming to have been "chosen by the gods," once he became the Aztec ruler he was unwilling to tolerate power sharing with those who claimed to be of equal rank. He ended the federalist order that had been functioning well for fifty years. He launched vicious attacks against the Tlaxcaltecan and Huejotzingan people who inhabited the present day states of Puebla and Tlaxcala.

Superstitious and fanatically religious, he interpreted the arrival of the Spaniards to Mexico as the predicted return of the high priest Quetzalcoatl. He later paid for his ruthless behavior toward the neighboring towns and for his astonishing weakness in confronting the Iberian conquerors. He mistakenly sought to buy the Spaniards with valuable presents, which, if anything, heightened their greed even more. By lodging Hernán Cortés in the palace, he denied himself the possibility of confronting him in the battlefield.

The arrival of the Spanish conquistadors and their effective military alliances with tribes who considered the Aztecs their worst enemy, combined with Moctezuma's own superstitions and mistakes in judgment, ended the Mexica Empire.

In an attempt to persuade his people to make peace with the Spaniards, he was stoned by the mob and suffered a head injury. A few weeks after the incident, he died in his palace.

CUITLAHUAC (?–1520). "Pile of Dung" or "Pillar of Ordure." *Position: Grand Tlatoani; Term: 1520.*

Cuitlahuac, the brother of Moctezuma II, was chosen as grand *tlatoani*, in charge of the Aztec military forces when Emperor Moctezuma II died. He fought bravely, trying to expel the Spaniards from the city, but did not succeed. He became ill with smallpox and died after a brief eighty days of rule in December 1520.

The Spaniards, however, thought it was wise to leave the city. The withdrawal supposedly caused Hernán Cortés to cry upon his own defeat during the famous *La Noche Triste* (The Sad Night).

CUAUHTEMOC (1502–FEBRUARY 28, 1525). "The Swooping Eagle." *Place of death*: Itzancanac, in the jungles of Petén, in the West of Guatemala; *Position*: Emperor; *Term*: 1520–1525.

Cuauhtemoc, the nephew of Cuitlahuac, was appointed ruler by Hernán Cortés. He was the last emperor of the Mexica Empire. According to the conqueror's explanation, the main reason to appoint him emperor was "to honor him and to fulfill Cortés' commitment." Cortés had many other practical reasons to appoint him ruler—mainly to use Cuauhtemoc as a shield against a possible uprising.

Cuauhtemoc refused to play the same role Moctezuma II had played. He fought bravely against the Spaniards and other enemies of the Aztecs, and was made a prisoner while trying to escape from his city. He was tortured and mutilated by the Spaniards, who wanted to know where the Mexica treasure was hidden. He never revealed the secret. Cuauhtemoc was later taken along on an expedition with Cortés to Honduras, and while in route, he was charged with plotting and hanged.

This last of the Mexicas' emperors is considered a great national hero in Mexico.

2

ENCOUNTER, CONQUEST, AND THE COLONIAL PERIOD, 1502–1821

THE INITIAL ENCOUNTER AND THE CONQUEST, 1502–1535

Three consecutive and different periods define the encounter of the Spanish and Mexican civilizations: the initial encounter, the conquest, and the colonization.

The first known contact between the European and the Mesoamerican cultures took place in 1502, when Christopher Columbus was on his fourth expedition to the so-called "new world" and crossed the path of an Indian merchant vessel. The quality of some of the products exchanged surprised him and, according to chronicles, made him think there must have been a more sophisticated world inland. He did nothing about it. He sailed south with the wind, coasting to the Yucatan, Central America, as far southeast as Panama, and back toward the Cuban coast on his way to Spain. He died in Valladolid, Spain, a few years later.

There were other navigators, such as Vicente Yáñez Pinzón and Juan Díaz de Solís, who probably sailed along the coast of Mexico (Yucatan, Tabasco, Veracruz, and even up to Tamaulipas), but did not explore the land in a systematic way. Jerónimo de Aguilar and Gonzalo Guerrero, however, did make it ashore well before Hernán Cortés landed on the Yucatan peninsula on February 10, 1519. Both sailors were captured by the Mayas, and for eight years they lived among them. Aguilar was interested in the Indian culture and learned the language. His curiosity would later prove invaluable to Cortés. Juan de Grijalva was another navigator who explored the region, naming it New Spain. Later on, Cortés would refer to the whole conquered territory by the same name.

Cortés' expedition was the one that truly explored and later conquered the new lands for the Spanish Crown. During his trip to the unknown, Cortés freed Jerónimo de Aguilar in Cozumel. Traveling further northwest, Cortés arrived in Tabasco where the natives presented him with Doña Marina, a woman with an extraordinary gift for languages. Together, Aguilar and Doña Marina would become Cortés' indispensable tools and main interpreters. Continuing his journey along the coast of what is now the Gulf of Mexico, Cortés founded the first Spanish settlement on the new land, the Villa Rica de la Vera Cruz.

In spite of the evident progress of their expedition, not everything was fine within the Spanish forces. Tired of the hardships and fearing the unknown, some soldiers began talking about returning to Cuba. Determined to go on, Cortés' answer was to scuttle the ships, thus rendering a retreat impossible.

Meanwhile, the Aztec Emperor Moctezuma II learned about Cortés' arrival and showered him with valuable gifts. Greed gave the Spaniards and their Totonac allies the incentive to march on toward wealth, fame, and glory. By the time they arrived in Cempoala, still near the coast, Cortés began sending generous samples of the initial booty to Charles V, the king of Spain.

Arriving at Tlaxcala, in central Mexico, Cortés became aware of the strong rivalry between the Tlaxcalans and the Aztecs, and later forged a military alliance with the former. His army grew larger and stronger as he marched toward Tenochtitlan. While camping in Cholula, Cortés believed Moctezuma II was trying to trap him and responded by slaughtering many Cholulan people.

Finally, on November 3, 1519, Cortés arrived in Tenochtitlan. Moctezuma II received him with precious gifts and housed the Spaniards at the Axayacatl Palace.

On November 14, Cortés seized Moctezuma II and ordered the destruction of all the religious relics of the Aztecs. In a defiant act of courage, he ordered a Catholic cross placed at the Great Temple in Tenochtitlan.

Meanwhile, having learned that, bypassing Diego Vélazquez, Cortés was sending large amounts of gold and other gifts to the king, Diego Velázquez, the governor of Cuba, sent Pánfilo de Narváez to supersede Cortés' authority. When Cortés heard of Narváez's arrival in San Juan de Ulúa, he rushed to meet him and left Pedro de Alvarado in charge of military operations in Tenochtitlan. During a religious celebration in the Great Temple of Tenochtitlan on May 23, 1520, Pedro de Alvarado ordered and participated in a massacre of huge proportions in which thousands of Indians were killed. Furious, the population rose up in arms against the Spaniards who took refuge in the palace of Axayacatl.

In the meantime, Cortés convinced Narváez and his men to side with him and proceed with the conquest. He rushed back to the city to help his people come out of the sieged palace. Cortés and his men were able to go inside the palace without suffering casualties, but once inside the battle reignited. Trying to calm them down, Cortés ordered Moctezuma to come out on the roof of the palace and make a plea for peace. The people reacted with insults and hurled stones at him, slightly injuring him in the head. Profoundly depressed, he died a few weeks later.

The situation with the Spaniards was becoming desperate. Realizing they were short of food and water, Cortés decided to evacuate the city by night. The proud Spanish army was trying to sneak out, but was discovered by the people. A battle ensued that caused many casualties on both sides. At the break of dawn Cortés is said to have cried under the shade of an old tree in an episode that has been described as *La Noche Triste* (The Sad Night).

Cortés retreated to Tlaxcala to heal his wounds and to prepare for a return to Tenochtitlan. Meanwhile in the city, a terrible epidemic of smallpox decimated the population, including Cuitlahuac, Moctezuma's successor. While in Tlaxcala, the Spaniards built a fleet of boats that would prove helpful in reconquering the city on the lake. After several bloody encounters between the Spanish conquistadors and the Indian Aztecs, finally on July 20, 1521, the Spanish and their allies captured Tenochtitlan.

The city, however, was no longer the jewel it had been and was instead in ruins. That day, the exhausted troops of the last Aztec Emperor Cuauhtemoc left Tenochtitlan without surrendering. A semifeudal European society was established in New Spain, where the Spaniards ruled and the indigenous people were converted into slaves and servants.

THE CONQUEST: AN INTERPRETATION

The conquest was a time of violence. The cities, temples, gods, and beliefs of the indigenous tribes were destroyed. Their land was taken, and a new government, a new religion, and a new system of values was imposed on them.

The conquest was accomplished through a well-organized mix of violence, strength, ambition, and greed. Military discipline lingered in the air, and everyday life was regimented in a military fashion. The new cities were planned from a military perspective and strategically placed. The central plaza was built with defense in mind, with a gallows pole, a church, and a cross in the plaza. The conquest was also the result of expeditions in search of wealth.

There is much speculation as to how a handful of Spaniards (roughly 500) were able to conquer Tenochtitlan, which had a population of at least 200,000 inhabitants. There is no definitive explanation of this, but there are many theories. It is a fact that the entire territory of what is now Mexico was made up of many different tribes, all of which held a tremendous resentment against the Aztecs. They believed the Aztecs ruled with a cruel hand. Thus, when the Spanish came, they aligned themselves with them, the unknown, against those they knew too well, the Aztecs. Their alliance was critical to the Spanish success.

Doña Marina (a k a La Malinche) played an important role in the conquest. Near Tabasco, as part of a peace offering, she came in contact with Hernán Cortés. She was a woman of exceptional intelligence. She assisted Cortés in matters of indigenous culture, mentality, and language, and turned herself into an invaluable resource in dealing with the tribes Cortés met. She served as the link between two cultures. In time, she also became Cortés' lover and gave him a son, in addition to her advice and guidance. The Mexicas referred to the Spaniards as "Malinches," meaning the people of Doña Marina.

Another crucial factor that can help explain the conquest was the military use of the horse and the mastiff. When the conquistadors appeared on horseback, the Mexicas were awestruck because they had never seen anything like that, as there were no horses on the American continent before the Spanish brought them. The Mexicas believed that the Spaniards were centaurs, mythical entities no one could fight.

The armor, cannon, and musket made the Spaniards seem invincible since the Mexica spears could not penetrate the armor that shielded the Spaniards. The Mexicas' belief that the Spaniards were supernatural beings, combined with this, created an unbeatable force.

At first the Aztecs also believed that the arrival of the Spaniards was related to the return of their god Quetzalcoatl. When Moctezuma II heard of the landing of the Spaniards, he remembered a dream he had had in which Quetzalcoatl relayed the prophecy that a white, bearded man would soon return. When Cortés and the other Spanish warriors arrived, Moctezuma believed the prophecy was being fulfilled.

THE LEGACY OF THE CONQUEST

The legacy of the conquest had both positive and negative aspects. The Spanish language was one of the major contributions brought by the conquest. The new language reduced the fragmentation caused by the many varied indigenous languages and brought a new, cohesive, and common language to the land. On the other hand, it should also be noted that establishing a common language impoverished the linguistic varieties prevalent among the Indians.

Another positive feature of the conquest was the mixture of the indigenous race and the western European Spanish race that created the *mestizo*, the Mexican. Last among the positives was the Catholic religion. Although sometimes forced upon the people, in time the population adopted it with absolute fervor. The conquest also brought about a much needed change in some of the more barbaric traditions of the Mexicas. No longer would such abhorrent and uncivilized practices as human sacrifices be tolerated. Slowly but surely, the Catholic religion uplifted the spirits of the new Mexicans. A new identity was born, and a country that loosely resembled Europe in its infrastructure and communication was created.

There were also several negative aspects brought on by the conquest. Among the worst was genocide. The Indians had not developed immunity to European diseases like measles and smallpox. The death toll of the conquest was high and for some people still unforgivable. At the time the Spanish arrived in Mexico, it is believed that there were between 12 and 25 million indigenous peoples. One hundred years after the conquest, it is estimated that only about 1 million Indians existed. Disease, battle, and abusive labor had taken its toll.

The Spanish conquistadors ransacked the land in the name of the king of Spain, and the natives were economically exploited with extreme brutality and abuse. The Spanish denied most natives the possibility of upward mobility. The political subjugation to the metropolis built up a social hierarchy that had the Spaniards at the top, followed by *criollos, mestizos*, and the Indians at the bottom of society. The majority of the population of the new city and the only native-born people on the land had no political, economic, or social rights.

Rulers of the Conquest, 1521–1535

CRISTÓBAL DE TAPIA. *Position*: Governor; *Term*: 1521.

De Tapia was named governor by the king of Spain. However, he could not handle the intense pressure that Hernán Cortés and his troops exerted on him, and he returned to Santo Domingo (La Hispaniola) in 1522.

HERNÁN CORTÉS (1485–1547). "Marquis of the Valley of Oaxaca."
Place of birth: Medellín, Extremadura, Spain; *Place of death*: Castilleja de la Cuesta, Spain (close to Seville); *Wives*: Catalina Juárez and Juana Zú-

ñiga; *Parents*: Martín Cortés of Medellín, Extremadura, and Catalina Altamirano Pizarro; *Position*: Governor and Captain General; *Term*: 1522–1524.

Hernán Cortés, the conqueror of New Spain, was a brave and clever man whose political genius allowed him to forge several alliances with the different tribes that had resisted the Mexica domination. Seeking wealth and power, this ambitious man kept intact his belief in God and his loyalty to the king of Spain.

Cortés reached the Mexican coast with 100 sailors, 508 soldiers, a herd of mastiff dogs trained to kill, 16 horses, and a small arsenal. Cortés was both victorious and defeated in battle, but almost always in a grand style.

When the last emperor of the Mexica Empire passed away, Cortés managed complete domination over the Aztec tribes and initiated the government of New Spain. He enforced the evangelization of the Indians and the instillation of Christian morals into society. He ordered the exploitation of the mines in the region, promoted agriculture, and developed cattle raising. He sent explorers to the north, and he commanded the expeditions to the south to conquer new lands and search for new treasures. He managed to make himself very prosperous and also managed to give untold wealth to Spain and the Crown.

The envy of Cortés enemies, both in Cuba and in Spain, made the king of Spain distrust him. He returned to Spain where he died pretty much in disgrace. In his will he requested that he be buried in Mexico City, in the crypts of the Jesus of Nazarene Hospital, one of the many institutions that he founded.

PROVISIONAL GOVERNMENT OF ALFONSO ZUAZO, ALONSO DE ESTRADA, AND RODRIGO DE ALBORNOZ (1524–1527).

Alfonso Zuazo—*Position*: Governor. Zuazo governed when Hernán Cortés departed on his expedition to Las Hibueras.

Alonso de Estrada—*Position*: Governor and Treasurer. De Estrada was one of the first royal representatives appointed by King Charles V to come to New Spain. It is alleged that he was an illegitimate son of Ferdinand the Catholic. He was Cortés' representative when Cortés was away on expeditions.

Rodrigo de Albornoz—*Position*: Accountant of New Spain. De Albornoz was the secretary of Charles V. He was one of the worst enemies Cortés had in the Spanish court. He was another of Cortés representatives while the latter was away on expeditions.

LUIS PONCE DE LEÓN (?–1526). *Position*: Judge in Residence; *Term*: July 4–20, 1526.

Ponce de León arrived in New Spain with Marcos Aguilar in 1526. After a big welcoming dinner, he became very sick and died a few days later apparently of typhus. He named Aguilar as his successor.

MARCOS AGUILAR (?–1527). *Position*: Judge in Residence; *Term*: July 20, 1526–February 28, 1527.

After the death of Luis Ponce de León, Aguilar took over as judge, not without some difficulties with the political establishment. Aguilar was an old man with an advanced case of syphilis; he governed until his death a few months later.

ALONSO DE ESTRADA (2ND TERM. SEE PROVISIONAL GOVERNMENT.) *Position*: Judge in Residence; *Term*: 1527–1528.

THE FIRST *AUDIENCIA* OF NUÑO BELTRÁN DE GUZMÁN, JUAN ORTIZ DE MATIENZO, DIEGO DELGADILLO, FRANCISCO MALDONADO, AND ALONSO DE PARADA (DECEMBER 6, 1528–DECEMBER 23, 1530).

The *audiencia*, a judicial and administrative council named by the king to rule in the colony, consisted of a president and *oidores*. The number of *oidores* changed from *audiencia* to *audiencia*.

Nuño Beltrán de Guzmán (?–1550)—*Place of death*: Valladolid, Spain; *Position*: Judge in Residence. Beltrán de Guzmán was considered a bad governor and president of the first *audiencia*. He was cruel to the Indians and abused his power. Removed from office, he ran away to the western part of the country on an expedition in search of personal wealth. Beltrán conquered New Galicia (today Jalisco). He was such a cruel man that the Indians depicted him as a serpent in their codes. There were so many complaints filed against him that he was arrested, tried, and found guilty. He was sent back to Spain in chains, and he died while in prison in Valladolid, Spain.

Juan Ortiz de Matienzo—*Position: Oidor*. Not much is known of Matienzo's rule except that he, like his predecessor, performed terrible acts of oppression and injustice against the Indians.

Diego Delgadillo—*Position: Oidor*. Under Delgadillo's rule, the natives of New Spain suffered through another one of its most cruel, oppressive, and unjust governments. Delgadillo didn't go unpunished; he was accused of several abuses, tried, and dispossessed of all his properties.

Francisco Maldonado—*Position: Oidor*. Maldonado conquered and pacified the Zapotec and Mijes indians, in what is today the state of Oaxaca, and the Chontales, who inhabited the zone of Tabasco. The king of Spain, Charles V, rewarded him with a prestigious coat of arms.

Alonso de Parada—*Position: Oidor*. De Parada died soon after he was appointed.

THE SECOND *AUDIENCIA* OF SEBASTIÁN RAMÍREZ DE FUEN-
LEAL (OR FUENTELEAL), FRANCISCO CEINOS, JUAN DE SALME-
RÓN, ALVARO MALDONADO, AND VASCO DE QUIROGA
(DECEMBER 23, 1530–NOVEMBER 14, 1535).

Sebastián Ramírez de Fuenleal (or Fuenteleal) (?–1547)—*Position*: Judge
in Residence. Fuenleal was a bishop and the president of the second *audiencia*. He is famous for his attempts at restoring peace and justice in New
Spain. He was responsible for the construction of many monasteries,
schools, and churches in New Spain. He died in Spain as the president of
the city council of Valladolid.

Francisco Ceinos (?–1570)—*Place of birth*: Zamora, Spain; *Place of
death*: New Spain; *Position*: Prosecutor and *Relator del Consejo de Indias*.
It has been written that thirty years after the second *audiencia*, Ceinos
participated in Martín Cortés (the legitimate son of Hernán Cortés) conspiracy of 1565, which attempted to make New Spain an independent
country.

Juan de Salmerón—*Position: Oidor.*

Alvaro Maldonado—*Position: Oidor.*

Vasco de Quiroga (1470?–1565)—*Position: Oidor.* Vasco de Quiroga
was the bishop and peacemaker of the state of Michoacán. At the shores
of Lake Pátzcuaro he made a reality out of the ideas expressed in Thomas
Moore's *Utopia*. He founded two hospitals, the Santa Fe of Mexico and
the Santa Fe of the Lagoon of Uayámeo. He was tireless in his defense of
the indigenous people. He wrote several literary works, and the Indians of
the region still refer to him as "Tata Vasco." Tata means "father" in Indian
language.

VICEROYALTY, 1535–1821

The encounter of civilizations that followed the European "discovery"
of America transformed both Europe and Mesoamerica. The Spanish
Empire transplanted its laws, customs, language, art, science, and religion
to the old civilizations that already flourished in what would later be called
the Americas. The Europeans also brought along their methods of cultivation of the land and their ideas on trade. The natives gave this transcul-
turation their own interpretation.

Throughout the era of the viceroyalty, the Spanish Crown held the political control of the new entity now called the New Spain. It was the king's
prerogative to appoint viceroys, residence judges, *audiencia* presidents, and
oidores. The list of viceroys is long. Some were considered good and some
bad. All together, they ruled New Spain for approximately 286 years. There
were many human and natural disasters during the years of the viceroyalty.

The Catholic Church and the Spanish Crown worked closely toward common goals. The expansion of the Spanish Empire meant a wider propagation of the Catholic faith and growth in the church's wealth. In New Spain the church was part benefactor and part tyrant for the indigenous people. New administrative institutions played a major role in the public and private life of all the people. Some, like the courts, were positive; others were intolerant, like the Holy Inquisition. Some were neutral, like the Council of the Indies and the *Casa de Contratación*.

During the viceregal period, the *mestizo* was born: a person of mixed blood whose ancestry can be traced to the European and Asian continents. From Spain the mix included Phoenician, Greek, Roman, German (from the Goths), Arab, and Jewish blood. From its indigenous roots, the *mestizo* is said to have descended from Asians and Polynesians, but was made of Aztec, Toltec, Mixtec, Zapotec, Tlaxcaltecan, Otomi, Mayan, and many other ancient tribes' blood.

Palaces, cathedrals, churches, monasteries, schools, hospitals, and universities were built at a fast pace. The mining and agriculture of New Spain thrived. Social classes became polarized, and one could walk down a city street and see extreme wealth on one side and extreme poverty on the other. The three centuries of colonial rule brought both splendor and shame to New Spain.

Rulers of the Viceroyalty, 1535–1821

Population of New Spain 1742: Approximately 3,865,529 Inhabitants

In 1794 there were 5.2 million, and in 1808 there were 6.5 million

THE HOUSE OF AUSTRIA—THE HAPSBURGS DURING THE REIGN OF CHARLES V (1500–1558): 1516–1556

Charles V of the Holy Roman Empire (Charles I of Spain) was born in the city of Ghent in Flanders, in 1500. He was the son of Queen Juana of Castile (Joan the Mad) and Prince Philip the Handsome, of the House of Hapsburg. He was the grandson of Ferdinand and Isabella of Spain, and the most powerful monarch of the century. Through conquest, he built such a vast dominion that it was said the sun never set on his empire. He was called the "lord of two worlds."

He married Isabella of Portugal. He abdicated in 1556 in favor of his son Philip II, and retired to the monastery of the order of St. Jerome at Yuste, where he died in 1558.

Charles ruled with two basic principles in mind: the Catholic faith and warfare in the defense of the Spanish Empire. During his rule he appointed only two viceroys to New Spain.

ANTONIO DE MENDOZA (1495–1552). "Count of Tendilla." *Place of birth*: Granada, Spain; *Place of death*: Lima, Peru; *Position*: Viceroy; *Term*: November 14, 1535–November 25, 1550.

Mendoza was a cultured, temperate, intelligent, and honest man. He had distinguished himself as a military commander during the Spanish reconquest of the territories occupied by the Moors in southern Spain.

Impressed with his abilities, Charles V assigned him to several diplomatic missions. His success led to his appointment as viceroy for New Spain. Once in the job, he promoted the development of agriculture and stockbreeding. His government was very good for New Spain. He brought the first printing press to America. He inaugurated the Casa de la Moneda and started coining (minting) in 1536. He ordered the road to Veracruz repaired and started the road to Guadalajara. He was cofounder of the schools of Santa Cruz de Tlaltelolco and of San Juan de Letrán.

He organized several expeditions to the interior of the viceroyalty. In one of these, Cape Mendocino, in California, was discovered. He ordered the history of the Mexicas (Aztecs) to be recorded in the Mendocino Codex. Mendoza sent the codex to Charles V, but the ship that carried the codex never made it to Spanish soil. In 1551 he was promoted to the viceroyalty of Peru. The following year he died in Lima.

LUIS DE VELASCO I (1511–1564). "Count of Santiago." *Place of birth*: Carrión de los Condes, Palencia, Spain; *Place of death*: New Spain; *Position*: Viceroy; *Term*: November 25, 1550–July 31, 1564.

Velasco began working at the Spanish Court when he was fourteen years old. He even participated along with King Charles V in the wars against France around 1530. As viceroy he followed progressive policies and was considered a very compassionate person. He issued many decrees protecting the indigenous people. Velasco abolished slavery in New Spain and freed more than 15,000 natives, including women and children.

He inaugurated the Royal and Pontifical University of Mexico in 1553. During his term, the mining industry flourished and progressed with discoveries such as the process for recovering silver from ore by amalgamation with mercury.

There were also many natural disasters during his tenure. The biggest was the first big flood after the conquest; it took place in Mexico City in 1552. Then the plague hit the New Spain in 1555.

Velasco's government, like that of his predecessor Antonio de Mendoza, was considered a very good one for New Spain. He died in office in 1564.

DURING THE REIGN OF PHILIP II OF SPAIN (1527–1598): 1556–1598

Philip II was known as the "Prudent King." He was born in Valladolid, Spain, in 1527 to Charles V and Isabella of Portugal. He had a reputation as a good public administrator. He was very interested in New Spain, and during his reign the viceroyalty was consolidated. Several successful conquests began at this time: La Florida, Philippines, New Mexico, and so on.

He encouraged the consecutive governments of New Spain to promote the development of agriculture, cattle raising (stockbreeding), and mining. He assembled all kinds of data regarding New Spain and its history. He sent his personal physician to learn about America's flora and fauna for medical purposes. He encouraged trade with the Orient by way of the so-called Nao of China, or Manila Galleon. He implemented a courageous defense of New Spain against pirates and filibusters.

He was married four times, and his wives were Mary of Portugal, Mary Tudor, Isabella of Valois, and Anne of Austria. Overall, his reign benefited New Spain. He died in 1598 in the Escorial monastery of Spain. During his rule he appointed seven viceroys to govern New Spain.

THE THIRD *AUDIENCIA* OF FRANCISCO CEINOS, PEDRO VILLA-LOBOS, JERÓNIMO OROZCO, AND VASCO DE PUGA (1564–1566).

Francisco Ceinos (or Ceynos) (2nd term)—*Position*: President. As a senior member of the *oidores*, Ceinos was left in charge of the government when Viceroy Luis de Velasco I died in office. This *audiencia* continued Velasco's program. At this time, the trial against Martín Cortés, the Marquis of the Valley of Oaxaca, took place.

Pedro Villalobos—*Position: Oidor.*

Jerónimo Orozco—*Position: Oidor.*

Vasco de Puga (?–1576)—*Position: Oidor.* Little is known about Villalobos, Orozco, and De Puga. In the case of De Puga, however, it is known that he was from Granada, Spain, and married Francisca de Baena. He held a Ph.D. from the Royal and Pontifical University of New Spain. One of his daughters married Pedro Quesada, a grandson of the *Malinche* (Doña Marina). He had several writings published.

GASTÓN DE PERALTA (?–1587). "Marquis of Folces." *Place of birth*: Pau, Baja Navarra, France; *Place of death*: Valladolid, Spain; *Position*: Viceroy; *Term*: 1566–1567.

Peralta proceeded slowly and carefully during his government because of the unrest present due to the trial and execution of some who participated in the alleged Conspiracy of 1565 by Martín Cortés.

He was considered a person of weak character. He suspended the execution of Cortés illegitimate son, Martín Cortés. This act led to a critical report from the *audiencia* that caused the king to order him back to Spain. To replace him in the meantime, the king sent a new representative, Alonso de Muñoz. This whole period could be characterized as one of unrest, terror, and cruelty.

AUDIENCIA GOBERNADORA OF LUIS CARRILLO AND ALONSO DE MUÑOZ (1567–1568 [SEVEN MONTHS]). *Position: Visitadores.*

MARTÍN ENRÍQUEZ DE ALMANZA. *Position*: Viceroy; *Term*: November 4, 1568–October 4, 1580.

Upon his arrival at Veracruz, Enríquez de Almanza began dealing with big problems. First he had to fight and oust the English pirates who had settled on the Island of Sacrificios.

Then, faced with the conflict between the secular clergy and the Franciscan order, he had to prove himself as a peacemaker. After long rounds of negotiations and granting several concessions to both groups, he was able to work out a truce.

The Jesuit order arrived in New Spain during his term. He worked to preserve and enforce the laws protecting the population against the invasion of barbarian Indians called Huachichiles. He even engaged them in battle. As part of his program of law and order he inaugurated the prisons of San Felipe in Guanajuato, and Ojuelos and Portezuelos on the road to Zacatecas in 1570.

In 1571 the Tribunal of the Holy Inquisition was established. In 1573 the first stone was set in the construction of the cathedral in Mexico City, and a special General Indian Court was created. Taking into consideration the abysmally poor condition of the Indians, during the epidemic of 1576 he excused them from paying tribute.

LORENZO SUÁREZ DE MENDOZA (?–1583). "Conte of the Coruña." *Place of birth*: Guadalajara, Spain; *Place of death*: New Spain; *Position*: Viceroy; *Term*: October 4, 1580–June 19, 1583.

Suárez was born a member of the old Spanish nobility. He was interested in literature and was a firm believer in education. He was honest, amicable, and a hard worker. As viceroy, he tried unsuccessfully to fight corruption through the creation of institutions like the Commerce Tribunal. The increasing power of the *audiencia*, the landowners, and the religious orders were obstacles to the viceroy's ability to rule. He asked for a *visitador*, a special envoy sent by the court with powers to investigate issues and report back to the king, and Pedro Moya de Contreras was sent. Later on, Moya became his successor.

Suárez, who by now was an old man, died suddenly, and the *audiencia* took over the government. Because Suárez was a good friend and protector of the Franciscan order, he was buried in a Franciscan Convent.

THE FOURTH *AUDIENCIA* OF LUIS DE VILLANUEVA Y ZAPATA, SANCHEZ PAREDES, PEDRO FARFÁN, FRANCISCO DE SANDE, AND DR. ROBLES (1583–1584).

Luis de Villanueva y Zapata (?–1583)—*Place of death*: New Spain; *Wife*: Mariana de Sandoval; *Position*: President.
Sánchez Paredes—*Position: Oidor.*
Pedro Farfán—*Position: Oidor.*
Francisco de Sande —*Position: Oidor.*
Dr. Robles—*Position: Oidor.*
In this *audiencia*, the *oidores* tried to maintain order in the colony. They increased trade between the metropolis (Madrid), New Spain, and the Philippines through the ports of Veracruz and Acapulco.

PEDRO MOYA DE CONTRERAS (?–1591). "Archbishop." *Place of birth*: Pedroche, Cordoba, Spain; *Place of death*: Madrid, Spain; *Position: Visitador*, Inquisitor, and Viceroy; *Term*: September 25, 1584–October 17, 1585.

Moya was a firm believer in the Catholic faith. As viceroy he governed with a strong hand, and he knew how to wield the immense power of the Inquisition. He sent many prisoners charged with embezzlement to the gallows pole.

On the other hand, as a bishop he traveled to the small towns of New Spain on pastoral visits. He wanted the Indians to learn the Catholic gospel, as well as reading, writing, music, and crafts, as did most of the early missionaries.

In 1585 he presided over a provincial council that decreed Indians could not be made slaves.

During his term, the viceroyalty sent more gold to Spain than all his predecessors combined. He went back to Spain where he was appointed president of the Council of Indies.

ALVARO MANRIQUE DE ZÚÑIGA. "Marquis of Villamanrique." *Place of death*: Madrid, Spain; *Wife*: Blanca de Velasco; *Position*: Viceroy; *Term*: October 17, 1585–January 27, 1590.

Manrique's rule was plagued by frequent pirate invasions. During his tenure the old conflict between the secular clergy and the orders resurfaced, and Manrique took sides with the seculars. The Dominican, Franciscan, and Augustinian orders were not pleased with him, and the quarrels brought New Spain to the brink of a civil war.

He was tried by the church courts, all his belongings were seized, and he was removed from office. Returning to Spain, he fought unsuccessfully to recover his wealth and prestige.

LUIS DE VELASCO II (1ST TERM) (1539–1617). "Marquis of Salinas." *Place of birth*: Carrión de los Condes, Palencia, Spain; *Place of death*: Seville, Spain; *Position*: Viceroy; *Term*: January 27, 1590–November 5, 1595.

Velasco II was the son of the second viceroy of New Spain. Having lived in Mexico City during his childhood and youth, he was familiar with the indigenous culture. His arrival in his beloved Mexico City was celebrated by all social classes.

Among the first accomplishments of his rule was the pacification of the feared Chichimec tribes, which inhabited the northern regions. Under the direction of the Franciscan order, several Tlaxcalan Indian families were transferred to the north to live with the Chichimecs in settlements surrounding the city of Zacatecas.

Velasco founded the *Hospital Real*, created the Alameda, a magnificent park in Mexico City, and opened many mines in San Luis de Potosí.

Sent to Peru in 1595, he asked for and was given permission to return to Mexico City to administer his businesses. He later went back into government.

GASPAR DE ZÚÑIGA Y ACEVEDO (1560–1606). *Place of birth*: Monterrey, Orense, Spain; *Place of death*: Peru; *Position*: Viceroy; *Term*: November 5, 1595–October 27, 1603.

Zúñiga served in Philip II's court and distinguished himself as a man of arms. As a viceroy, he was very friendly with the indigenous people. He sought to protect the Indian towns from miners and rich land owners and encouraged the Indians to form congregations for their own defense.

He organized an expedition to California and another one to New Mexico. The city of Santa Fe was founded during the latter expedition. Many Jesuit missions were established, and the port of Veracruz was moved to its present location under Zúñiga's rule. In New Spain, Zúñiga was respected by the indigenous peoples—*criollos, mestizos*, and *peninsulares* alike—and he later became a viceroy in Peru.

DURING THE REIGN OF PHILIP III OF SPAIN (1578–1621): 1598–1621

Philip III was born in Madrid, Spain, in 1578. His parents were Philip II and Anne of Austria. His ascension to the throne in 1598 was celebrated in New Spain with the usual *fiestas*, bullfights, fireworks, and extravagant balls. The new king never matched the greatness of his predecessors, and opted for a life of leisure, partying, hunting, and seeking pleasure. He married the Archduchess Marguerite of Austria. The power behind the throne was his counselor Francisco Rojas Sandoval, Duke of Lerma.

During his reign, explorations to the South Seas were expanded. In New Spain the impetus to promote higher education led to the founding of the schools of San Ildefonso and San Pedro y San Pablo. Several Indian tribes submitted to Spanish control. He died in Madrid, Spain, in 1621. Thus began an era of decadence of the Spanish Empire. Philip III sent four viceroys to govern New Spain, and all of them were fair and honest men.

JUAN DE MENDOZA Y LUNA (1571–1628). "Marquis of Montesclaros." *Place of birth*: Guadalajara, Spain; *Place of death*: Madrid, Spain; *Position*: Viceroy; *Term*: October 27, 1603–July 2, 1607.

Due to the severe floodings that affected Mexico City, Mendoza wanted to move the capital of New Spain to firmer ground in the nearby city of Tacubaya. When it was realized that the cathedral, the Palace of the Viceroys, and other great buildings were worth nearly 20 million pesos, Mendoza changed his mind. Instead he ordered the construction of dams, canals, and avenues such as the *calzadas* of Guadalupe, San Cristóbal, and Chapultepec. He also ordered improvements to the old drainage system. Juan de Mendoza was an upright and honest administrator. He promoted prosperity, gave aid to the natives, and enhanced the city by paving its streets with cobblestones. He was named viceroy of Peru and departed from Acapulco.

LUIS DE VELASCO II (2ND TERM). *Position*: Viceroy; *Term*: July 2, 1607–June 19, 1611.

After spending a few years as viceroy in Peru, Luis de Velasco II returned to the viceroyalty of Mexico. He continued work on the Huehuetoca drainage system which was inaugurated in 1608. During his second term, he tried to follow the same path he had followed in the first, and devoted himself to improving the standard of life and working conditions of the Indians.

His wish to retire and die in Mexico was not fulfilled because the king promoted him to the presidency of the Council of Indies. He sailed from Veracruz on June 11, 1611, and died in Spain.

FRAY GARCÍA GUERRA (1545–1612). "Archbishop." *Place of birth*: Fromista, Palencia, Spain; *Place of death*: Mexico City; *Position*: Viceroy; *Term*: June 19, 1611–February 22, 1612.

García substituted for Luis de Velasco II when he was sent back to Spain. García was a Dominican friar who rose up through the hierarchy to become a bishop. His rule was short but fair. He tried to put an end to abuses committed against the indigenous people. He even returned ownership of their land to many Indians who, in his judgment, had been unjustly dispossessed.

His rule was disturbed by a violent earthquake, which caused heavy damage to many of the capital's buildings. Also, one day while boarding his carriage, he suffered an unfortunate accident from which a tumor developed on his forehead and led to his death. He was buried in the cathedral of Mexico City.

AUDIENCIA GOBERNADORA OF PEDRO OTÁLORA. *Position: Oidor; Term*: February 22, 1612–October 18, 1612.

DIEGO FERNÁNDEZ DE CÓRDOBA (1578–1630). "Marquis of Guadalcazar." *Place of birth*: Seville, Spain; *Place of death*: Guadalcazar, Cordoba, Spain; *Position*: Viceroy; *Term*: October 18, 1612–March 14, 1621.

Fernández de Córdoba continued the drainage system project. He also established the prosecutor's tribune. He built the San Diego fortress in Acapulco, and founded the city of Lerma, expelling the thieves that had been living there for some time. During his administration famine raged, droughts were severe, and many political and religious disputes erupted. Fernández de Córdoba also had to deal with a revolt of the Tepehuanes Indians.

THE FIFTH *AUDIENCIA* OF PAZ DE VALECILLO, JUAN GARCÍA GALDÓS Y GALDOCHE DE VALENCIA, AND GÓMEZ CORNEJO (MARCH–SEPTEMBER 1621 [SIX MONTHS]).

Paz de Valecillo—*Position*: President and Governor.

Juan García Galdós y Galdoche de Valencia—*Place of death*: Lima, Peru; *Position: Oidor*.

Gómez Cornejo—*Position: Oidor*.

DURING THE REIGN OF PHILIP IV OF SPAIN (1605–1665): 1621–1665

Philip the IV was born in Valladolid, Spain, in 1605. He was son of Philip III and Marguerite of Austria, and father-in-law of Louis XIV of France. He had an apathetic character, and left the tedious business of government to his favorite Gaspar de Guzmán, Duke of Olivares. His reign was rich in artistic and literary accomplishments. Politically, he faced serious problems, including a major revolt in Catalonia. During his reign, Spain lost part of the supremacy and influence it had once held in Europe.

In New Spain the viceroyalty was coming of age. The cathedral was finished, and new classes were inaugurated at the university. The work in the drainage system project continued, and government support for the arts grew more generous.

Philip IV was married twice—first to Isabelle of Bourbon and then to Maria Anna of Austria. He died in Madrid, Spain, in 1665. During his rule he appointed twelve viceroys to govern New Spain.

DIEGO CARRILLO DE MENDOZA Y PIMENTEL. "Marquis of Gelves." *Place of birth*: Reino de Aragón, Spain; *Position*: Viceroy; *Term*: September 12, 1621–January 15, 1624.

Carrillo de Mendoza was a stern believer in law and order and showed great determination in putting down banditry in cities and in the countryside. He followed legal proceedings against a number of influential and prominent citizens, on charges of having committed many abuses. By doing so he made many enemies, one of whom was the Archbishop Pérez de la Serna. The archbishop created such strife between them that the quarrel led to a riot. The viceroy was forced to seek asylum in the Convent of San Francisco, and he then departed for Spain.

AUDIENCIA GOBERNADORA **(OCTOBER 1, 1624).** Files regarding this government could not be found.

RODRIGO PACHECO Y OSORIO (?–1652). "Marquis of Cerralvo." *Place of death*: Madrid, Spain; *Position*: Viceroy; *Term*: October 3, 1624–November 16, 1635.

Pacheco arrived in Mexico at a time when there were a series of riots in the city. The king had instructed him to investigate the cause of the riots and punish those who provoked them. However, Pacheco became immediately involved in the combat against French and Dutch pirates who were assailing Spanish ships in the Gulf of Mexico. Piet Heyn, a famous Dutch pirate, was credited with the capture, in 1628, of an entire Spanish silver fleet worth 8 to 12 million pesos.

Meanwhile, in 1629, with the work in the drainage system abandoned, the valley and the city suffered the worst flood in their history. Many people in Mexico City and lake shore dwellers were drowned. The water rose up to six feet in some parts of the city, and did not recede completely for the next four years. It was only toward the end of his administration that the work on the drainage system was finished.

To contain the incursions of the marauding Indian tribes in the northern regions of New Spain, he ordered the construction of the Cerralvo fortress in the state of Nuevo León.

The Marquis of Cerralvo's honesty was seriously questioned in his time. It has been alleged that he got a percentage of every public work he ordered. That would explain why he returned to Spain immensely rich.

LOPE DÍEZ DE ARMENDÁRIZ. "Marquis of Cadereyta." *Place of birth*: Quito, Viceroyalty of Nuevo Toledo, Peru (today Ecuador); *Position*: Viceroy; *Term*: September 16, 1635–August 28, 1640.

Born in Quito in the viceroyalty of New Toledo where his father was the president of the *Real Audiencia*, Díez de Armendáriz was the first *criollo* who ruled in New Spain. He studied to be a navigator, and had a very distinguished career as a navy commander.

The Marquis of Cadereyta governed with moderation, watched over the prosperity of the colony, and steered the state's course with ease. When an earthquake destroyed part of the drainage system of Mexico City, he had it repaired. He founded the cities of Cadereyta and Querétaro. The former had been built originally as a presidio to contain the incursions of Apache and Comanche tribes.

Having finished his term as viceroy, he went back to his old career and organized the Barlovento fleet that patrolled the waters of the Gulf of Mexico, protecting Spanish ships and chasing pirates away. He was based in Veracruz.

DIEGO LÓPEZ PACHECO DE CABRERA Y BOBADILLA (1599–1653). "Marquis of Villena." *Place of birth*: In the Alcazar of Belmonte, La Mancha, Spain; *Place of death*: Pamplona, Spain; *Position*: Viceroy; *Term*: August 28, 1640–June 10, 1642.

López Pacheco was a member of an aristocratic family in Spain. He studied at the University of Salamanca, and later became an infantry colonel in the royal army. He was a congenial man who enjoyed social occasions, parties, and celebrations. He came to New Spain with the bishop of Puebla, Juan de Palafox, with whom he later had serious difficulties. His first concern as viceroy was to reinforce the Barlovento fleet. He ordered the construction of warships and the manufacturing of gun powder, cannons, and other weapons.

Meanwhile, in Mexico City he was the subject of a complicated palace intrigue that accused him of trying to separate New Spain from the Spanish Crown. The fact was that one member of his family led a revolt in Portugal seeking to separate it from Spain. This lent credence to the unjustified suspicion.

On June 9, 1642, Bishop Palafox surrounded the viceroy's palace with troops, removed Pacheco, and appointed himself as the next viceroy. Palafox also ordered the confiscation of Pacheco's property in New Spain.

Upon his return to Spain, Pacheco informed the king of his troubles, and the king offered to return him to his job in New Spain. The Marquis of Villena declined the offer, but accepted compensation for his confiscated wealth. He became governor of Sicily and later of the kingdom of Navarra. He died in Spain.

JUAN DE PALAFOX Y MENDOZA (1600–1659). "Bishop of Puebla." *Place of birth*: Fitero, Navarra; *Place of death*: Burgo de Osma, Soria; *Position*: Viceroy; *Term*: June 10, 1642–November 23, 1642.

Palafox studied jurisprudence in Salamanca, Spain, and was prosecutor of the Council of War and of the Supreme Council of Indies. Later, he studied for the priesthood and became a bishop. He was an upright man with a conflictive, aggressive personality. He arrived in New Spain as Judge of Residence, and ousted Viceroy Diego López Pacheco from the government in a very dubious move (see Diego López Pacheco de Cabrera y Bobadilla).

Once viceroy, Palafox devoted most of his tenure to helping the church. He ordered the acceleration of the construction of Mexico's cathedral, and built several convents and houses for clerics.

He also began the construction of a new cathedral in Puebla and founded in the same city a remarkable library named after him.

GARCÍA SARMIENTO DE SOTOMAYOR (?–1659). "Count of Salvatierra." *Place of death*: Lima, Peru; *Position*: Viceroy; *Term*: November 23, 1642–May 14, 1648.

Viceroy García Sarmiento was a good administrator who proved to be a practical man able to restore the power equilibrium between church and state that had tilted so much in favor of the church during the previous administration.

During his tenure, Mexico City suffered more floods, and Sarmiento had to order new work in the drainage system. He also ordered the reconstruction of the aqueducts that supplied fresh water to the city.

When his term ended he was sent to Peru as viceroy, and remained there until his death.

MARCOS DE TORRES Y RUEDA (1588–1649). "Bishop of Yucatan." *Place of birth*: Almazán, Soria; *Place of death*: New Spain; *Position*: Viceroy; *Term*: May 13, 1648–April 22, 1649.

Torres was the first viceroy who refused the title of viceroy and asked to be addressed as governor. During his term, the Inquisition executed 12 people and punished another 107 in an *Auto de Fe* (Act of Faith). The viceroy, who had governed for barely a year, was so sick that he was not able to witness the *Auto de Fe*. He died a short while later.

After his death all his property was sequestered by the authorities who were suspicious of illicit business done through his secretary, Juan de Salazar, who was married to the viceroy's niece, Petronila Rueda. Salazar was jailed. Much later, Torres's honor was cleared, and Salazar was freed.

THE SIXTH *AUDIENCIA* OF MATÍAS DE PERALTA (APRIL 22, 1649– JUNE 28, 1650).

Matías de Peralta—*Position*: President. Peralta began his term following Bishop Torres Rueda's death. He was the one responsible for sequestering the latter's possessions, and sentenced his family to incarceration. He was in power for a short period of time until superseded by the next viceroy.

LUIS ENRÍQUEZ DE GUZMÁN. "Marquis of Villaflor." *Position*: Viceroy; *Term*: June 28, 1650–August 15, 1653.

As a mining expert, Enríquez de Guzmán promoted the industry, which enjoyed great prosperity during his tenure. His financial ability allowed him to improve the collection of taxes, custom duties, and sales taxes. The money was sent to the Spanish crown.

During his term, a rebellion by the Tarahumara Indians was promptly suffocated and the leader of the Indians was hanged.

He was appointed viceroy of Peru in 1653.

FRANCISCO FERNÁNDEZ DE LA CUEVA (1619–1676). "Duke of Albuquerque." *Place of birth*: Barcelona, Spain; *Place of death*: Madrid, Spain; *Position*: Viceroy; *Term*: August 15, 1653–September 16, 1660.

Fernández de la Cueva was a distinguished military officer and an aristocrat. He was a patron of poets, painters, and sculptors.

He ordered the colonization of the northern regions, sending approximately 100 Spanish families to found Albuquerque in the territory of New Mexico. He also sent arms and ammunition to Jamaica, which had fallen into English hands. Concerned with security, he reinforced the Barlovento Fleet that had been created to protect the Spanish ships from pirates.

He was very active in trade matters, ordered the minting of gold coins, and followed the steps of his predecessor in improving tax collection.

He was a profoundly religious and generous man, and one day as he was praying inside the cathedral, he was involved in an ugly incident. A soldier of his guard attacked him. The soldier was summarily tried, judged insane, sentenced, and executed the following day. This type of swift—but not always fair—justice was a sign of the times.

After his tenure in New Spain he was named ambassador to Vienna and later on returned to die in Madrid, Spain.

JUAN DE LEYVA Y DE LA CERDA (1604–1678). "Count of Baños." *Place of birth*: Alcalá de Henares, Spain; *Place of death*: Monastery of San Peter Pastrana, Guadalajara, Spain; *Position*: Viceroy; *Term*: September 16, 1660–June 29, 1664.

Leyva was a nobleman and soldier. He fought Algerian pirates in the Mediterranean and rebel Catalonians in Tarragona before being named viceroy.

He was a devout man, but he was also arrogant, edgy, and greedy. Upon his family's arrival in Mexico, his son Pedro had an argument with a servant of the count of Santiago and killed him on the spot. Upset, the count demanded an explanation from Pedro who, unrepentant, responded by hiring assassins to kill the count. The attempted assassination did not succeed, and it tainted the record of his father the viceroy.

These were not the only difficulties of the viceroy. Leyva seized land, goods, and money of other people, transferring land titles to his family and friends. His abusive rule led to several Indian uprisings. The viceroy's response in some cases, as in Tehuantepec, was brutal repression.

There were so many complaints against Leyva that the crown finally dismissed him and named Bishop Diego Osorio de Escobar as viceroy. Leyva, however, intercepted the communiqué and remained in power a bit longer. When the bishop eventually learned of his appointment, Leyva sneaked out of the capital.

Back in Spain, Leyva was severely reprimanded by the king and was forbidden to hold a public post ever again. Toward the end of his life, Leyva joined the Carmelite order and died in one of their convents.

DIEGO OSORIO DE ESCOBAR Y LLAMAS (?–1673). "Bishop of Puebla." *Place of birth*: La Coruña, Spain; *Place of death*: Puebla, Mexico; *Position*: Viceroy; *Term*: June 29, 1664–October 15, 1664.

Osorio was a religious man with no interest in public office. He became a reluctant viceroy only after his predecessor was deposed. His term was extremely short. He basically tried to redress the problems created by the preceding administration. He encouraged a faster pace in the construction of the cathedral in Puebla, and procured funds to build other churches. He sent all the money he could scrape up to Spain, and he fortified Cuba to help keep the pirates away. He also ordered the fortification of the port of Campeche to protect it against pirates and supplied money and weapons to strengthen the Barlovento Fleet. He resigned his post on October 15 and retired in Puebla.

ANTONIO SEBASTIÁN DE TOLEDO MOLINA Y SALAZAR. "Marquis of Mancera." *Position*: Viceroy; *Term*: October 15, 1664–November 20, 1673.

Toledo Molina had prior knowledge of life in New Spain because he had lived in Peru while his father was viceroy there in 1639. He was a protégé of King Philip IV. He governed during a time of economic difficulties, and his rule was very austere. He used the little money available to expand the defenses of the Caribbean islands, which were being harried and looted by pirates.

But there were also many problems in the land. The indigenous peoples fled to the hills to escape their *encomenderos*, and the *mestizos* preferred highway robbery and banditry to working like serfs.

In bad health, overwhelmed by severe economic problems and petty arguments with the *audiencia*, Toledo asked the crown to relieve him of his duties. It took several years before the petition was granted. His return to Spain was painful as his wife died during the trip. Back in Spain, he was hired as majordomo for the Queen of Spain and was appointed ambassador to Venice and Germany.

DURING THE REIGN OF CHARLES II OF SPAIN (1661–1700): 1665–1675 UNDER THE REGENCY OF HIS MOTHER, MARIANE OF AUSTRIA; 1675–1700 BY HIMSELF

Charles II was born in Madrid, Spain, in 1661. He was the son of Philip IV and Maria Anna of Austria. He was a very weak and sickly child.

During his tenure, Spanish America was constantly attacked by pirates and corsairs. Spain's response was limited. The spirit of the conquest had diminished considerably, and to make things worse, famines and riots plagued the colonies. During one of these disturbances, the palace of the viceroys in Mexico City was burned to the ground. The discovery of gold and pearls in Baja California (Mexico) led Charles II to order new expeditions to colonize it and California.

Charles II married twice—to Marie Louise d'Orléans and to Marie Anne of Neuburg. During his rule he appointed seven viceroys to govern New Spain. He died in Madrid in 1700, and as he had no children to inherit the Spanish throne, his reign marked the end of the Hapsburg dynasty in Spain. The Bourbon dynasty began when Louis XIV of France placed his grandson Philip of Anjou as king of Spain.

PEDRO NUÑO COLÓN DE PORTUGAL Y CASTRO (?–1673). "Duke of the Veragua." *Place of death*: New Spain; *Position*: Viceroy; *Term*: November 20, 1673–December 13, 1673.

Viceroy Colón was a descendant of Christopher Columbus, and his reputation was that of a kind and prudent man. His health, however, was in a precarious state, and his tenure lasted for a very short time.

Aware of the insufficiencies in the indigenous diet and determined to improve it, he issued an important decree lowering the price of grain. His term of less than one month was the shortest viceregal period in New Spain's history.

FRAY PAYO ENRÍQUEZ DE RIVERA (?–1684). *Place of birth*: Seville, Spain; *Place of death*: Convent of the Risco, Avila, Spain; *Position*: Viceroy; *Term*: December 13, 1673–November 7, 1680.

Friar Enríquez, of the Augustinian Order, was a graduate of the University of Osma. As the bishop of Guatemala, he was selected to become the bishop of Michoacán, and later became archbishop of the capital of New Spain.

He was honest and humane, as well as a capable and hardworking politician. He is remembered for his virtuous measures, which helped protect the indigenous people. He also fought to eliminate clerical abuse of the indigenous people.

Friar Enríquez was also known for his interest in developing Mexico City's infrastructure, ordering, for example, the reconstruction of the *calzada* of Guadalupe, the installation of a drainage system in the village of Guadalupe, and rebuilding the convent of Saint Augustine, which had burned down.

TOMÁS ANTONIO DE LA CERDA Y ARAGÓN (1638–1692). "Marquis of the Laguna." *Place of birth*: Cogolludo, Guadalajara, Spain; *Place of death*: Madrid, Spain; *Position*: Viceroy; *Term*: November 7, 1680–June 16, 1686.

De la Cerda was born into an illustrious noble family. He was considered an intellectual, and he and his wife became protectors, admirers, and faithful friends of Sor Juana Inés de la Cruz, Mexico's greatest poet, hailed in Mexico as "the tenth muse."

At the beginning of his term there was a serious uprising in New Mexico, the Popé Revolt, and many Spanish subjects, soldiers, and missionaries were killed by the natives. Those who survived were forced to flee New Mexico. De la Cerda sent troops to pacify the region and pursue the Indians, along with a new wave of colonizers to repopulate New Mexico.

Another disaster De la Cerda had to endure in his term was the looting and destruction of the port of Veracruz by a pirate known as "Lorencillo." The viceroy himself traveled to Veracruz and ordered an investigation of the circumstances that led to the looting. The governor was found guilty of negligence and sentenced to death, but he appealed the sentence and was sent back to Spain instead.

Three years later, De la Cerda returned to Spain where he became a member of the Council of Indies and a majordomo for the queen.

MELCHOR PORTOCARRERO LASSO DE LA VEGA (1636–1705). "Count of Monclova." *Place of birth*: Madrid, Spain; *Place of death*: Lima, Peru; *Position*: Viceroy; *Term*: June 16, 1686–November 20, 1688.

Portocarrero was a stalwart soldier. It was said that he had lost an arm in battle and wore a silver replacement. This peculiarity won him the nickname "Silver Arm."

Believing reports that there were French pirates in the Gulf of Mexico, he sent expeditions to look for them. The French were never found, but the remnants of two ships were located in the Bay of San Bernardo, in Texas. In the meantime, the Spanish soldiers did capture three English pirates who had found refuge in the Laguna de Términos, near Veracruz.

Always concerned about French pirates landing in New Spain, Portocarrero ordered the construction of several garrisons, called *presidios*, in the northern provinces. The first one was established in a place that was named Monclova in his honor (he was the count of Monclova). Some 150 families were sent to live there.

He expelled all unlicensed foreign priests from New Spain. With his own money he financed the piping of potable water from Chapultepec hill to a fountain in downtown Mexico City called *Salto del Agua*. He also accelerated urgent projects, such as the drainage of the valley.

Appointed viceroy in Peru, he had to wait for one year for the boat that would take him to his new post.

GASPAR DE LA CERDA SANDOVAL SILVA Y MENDOZA (1653–1697). "Count of Galve." *Place of death*: Port of Santa María de Cadiz, Spain; *Position*: Viceroy; *Term*: November 20, 1688–February 27, 1696.

De la Cerda was one of the youngest viceroys to rule in New Spain. He was thirty-five years old when he arrived in Mexico. He was hindered by much internal turmoil, which required military response. He had to battle the French, who came from the north, and the British, who came from the south. To this end, he order the construction of a fleet of Spanish ships that were sent to defend the Caribbean seas and the Gulf of Mexico. The port of Veracruz was eventually fortified as well.

He also had to deal with the riots of 1690 and 1691 in which desperate farmers who had lost their harvests in a series of droughts in Mexico burned many buildings, including the Viceroy's palace and the city hall. When De la Cerda discovered who the organizers of these riots were, he sent them straight to the public plaza and had them hanged without trial.

He sent Mexican troops to fight in La Hispanola where they defeated a French garrison. This marked the first time that troops from New Spain were sent to fight abroad.

Through peaceful means, he was able to recover the territory of New Mexico. He began construction of the *Seminario Conciliar* and the Guadalupe Sanctuary. He was also the first viceroy to order Spanish language classes for the indigenous people. These classes proved to be a major success.

JUAN DE ORTEGA MONTAÑÉS (1ST TERM) (1627–1708). *Place of birth*: Siles, Murcia, Spain; *Position*: Viceroy; *Term*: February 27, 1696–December 18, 1696.

Before being named viceroy, Ortega Montañés served as the bishop of Michoacán, archbishop of Mexico, member of the Inquisition, and bishop of Guatemala. He was known as a strong man who held no sympathy for deviant or lazy people. He built several convents, inaugurated the cathedral of Guatemala City, and pushed for the completion of Morelia's cathedral. His rule lasted less than one year.

JOSÉ SARMIENTO VALLADARES (1643–1708). "Count of Moctezuma and Tula." *Place of birth*: San Roman de Sajamonde, Pontevedra, Spain; *Place of death*: Madrid, Spain; *Wife*: María Andrea Moctezuma Jofre de Loaiza (Third Countess of Moctezuma); *Position*: Viceroy; *Term*: December 18, 1696–November 4, 1701.

Valladares was the husband of Moctezuma II's great-great-great-granddaughter, María Andrea Moctezuma. This viceroy was the first *mestizo* to govern New Spain. He was a very efficient viceroy whose main interest was to improve the living conditions in the country, especially in the capital, which was in a ruinous state due to fires, riots, and floods.

Under his rule churches, palaces, and buildings in Mexico City were luxuriously remodeled following the baroque style. He assisted the people, giving away grain in times of scarcity. He was also responsible for sending the Jesuit Juan María Salvatierra on an expedition that founded several missions in Baja California.

His marriage to the great-great-great-granddaughter of Moctezuma II allowed the Moctezuma family to regain prestige in New Spain approximately two centuries after the Aztec Emperor's death.

When Valladares and his wife returned to Spain, they were greeted by the king of Spain with great accolades and honors.

THE BOURBON DYNASTY: During the Reign of Philip V of Spain (1683–1746): 1700–1746 (Philip V abdicated in favor of his son Louis I in 1724, but when Louis died of smallpox a few months later, Philip resumed the crown)

Philip of Anjou, or Philip V of Spain, was the son of the dauphin Louis and Marie Anne of Bavaria and the grandson of Louis XIV of France. He was born in Versailles, France, in 1683. When Charles II of Spain died without heirs, he left Philip all his possessions, which included Spain, New Spain, the Spanish part of the Netherlands, and some parts of Italy. On the other hand, Louis XIV not only accepted the will but kept firm on his refusal to exclude Philip from the line of succession to the French throne, thus provoking the Spanish Succession War.

Philip was the founder of the Bourbon dynasty in Spain, and during his rule French ideas and customs gained ascendancy. He was married twice, to Marie Louise of Savoy and to the Princess Isabelle of Parma.

Philip V suffered from a mental illness and his wife, Isabelle, had to take charge of the government. To handle the administration of the kingdom she leaned on her minister, José Patiño. However, the combination did not prove effective, and Spain was severely impoverished during their administration.

In America, meanwhile, the situation with the pirates worsened, forcing the government of New Spain to turn the coastal cities into fortresses to defend themselves. French ideas and customs that had made their way to Spain were also brought to New Spain, thus greatly broadening the country's culture.

Philip V instituted the *Real Cofradía de Guadalupe* in Madrid, the city where he died in 1746. During his rule, eight viceroys were sent to New Spain.

JUAN DE ORTEGA MONTAÑÉS (2ND TERM). "Archbishop." *Position*: Viceroy; *Term*: November 4, 1701–November 27, 1702.

Arriving for his second term, Ortega Montañés faced the serious problem of the abuse of black slaves that had been brought to New Spain as a source of cheap labor. The viceroy, who was a kind man, sided with the Indians, *mestizos*, and blacks, who lived in terrible conditions, and he issued decrees to protect them.

He was also a firm man who did not hesitate to act swiftly against a group of students who were holding a demonstration against the monarchy and threatened to burn the pillory located in the city's main square.

He was so impatient with idleness that he would prosecute and jail those who were caught doing nothing. He was also very religious, and instructed the Jesuit order to proceed with the evangelization of Baja California.

He turned his office over to his successor in 1702 and retired in Michoacán. He died a few years later and is buried in the cathedral of Mexico City.

FRANCISCO FERNÁNDEZ DE LA CUEVA ENRÍQUEZ (?–1733). "Duke of Albuquerque." *Place of birth*: Geneva, Italy; *Place of death*: Madrid, Spain; *Position*: Viceroy; *Term*: November 27, 1702–November 13, 1710.

Fernández was a blood relative of the first Duke of Albuquerque. He governed for a long period, but did nothing remarkable. He was a vain man and warmly supported the introduction of French styles and manners into his court and army. Furthermore, he seems to have been implicated in a scheme to traffic with black slaves. He was a big supporter of the Bourbon House, and assisted them monetarily in the war of the Spanish Succession. He demanded from the secular clergy a tax based on 10 percent of their income. The measure created an enormous conflict between the archbishop and the civil authorities.

The cruelty used during his tenure to repress a Pima Indian rebellion in

Nueva Vizcaya created a long-lasting mistrust in the Indians that delayed their conversion to the Catholic faith. Before his return to Spain, he dedicated himself to the construction of the Shrine of Guadalupe.

FERNANDO DE ALENCASTRE NOROÑA Y SILVA (1641?–1717).
"Duke of Linares." *Place of death*: New Spain; *Position*: Viceroy; *Term*: November 13, 1710–July 16, 1716.

De Alencastre was one of the most powerful men in Spain and France. In New Spain he gained even greater stature because of his intelligence and warm human qualities. Upon his arrival, he experienced the famous thirty-minute earthquake in 1711, which devastated the city and caused much suffering. It has been written that he used his own money to repair buildings and to assist victims of the quake.

He prohibited the distilling of rum in the city in an effort to prevent further debasement of the poor. He also put a check on the unbounded ambitions of the regular clergy.

Of the many public works inaugurated during his term, the first public library and the first zoo and botanical gardens in New Spain stand out. He also engaged in the construction of the aqueduct of Arcos de Belén, which brought water from Chapultepec, and reconstructed the Viceregal palace.

Outside Mexico City, he founded the city of Linares in Nuevo León and, concerned with piracy in the Gulf of Mexico, ordered the construction of four light ships to reinforce the Barlovento Fleet. At the same time, the watch over the Laguna de Términos was reinforced.

During De Alencastre's rule, an unexpectedly long and cold winter ruined much of the harvest. This brought famine and starvation, and urgent measures were necessary. During these years the population diminished considerably. The viceroy acted by lowering the price of imported seed to make it more accessible.

He created the so-called *Acordada*, a tribunal with a police force devoted to bringing law and order in cities and on roads. But perhaps his greatest achievement as viceroy was the commissioning of a study on the social condition of the country called *"Instrucción."* This manual served as an accurate introduction to the country for the succeeding viceroys.

In spite of all the natural and human disasters that his administration experienced, he governed wisely and was considered a good ruler and a benefactor of the poor.

BALTASAR DE ZÚÑIGA GUZMÁN SOTOMAYOR Y MENDOZA (1658–1727). "Marquis of Valero." *Place of death*: Madrid, Spain; *Position*: Viceroy; *Term*: July 16, 1716–October 15, 1722.

De Zúñiga was the first unmarried viceroy to govern New Spain. He had served in the Council of Indies and was viceroy in Navarra and Sardinia. He sent an expedition bringing food and supplies to colonists in Texas, who were threatening to abandon their settlements due to an imminent famine. Once there, the Spanish expedition members taught the colonists how to better cultivate the land and raise cattle, while the soldiers expelled the French settlers who had established themselves in parts of Texas and Coahuila. At the same time, another regiment of Spanish soldiers were expelling English pirates from the Laguna de Términos in the state of Veracruz.

Also during de Zúñiga's rule, he made peace with the Indian leaders in Florida, bringing them to Mexico City and giving them such an splendid reception that they swore unconditional allegiance to the Spanish crown. He also incorporated the present day state of Nayarit into New Spain.

During De Zúñiga's tenure, the crown decreed the tobacco industry to be a monopoly administered by the state. This became a very profitable business for the crown.

He was considered an excellent governor and a patriot who deeply loved New Spain. He returned to Spain to serve as majordomo in the court in Madrid.

JUAN DE ACUÑA (1658–1734). "Marquis of Casafuerte." *Place of birth*: Lima, Peru; *Place of death*: New Spain; *Position*: Viceroy; *Term*: October 15, 1722–March 17, 1734.

Acuña was born in Lima, Peru. He joined the armed forces and was the military commander in Aragón and Majorca when he was appointed viceroy of New Spain. He had governed in Sicily and had been Captain General of Armies in His Majesty's War Council.

Under his rule, New Spain progressed greatly. He improved the prison systems in many provinces. Acuña took a personal interest in the development of the Pachuca silver mines and ordered that all silversmiths be located on the street of San Francisco, in Mexico City. Soon the name was changed to Plateros (Silversmiths) and now is called Madero.

He sent several galleons loaded with more than 11 million silver pieces back to Spain, but managed to keep enough at home. His well-armed galleons always arrived safely at Cadiz. He authorized the first minting of round coins, and the work done at the mint in Mexico set the example for the rest of the continent.

He built the first customs house in New Spain and the first cannon factory in Orizaba. *La Gaceta de México*, the first Mexican newspaper, was also published during his tenure.

Acuña improved the ports of New Spain and gave special attention to the port of Veracruz. He is remembered for fighting stubbornly against British intruders. He asked the pope for permission and was granted a bull to build the Collegiate Church of Our Lady of Guadalupe.

He was respected and beloved by all, and he ruled until his dying day.

His body was buried in the Convent of the Recolectos Franciscans in the barrio of San Cosme in Mexico City.

JUAN ANTONIO DE VIZARRÓN Y EGUIARRETA (?–1747). "Archbishop." *Place of birth*: Port of Santa María de Cadiz, Spain; *Place of death*: New Spain; *Position*: Viceroy; *Term*: March 17, 1734–August 17, 1740.

During De Vizarrón's tenure, a terrible epidemic called "the great *matlazahuatl*" struck New Spain. Close to 40,000 people died in Mexico City, and around 200,000 died in all of New Spain. To cope with the emergency he established hospitals and declared the Virgin of Guadalupe the patron of the city and of New Spain.

He launched a very successful law and order campaign to capture bandits. He was very active in the reconstruction of the Episcopal Palace and other buildings in Mexico, and provided a generous sum for the reconstruction of the Royal Palace in Madrid, which had been burnt in 1734. He also sent vast amounts of silver to Spain to help with its war against the British.

He was considered an effective viceroy and is buried in the cathedral of Mexico City.

PEDRO DE CASTRO FIGUEROA Y SALAZAR (?–1741). "Duke of la Conquista." *Place of birth*: San Julián de Cela, Coruña, Spain; *Place of death*: New Spain; *Position*: Viceroy; *Term*: August 17, 1740–August 22, 1741.

De Castro arrived in New Spain not only accompanied by many noble titles, but also pursued by English ships. While in government, he sent many shipments of coined silver to some provinces, particularly to Havana, where warships were being built to fight against the British in the Caribbean. He reinforced the country's defense forces, especially in Veracruz and San Juan de Ulúa. He is buried in the Altar of Kings in the cathedral of Mexico City.

THE SEVENTH *AUDIENCIA* OF PEDRO MALO DE VILLAVICENCIO (AUGUST 1741–NOVEMBER 2, 1742). Pedro Malo de Villavicencio— *Position*: President. In 1742 there was an extensive fire in the capital of New Spain that caused widespread damage to the city.

PEDRO CEBRIÁN Y AGUSTÍN (1687–1752). "Count of Fuenclara." *Place of birth*: Luceni, Zaragoza, Spain; *Place of death*: Madrid, Spain; *Position*: Viceroy; *Term*: November 3, 1742–July 9, 1746.

Like his predecessor, Cebrián brought with him a trunk full of titles. Even before he arrived in Mexico City, he heard of an Italian named Lorenzo Boturini who was collecting funds to make a gold crown for the Virgin of Guadalupe.

For unknown reasons, Cebrián did not like Boturini and his project. After a brief investigation, Boturini was first imprisoned and later exiled to Spain. All the maps, plans, documents, codexes, and objects Boturini had collected in an Indian museum were confiscated and destroyed with the sole exception of the "Strip of the Wanderings of the Aztec People."

Cebrián's stubbornness and animosity toward Boturini cost Mexico the loss of this promising museum, which today would have been a valuable resource for all America.

Many great works, including the work containing accounts of the apparition of the Virgin of Guadalupe, were sent to Spain and lost to pirates attacks.

In 1743 Cebrián decided to send a treasure to Spain via the Philippines in a ship called *Nuestra Señora de Covadonga*, which belonged to the fleet of the Nao of China. The ship was captured by English pirates, and the cargo, estimated at more than one and a half million pesos, was lost.

The ambition of the viceroy had no limits. He placed heavy bets on cock fights and sold some of his titles. Ironically, he also became involved in a campaign to strengthen moral values, and ordered the paving of several streets in Mexico City.

A few years later the viceroy fell sick and asked to be relieved from the post. His petition was granted, and he returned to die in Spain.

DURING THE REIGN OF FERDINAND VI OF SPAIN (1713–1759): 1746–1759

Ferdinand was born in Madrid in 1713. He was the son of Philip V and Marie Louise Gabriella of Savoy. During his father's reign, he never got involved in politics because his relationship with his stepmother, Isabelle of Parma, was bad. She had always wanted him out of the picture because she wanted her own children to inherit the throne and acquire the wealth of Spain.

His reign lasted thirteen years, but with him Spain underwent a rebirth. During his reign, Spain enjoyed prestige, tranquility, and abundance. He married Barbara of Braganza, but when his wife died, Ferdinand VI lost his mind and died shortly thereafter in Villaviciosa de Odón on August 10, 1759. It is interesting to note that his father, Philip V, died of the same type of madness.

During his rule he appointed two viceroys to govern New Spain.

FRANCISCO DE GÜEMES Y HORCASITAS (1682–1768). "First Count of Revillagigedo." *Place of birth*: Reinosa, Santander, Spain; *Place of death*: Madrid, Spain; *Position*: Viceroy; *Term*: July 9, 1746–September 9, 1755. Güemes had a distinguished career in the military, and his record indicates he was a courageous, intelligent, and skillful administrator. During his term as viceroy, he displayed these qualities and many more.

His knowledge in mining brought badly needed revenue to the national treasury and some prosperity to the nation. Trade was promoted, and general commercial activity in the country grew notably. He founded eleven new towns and a colony named New Santander in what is now Tamaulipas, a northeastern border state adjacent to the United States.

With the organizing vision of a man of state, he ordered the separation of civil and religious documents. Up until this time, the church handled all documents that pertained to civil and religious life. This separation led to Mexico's General Archives.

His tenure was very favorably rated by the crown, even though there were some unproved accusations of corruption against him.

In 1755 he returned to the Spanish Court and was appointed secretary of war.

AGUSTÍN AHUMADA Y VILLALÓN (?–1760). "Marquis of Amarillas."

Place of death: Cuernavaca, Mexico; *Position*: Viceroy; *Term*: November 10, 1755–February 5, 1760.

Ahumada was a hard worker and an extremely honest leader. He confronted the powerful clergy in Puebla, who had the authorization to grant permissions to manufacture alcoholic beverages like *aguardiente*, or to manage casinos.

Ahumada forced them to systematize the process by which they were granting these concessions, making sure that those who received them were respected citizens. He completed the valley's drainage system, continued the development of the mining industry, and sent troops to combat the Comanches in Texas.

In 1759, a volcano erupted in the state of Michoacán on the *hacienda* San Miguel Jorullo, and many nearby townships had to be evacuated. He aided the victims of this natural catastrophe and directed the process of their relocation in other towns. He died a very poor man. Ahumada is buried in the church of La Piedad in Mexico City. He was considered a successful ruler of New Spain.

THE EIGHTH *AUDIENCIA* OF FRANCISCO ANTONIO DE ECHAVARRI (FEBRUARY 5, 1760–APRIL 28, 1760).

Francisco Antonio de Echavarri—*Position*: President.

DURING THE REIGN OF CHARLES III OF SPAIN (1716–1788): 1759–1788

Charles of Bourbon was the son of Philip V of Spain and Queen Isabelle of Parma. He was born in Madrid in 1716. Charles III was married to

María Amalia of Sajonia. He was duke of Parma and king of Naples. When his half brother Ferdinand VI died, Charles III was named king of Spain. He handed the throne of Naples to his third child, Ferdinand.

The top priority of his reign was to regain the economic and political power Spain had once had. His style of governing was absolutist, and many people thought him to be a tyrant. When he believed the Jesuit order presented a potential threat to his rule, he expelled the order from Spain and all her colonies.

Among Charles III's best qualities was his ability to choose collaborators wisely. He excelled in naming very intelligent, wise, and valuable men for important posts. Trade, agriculture, and the arts flourished during his rule, and Spain was considerably more prosperous than before. His foreign policy, however, was not very fortunate. A war with the British ended with Spain losing Florida. Just as disastrous was the loss of Spain's naval power during his rule. He refused to recognize the independence of the new United States of America. He appointed nine viceroys to govern New Spain.

FRANCISCO CAJIGAL DE LA VEGA. "Knight of the Order of Santiago." *Position*: Viceroy; *Term*: April 25, 1760–October 5, 1760.

Cajigal ruled New Spain for just a few months in 1760, during which time he devoted his energy to raising funds for the treasury. He also increased the size of the army and named his son a commander of a platoon. There were charges of dishonesty leveled against him, but they did not have any effect on his career. After his service as viceroy in New Spain he became governor of Cuba.

JOAQUÍN DE MONSERRAT (1700–1771). "Marquis of Cruillas." *Place of birth*: Valencia, Spain; *Place of death*: Valencia, Spain; *Position:* Viceroy; *Term*: October 5, 1760–August 24, 1766.

Monserrat's grand plan to organize a very large army was never fulfilled. In 1761 there was a severe smallpox epidemic that killed more than 15,000 people in Mexico City and 80,000 in Puebla. This disaster drained the treasury, and Monserrat was forced to take emergency measures to avoid speculation in basic staples and food. He also had to cope with a rebellion by the Pima Indians in New Mexico, who charged mistreatment by the Spanish colonists. There was a flood in Guanajuato, which affected the mines, forced the miners to stop production, and brought about a new epidemic. As a result of a treaty with the British, Spain lost Pensacola in Florida and Belize in the Mayan territory.

In spite of all these calamities, Monserrat was finally able to put together his army, which became the first formal Mexican army with well organized infantry and cavalry regiments. He ordered further fortification of San Juan de Ulúa in Veracruz. The marquis had some problems with José de Gálvez, who had been sent as *visitador*, so he quit his job, and returned to Spain.

CARLOS FRANCISCO DE CROIX (1730–?). "Marquis of Croix." *Place of birth*: Lille, France; *Place of death*: Valencia, Spain; *Position*: Viceroy; *Term*: August 24, 1766–September 22, 1771.

De Croix was a man of arms. He had a reputation as an honest man, and he refused the gifts and presents brought to him by courtiers and religious orders. He also prohibited the ostentatious festivals that had become a part of New Spain's tradition.

During his rule, the king of Spain ordered the expulsion of the Jesuits from New Spain. The Jesuits refused to leave, and the way he carried out the royal orders made him famous. He told the Jesuits they were born to shut up and obey, not to argue or have opinions regarding complicated issues of government. Then he sent in the troops to remove them.

His quarrel with the Catholic church continued when he expropriated land belonging to the Holy Inquisition, and prohibited the church from staging public burnings. With the expropriated land, he enlarged and beautified the Alameda park in Mexico City. When he retired to Spain, he was awarded a prestigious position in the court.

ANTONIO MARÍA DE BUCARELI Y URSÚA (1717–1779). "Father of the People." *Place of birth*: Seville, Spain; *Place of death*: Mexico City; *Position*: Viceroy; *Term*: September 22, 1771–April 9, 1779.

A member of a noble family, Bucareli earned well deserved fame as a military officer in the field. He was first sent to Cuba to organize militias and build the *Príncipe* and *El Morro* fortresses to protect Havana.

He was appointed viceroy of New Spain while still in Cuba. He protected the indigenous, *mestizo*, and mulatto people of New Spain. He founded the Hospice of the Poor People, the *Casa de Cuna* (a place for foundlings), and the famed *Montepío* (the government pawnshop).

He ordered the customs house repaired and the forts of San Juan Ulúa, in Veracruz, and San Diego, in Acapulco, refurbished. He obtained a loan of 2 million pesos from city merchants in an attempt to increase the amount of money in circulation to stimulate the economy. His great administrative skills allowed him to repay every penny of the loan.

He refined the coin minting process. To handle disputes between miners he founded the Mining Tribunal, which was a great success. He allowed the miners the right to form an association, similar to that of the merchants, which gave them enough flexibility to handle their business and defend their interests. The famous Baron Alexander von Humboldt, who visited New Spain in 1803, wrote in his *Political Essay On The Kingdom Of New Spain* that the workers in the Mexican mining industry were the best paid miners in the world.

Bucareli ordered construction of the beautiful Bucareli promenade in Mexico City, and he eradicated the locust problem that had been plaguing

New Spain. On the battlefield, he sent troops to fight the Apaches, Seris, and Pimas on the northern frontier.

By popular acclaim, the *audiencia* declared Bucareli the "Father of the People," and Charles III of Spain showered him with honors and generously raised his stipend. He died of a pulmonary infection in Mexico City and was buried with great pomp.

THE NINTH *AUDIENCIA* OF FRANCISCO ROMA Y ROSSELL (APRIL 1779–AUGUST 1779).

Francisco Roma y Rossell—*Position*: First Mayor. Roma is famous for opening the sealed envelope, or Shroud Letter, which contained the name of the future viceroy and president of the Province of Guatemala.

MARTÍN DE MAYORGA. "Knight of the Order of Alcántara." *Place of birth*: Barcelona, Spain; *Place of death*: On the high seas; *Position*: Viceroy; *Term*: August 23, 1779–April 28, 1783.

Mayorga continued Bucareli's work and founded the Academy of Fine Arts. He brought valuable works of art from Spain—paintings and sculptures—as well as professors of literature and music to promote culture and the arts in New Spain. He fought tirelessly against a chicken pox epidemic that swept across the land. He departed for Spain and died aboard the ship near the port of Cadiz.

MATÍAS DE GÁLVEZ Y GALLARDO (1717–1784). *Place of birth*: Macharaviaya, Málaga, Spain; *Place of death*: Mexico City; *Position*: Viceroy; *Term*: April 28, 1783–October 20, 1784.

Born to a farm family, Gálvez became a man of letters. He was the brother of the *visitador*, José Gálvez, and the father of the viceroy, Count Bernardo of Gálvez. He was the last viceroy to enter Mexico City on horseback.

During his rule, he ordered that Mexico City be divided into quarters and repaved with cobblestones. He also brought many works of art from Spain to New Spain. He founded the San Carlos Bank and renewed publication of the first newspaper, *La Gaceta*.

Carriages became very popular in New Spain at this time, and according to a census taken by Gálvez' government, the number of carriages in New Spain totaled 637.

He died while in office and was buried at the convent of San Fernando.

THE TENTH *AUDIENCIA* OF VICENTE HERRERA (OCTOBER 20, 1784–JUNE 17, 1785). **Vicente Herrera**—*Position*: President. In a move to strengthen the judiciary power, he gave the *Acordada* (rural police) jurisdiction over the Marquisate of the Valley of Oaxaca.

BERNARDO DE GÁLVEZ (1746?–1786). "Count of Gálvez." *Place of birth*: Macharaviaya, Málaga, Spain; *Place of death*: Tacubaya, Mexico; *Position*: Viceroy; *Term*: June 17, 1785–November 30, 1786.

Gálvez was a much loved and admired viceroy. He was the son of the previous viceroy and the nephew of *visitador* José de Gálvez. Living in New Spain as a young officer, he participated in several forays against the Apache tribes. Back in Spain, he was sent to Algiers, where he was severely wounded in battle.

He was named military governor of Louisiana when it was under Spanish dominion. Then, back in Spain, he was sent to fight in Holland, and later on went to Cuba as captain general of the island. Throughout his rapid rise in the military, he was greatly admired and his ability was properly recognized.

Gálvez was appointed viceroy of New Spain in 1785, and made a good impression on the people from the very beginning of his rule. He was a humble, frank, and honest man who lived in accordance with his democratic ideas, never used bodyguards, and drove his own carriage. Once, during a winter frost, he used part of his own money to feed the poor. He ordered the construction of Chapultepec Castle and two *calzadas* (roadways), Vallejo and La Piedad. Beyond the urban improvement, he also put poor people to work in public projects, paving the streets and installing lighting, in order to help them out during the famine of 1786.

The praise and recognition of the viceroy from the court in Madrid did not sit well with the *audiencia*, which, without any foundation, accused Gálvez before the Spanish court of attempting to make New Spain an independent country. The Crown believed the *audiencia*, and Gálvez went into a melancholic mood and later died.

His death lies in a shroud of mystery, but it is believed that he was poisoned by the people who had accused him of wrongdoing. He died suddenly while at the archbishop's palace in Tacubaya, Mexico.

THE ELEVENTH *AUDIENCIA* OF EUSEBIO BELEÑO (NOVEMBER 30, 1786–MAY 8, 1787).

Eusebio Beleño—*Position*: President. Beleño divided the executive government into two branches. One included the ministries of war, treasury, navigation, and commerce. The other branch covered justice and religion. He also ordered the *encomiendas* of Tabasco and Mérida to be incorporated into the viceroyalty.

ALONSO NÚÑEZ DE HARO Y PERALTA (1729–1800). "Archbishop." *Place of birth*: Villagarcía, Cuenca, Spain; *Place of death*: Mexico City; *Position*: Viceroy; *Term*: May 8, 1787–August 16, 1787.

Núñez graduated from the universities of Toledo and Bologna, and received his doctorate in theology. He was a humanitarian and was also extremely pious. He supported construction of the cathedral and of the Shrine of Guadalupe. He converted the College of Tepoztlán into a retirement home for the clergy.

He gave up the political power of the viceroy, but held on to the ecclesiastical power, remaining the archbishop of Mexico. He was considered an able ruler.

MANUEL ANTONIO FLORES MALDONADO MARTÍN DE ANGULO Y BODQUÍN. "Knight of the Order of Calatrava." *Place of birth*: Seville, Spain; *Place of death*: Madrid, Spain; *Position*: Viceroy; *Term*: August 16, 1787–October 16, 1789.

As viceroy, Flores Maldonado was very interested in military affairs. He initiated a program that recruited young upper class youths into the armed services. He organized the army into three regiments—"*El México*," *El Puebla*," and "*El Nueva España*"—whose maintenance cost to New Spain was extremely high. He strongly advocated improving the manufacturing of weapons through new metallurgical techniques.

Flores Maldonado was very cruel and intolerant to the indigenous people, whom he considered idolatrous. Curiously, he also worked in programs to help urban centers where the indigenous people lived.

When Charles III passed away, Flores ordered the nation to mourn. Anyone caught not mourning was fined 50 pesos. The death of the king, who had always protected him, caused him great grief, leading to health problems and forced him to resign. He died with honors in Madrid in 1799.

DURING THE REIGN OF CHARLES IV OF SPAIN (1748–1819): 1788–1808

Charles IV was born to Charles III and Marie Amalia of Saxony in 1748 in Portici, Italy. He ruled under the influence of his wife, Marie Louise of Parma, and the minister of the Court, Marie Louise's lover Manuel Godoy.

At first, he ruled strongly, following his father's guidelines, but due to his weak nature, his wife and Godoy soon took over. Under Godoy's influence, Spain became an ally of France, though playing a very minor role. Soon the French occupied Spain, and Napoleon Bonaparte took it upon himself to decide who would be next in the Spanish succession.

By 1808 Charles's son Ferdinand, who opposed Godoy and the French occupation, led a revolt. Godoy was imprisoned, and Charles abdicated in favor of Ferdinand. However, pressured by the French, Charles traveled to Bayonne for an interview with Napoleon, retracted his abdication, and obtained Ferdinand's abdication in his favor. Charles in turn abdicated in favor of Napoleon, who appointed his brother Joseph Bonaparte as king of Spain. The Spaniards nicknamed their new king "Pepe Botella," or Bottle Joe, because of his problem with alcoholism.

This new development precipitated the end of the Spanish Empire in continental America because it led to a situation that sped up independence movements in the colonies.

Charles IV sent six viceroys to New Spain. He died in Rome, Italy, in 1819.

JUAN VICENTE DE GÜEMES PACHECO DE PADILLA HORCASITAS Y AGUAYO (1740–1799). "Second Count of Revillagigedo." *Place of birth*: La Havana; *Place of death*: Madrid, Spain; *Position*: Viceroy; *Term*: October 16, 1789–July 11, 1794.

Güemes Pacheco began his rule in the *Villa of Guadalupe*. He was a Cuban born *criollo*, who had been reared in the Spanish court and the Spanish military academy. As viceroy of New Spain, his tenure was marked by the incessant task of beautifying the country and improving the living conditions of its inhabitants. He fixed what could be fixed, and every half-completed structure was ordered completed. He reorganized the nation's archives and inaugurated the Mining College.

He ordered a thorough census of the country's population. He also ordered a written history of the Royal Treasury, an enterprise that required thirty volumes.

In Mexico City more streets were paved and lighted. He ordered the embellishment of strolling paths, streets, and avenues with flowers and grass. He established a new police system in New Spain, and pursued thieves, assassins, and crooks with a vengeance, while predicting New Spain would soon see a quick and efficient judicial system.

The viceroy, who was deeply committed to education, mandated free education for all and ordered the construction of new schools. He also tried to improve the quality of higher education, bringing teachers from Spain to teach subjects such as art, mathematics, botany, architecture, and many more.

He regulated commerce in such a manner that he was able to avoid the prevalent chaotic conditions in city streets, roads, and highways. To protect the city from fires, he ordered the installation of pump stations in different parts of the city. He issued orders to place graveyards in the outskirts of cities, away from population centers. His beautifying of Mexico City did not go unnoticed: In his writings Baron Alexander von Humboldt stated that the capital was "The City Made of Palaces."

Güemes Pacheco also ordered the construction of an extensive system of highways that included roads to Veracruz, Acapulco, Mazatlán, Toluca, Guadalajara, and San Blas. He also promoted the establishment of textile factories to weave cotton, linen and hemp.

In spite of the evident progress under his rule, or perhaps angered by his success, a group of envious officials within his administration unfairly accused Güemes Pacheco of acts that questioned his probity. He was forced to resign and was tried, but during the trial, the plot against him was uncovered. He was found innocent of wrongdoing, and the plotters were punished.

Güemes Pacheco's honor was vindicated, and the king of Spain named him "*Grande de España*." He is considered one of the best viceroys in the history of New Spain.

MIGUEL DE LA GRÚA TALAMANCA Y BRANCIFORTE. "Marquis of Branciforte." *Place of birth*: Palermo, Sicily; *Place of death*: Marseille, France; *Wife*: María Antonia Godoy (sister of Prime Minister of Spain, Manuel Godoy); *Position*: Viceroy; *Term*: July 11, 1794–May 31, 1798.

De la Grúa Talamanca owed his appointment to his marriage to María Antonia Godoy, sister of the Prime Minister of Spain. Following in the steps of his brother-in-law, a man with few virtues, Talamanca used power for his personal benefit. The contrast with his viceregal predecessor was pathetic.

Using the state of war between Spain and revolutionary France as a pretext, Talamanca expropriated the properties of the French citizens living in New Spain and in Louisiana, and awarded himself most of them. He also sold public offices and military ranks.

In what may have been his only good deed, he ordered architect and sculptor Manuel Tolsa to create a statue of Charles IV. The statue turned out to be a magnificent work of art that depicts Charles riding a horse. In Mexico City, the statue is known as "*El Caballito*," and may still be seen today.

When his poor reputation reached Spain, he was ordered to resign and return.

MIGUEL JOSÉ DE AZANZA (1746–1826). "Duke of Santa Fe." *Place of birth*: Aoiz, Navarra, Spain; *Place of death*: Burdeos, France; *Position*: Viceroy; *Term*: May 31, 1798–April 29, 1800.

As a young man, Azanza traveled to New Spain and visited a large part of the country while working as secretary to the *visitador* José de Gálvez. Back in Spain he joined the army, served as a diplomat, and later was also secretary of war. He was very critical of Prime Minister Manuel Godoy, and it was rumored that his appointment as viceroy to New Spain was a maneuver by Godoy to send an enemy far away.

New Spain's economic situation improved slightly during his rule. Azanza was neither as corrupt nor as inefficient as his predecessor, and there were several good things about him. The textile factories created by the second count of Revillagigedo experienced considerable growth and were creating jobs. Because the number of trips transporting Mexican gold and silver to Spain decreased for fear of the pirates, much of that wealth remained and was used in New Spain. Azanza took special care to keep the ports properly safeguarded from British naval forces. He organized expeditions to populate Alta California. During his rule, the Machete Conspiracy, headed by Pedro de la Portilla, took place. This failed conspiracy, which counted on about twenty people armed with machetes, aimed to kidnap the viceroy and declare Mexico's independence from Spain.

Azanza returned to Spain and worked for Joseph Bonaparte. When Ferdinand VII recovered the throne in 1814, most of Azanza's titles, properties, and fortune was taken by the crown.

FÉLIX BERENGUER DE MARQUINA (1738–1826). *Place of birth*: Alicante, Spain; *Place of death*: Alicante, Spain; *Position*: Viceroy; *Term*: April 29, 1800–January 4, 1803.

Berenguer was of humble origin. He served in the navy from an early age and later became a professor of mathematics at the academy of *Guardias Marinas*. He governed the Marianas Islands in the western Pacific, and went back to Spain and worked for the Navy Ministry. Then he was appointed viceroy to New Spain.

He was an honest man who made some improvements in the administration of justice in New Spain. His rule was considered very puritanical, and when he banished bullfighting in New Spain, his popularity with the people suffered a severe blow.

During his tenure, Spain and England agreed to make peace, and New Spain seriously began its quest for independence.

JOSÉ DE ITURRIGARAY (1742–1815). *Place of birth*: Port of Cadiz, Spain; *Place of death*: Madrid, Spain; *Position*: Viceroy; *Term*: January 4, 1803–September 15, 1808.

Iturrigaray became a cadet at age seventeen. He was a member of the Spanish forces stationed in Portugal and Gibraltar. He became the military chief in Andalucía. Thereafter, he was sent by his friend, Prime Minister Manuel Godoy, to be the viceroy of New Spain.

He was an ambitious, greedy man who indulged in self-serving schemes to make himself rich. He liked bullfights, and his promotion of the fiesta in New Spain made him popular with the people. He authorized the staging of a big bullfight festival in Celaya to raise funds for a bridge over the Laja River. The prestigious architect Francisco Eduardo Tresguerras was in charge of its construction. He also encouraged universal vaccination in New Spain.

At this time, as Carlos IV and Ferdinand VII were being held under Napoleon Bonaparte's control, local authorities denied the existence of a monarch in Spain, allowing the viceroy to continue in his post. The *au-*

diencia in Mexico City, however, did not approve the step, believing that it established some sort of temporary independence from the kingdom.

A councilman named Francisco Primo de Verdad y Ramos went a bit further. On August 9, 1808, he declared that state sovereignty was not an attribute of the throne but of the people, and that as long as Ferdinand VII was not on the throne, New Spain should act as a sovereign state. The most conservative members of the *audiencia* judged his rhetoric as subversive and insubordinate. The Inquisition called Primo's statement heretical, and pronounced an anathema.

The division within the power structure of New Spain became clearly visible. The *audiencia* represented the interest of the Spanish crown while the *ayuntamiento* (City Hall) expressed the new revolutionary mentality that characterized the American point of view. In the animated August 9 meeting at City Hall, Iturrigaray indicated he would resign. The *criollos* begged him to stay, and mass pandemonium ensued.

A powerful Spanish party and dozens of nobleman, headed by a man named Gabriel Yermo, organized a conspiracy that ended with the kidnapping of the viceroy and his family.

Once freed, Iturrigaray traveled back to Spain where he was charged with corruption. He was reprimanded and fined a considerable sum. He died before paying the fine, but the obligation had to be fulfilled by his family.

THE TWELFTH *AUDIENCIA* (SEPTEMBER 15–16, 1808).

This *audiencia*, which was dominated politically by the archbishop of Mexico, the *oidores*, and *hacienda* owner Gabriel Yermo, marked Francisco Primo de Verdad y Ramos as public enemy number one, and had him imprisoned and hung. The *audiencia* named Pedro de Garibay the new viceroy.

PEDRO DE GARIBAY (1727–1815). *Place of birth*: Spain; *Place of death*: Mexico; *Position*: Viceroy; *Term*: September 16, 1808–July 19, 1809.

Garibay was used merely as a puppet by the twelfth *audiencia*. He ruled under the power of Ferdinand VII, and he put on trial and persecuted those who favored independence. The Spanish Crown presented him with the order of Charles III, and upon finishing his short term, he was given a generous pension.

DURING THE REIGN OF FERDINAND VII OF SPAIN (1784–1833): 1808 (HE ABDICATED IN FAVOR OF NAPOLEON BONAPARTE)

Ferdinand VII was the son of Charles IV and Marie Louise of Parma. He was born at the Escorial Palace, near Madrid, in 1784. He was married four times to Marie Antoinete of the Two Sicilies, Marie Isabelle of Portugal, Marie Josefa Amalia of the Two Sicilies, and Marie Christine of Naples.

Ferdinand VII was the last Spanish king to rule over New Spain. In 1808, Ferdinand rebelled against Napoleon Bonaparte's adventure in Spain. King Charles of Spain, his father, abdicated in his favor but soon reversed himself and named Napoleon instead. Napoleon, in turn, appointed his brother Joseph as king of Spain.

During the short time he was in power, Ferdinand relentlessly persecuted the liberals of Spain and repudiated the liberal Constitution of 1812, promulgated by the *cortes* of Cadiz. (The *cortes* are the courts of law that were located in the Spanish port of Cadiz where the Spanish justices met and promulgated the famous liberal constitution of March 1812, which led to the 1820 revolution.) Perhaps his most important political action was to confirm the revocation of the Salic Law, thus allowing his daughter to succeed him to the throne as Isabelle II.

Both in Spain and in New Spain, the Inquisition strengthened under Ferdinand VII's rule. In Spain the Riots of Aranguez took place, and in New Spain (America) the struggle for independence began. Ferdinand VII died in Madrid in 1833.

FRANCISCO JAVIER DE LIZANA Y BEAUMONT (1750–1811). "Archbishop." *Place of birth*: Arnedo de la Rioja, Logroño, Spain; *Place of death*: Mexico; *Position*: Viceroy; *Term*: July 19, 1809–May 8, 1810.

Lizana received his ecclesiastical education at Calatayud and Zaragoza. He received doctorates in civil and ecclesiastical law. He was considered to be a kind man. He favored *criollo* policies, but became very unpopular when he imposed a 4-million-peso loan on the people to send the money to Spain to help fight the French.

His was a time of great political unrest in New Spain. There were many intrigues, such as the famous Valladolid Conspiracy. This was a plot headed by José Mariano Michelena, whose aim was to create a congress in Mexico on behalf of Ferdinand VII. The conspiracy was discovered before it materialized.

THE THIRTEENTH *AUDIENCIA* OF PEDRO CATANI (MAY 8, 1810–SEPTEMBER 14, 1810).

Pedro Catani—*Position*: President.

FRANCISCO JAVIER VENEGAS (1760–1838). "Marquis of the Reunion." *Place of birth*: Bujalance, Cordoba, Spain; *Place of death*: Madrid, Spain; *Position*: Viceroy; *Term*: September 14, 1810–March 4, 1813.

Venegas began his rule one day before Father Miguel Hidalgo y Costilla bellowed the famous *Grito* in Dolores, Guanajuato. Venegas was a very active military commander, leading the fight against the Mexican insurgents. He ordered General Félix María Calleja to pursue and kill the leaders of the Mexican independence movement. Venegas ordered the army to shoot all prisoners of war and to jail any person suspected of aiding the independent's cause.

In 1811, as the insurgents were heading north toward the United States, Calleja apprehended Hidalgo, Ignacio Allende, Juan Aldama, and Mariano Jiménez in Acatita de Baján. They were tried, found guilty, shot, and beheaded in Chihuahua. Their heads were later brought back to Guanajuato and exhibited in the main square to serve as a warning to other revolutionaries. Their decomposed heads, hanging on each corner of the *Alhondiga of Granaditas* (communal warehouse), remained on display until 1821.

Venegas was blamed by the Courts of Cadiz for delaying the peace process in New Spain. Meanwhile, the conservatives in New Spain accused him of not doing enough to crush the rebels. He resigned the viceroyalty and returned to Spain to give an account of the situation in New Spain. When he left New Spain, the Mexican people chanted gleefully: "Long live the Independence! Long live America! Long live *La Virgin de Guadalupe!*"

FÉLIX MARÍA CALLEJA DEL REY (1755?–1828). "Count of Calderón." *Place of birth*: Medina del Campo, Valladolid, Spain; *Place of death*: Valencia, Spain; *Wife*: Doña Francisca de la Gándara; *Position*: Viceroy: *Term*: March 4, 1813–September 20, 1816.

Calleja had a distinguished military record before he was sent to New Spain. The Crown hoped he would tilt the balance of the fighting in Spain's favor. He began service in New Spain when the count of Revillagigedo was viceroy in 1789. He married Francisca de la Gándara, a very wealthy *criolla* who owned the hacienda of Bledos. He remained in the army, fighting the insurgents, until he became viceroy.

His rule was marked by war; he fought with everything he had. He reorganized the treasury in Mexico. He raised funds for the war effort by selling the assets of the Holy Inquisition and by obtaining loans from the local merchants. He was very successful in reorganizing a demoralized army, and he almost succeeded in defeating the insurgent forces.

He was greatly feared, especially after he caught and shot Miguel Hidalgo's successor, José María Morelos y Pavón, who had inherited the leadership from Hidalgo. He was relieved of his position as viceroy in 1816 and returned to Spain. He was awarded the title of count of Calderón for defeating the insurgents at a place called Puente de Calderón, and was given other honors.

In Spain, he and Ferdinand VII spent many nights planning how to reconquer Mexico, an undertaking that never materialized.

JUAN RUIZ DE APODACA (1754–1835). "Count of the Venadito." *Place of birth*: Cadiz, Spain; *Place of death*: Madrid, Spain; *Position*: Viceroy; *Term*: October 20, 1816–July 5, 1821.

Apodaca's arrival in New Spain came at a critical time. Initially, his attitude toward the insurgents was conciliatory, and his amnesty offer was accepted by many. However, when Francisco Javier Mina traveled from Spain in 1917 to assist the Mexicans in their independence movement against the government of Ferdinand VII, Apodaca fought him with a vengeance.

Even though Mina and his 300-man army managed to win a few small skirmishes, Apodaca's forces proved to be too powerful for him. Mistrusted by the insurgents and hated by the Spaniards, Mina was captured by the royalist army and shot.

A revolution in Spain forced Ferdinand VII to restore the Constitution of 1812. Meanwhile, a group of Spaniards, Apodaca among them, was meeting at the church of La Profesa, plotting to declare the independence of New Spain and save the throne for Ferdinand. The plotters figured that Ferdinand could run an absolute monarchy in New Spain without the constraints of a constitution. To that end, Apodaca named Agustín de Iturbide supreme commander of the royalist army. Iturbide, who had his own plans, accepted the post and arranged a meeting with the commander of the insurgent forces, Vicente Guerrero.

During the meeting, which took place in the city of Iguala, both generals declared Mexico's independence and invited Apodaca to head the independence movement. Apodaca vehemently rejected the idea, declared Iturbide a traitor, and ordered the army to capture him. The army sided with Iturbide, and Apodaca was declared unsuitable. A while later, he was deposed and sent to Spain where he later died.

FRANCISCO NOVELLA. *Position*: Viceroy; *Term*: July–September, 1821.

Brought to power through a political negotiation to get rid of Juan Ruiz de Apodaca, Novella was neither respected nor accepted as viceroy in all quarters. He ruled for only two months.

JUAN O'DONOJÚ (1762–1821). *Place of birth*: Seville, Spain; *Place of death*: Mexico; *Position*: Viceroy; *Term*: August 3, 1821–September 28, 1821.

A Spaniard of Irish descent, O'Donojú was the last viceroy of New Spain. With him ended 300 years of Spanish rule in Mexico, which had begun with the fall of Tenochtitlan on August 13, 1521, and ended on October 8, 1821, the day the Act of Independence was signed (not officially though, since Spain did not accept the Act of Independence).

O'Donojú landed in the port of Veracruz on August 3, 1821. His task was to hand over the kingdom of New Spain to Agustín de Iturbide. He made a pact with Iturbide, who was the military chief of the so-called *Ejército Trigarante*, which led to the Treaties of Cordoba. The treaties, whose stated goal was "to undo, without severing, the ties between the two continents," were never accepted by Ferdinand VII, then king of Spain. The country, however, had already been liberated.

O'Donojú traveled to the capital where he was received with great honors. The Act of Independence was signed for the second time on September 28, 1821. O'Donojú signed for Spain. The celebrations were marred, however, by the viceroy's untimely death due to pleurisy. He was buried at the cathedral, under the Altar of Kings. Mexico's independence was finally recognized by Spain on December 28, 1836. The Treaty of Santa María-Calatrava was signed in Madrid, Spain. Miguel Santa María signed for Mexico and José María Calatrana for Spain.

3

FROM THE WAR OF INDEPENDENCE TO THE DÍAZ DICTATORSHIP, 1810–1910

WAR OF INDEPENDENCE AND FIRST EMPIRE, 1810–1824

There were many factors that propelled the Mexican people to free themselves from Spanish rule. The independentist army was composed of three kinds of people. At the top were the *criollos*, who saw in the movement the opportunity to reach equality with the peninsulars. The *mestizos*, who organized most of the fighting, thought independence would give them upward economic and social mobility. The Indians, who made up the largest contingent of troops, hoped independence would mark the fulfillment of a long cherished desire to finally expel the Spaniards from their land.

By the time the war of independence was over, the economic condition of the Indians and *mestizos* was at an all time low. These people lived under a severely oppressive regime, which marginalized them socially, economically, and politically as second- and third-class citizens.

The Napoleonic invasion of Spain played a key role in the struggle for independence. The French revolutionist ideals of liberty, equality, and fraternity reverberated strongly in the souls of many enlightened people in Mexico, but less among the *mestizos* and Indians.

There were indigenous uprisings from Durango, in the north, to Yucatan, in the southeast. Throughout the country there were also plots and conspiracies that proved to be significant in the outcome of the struggle. The main ones were the so-called conspiracies of Valladolid, Machetes, and Querétaro.

The times posed new challenges, and leaders like Miguel Hidalgo, José

María Morelos, Ignacio Allende, Ignacio López Rayón, Josefa Ortíz de Domínguez, and Leona Vicario rose up to meet them.

Behind the leaders there was also an impressive array of valuable people like attorney Primo de Verdad y Azcárate, newsmen like José Joaquín Fernández de Lizardi and Carlos María de Bustamente, churchmen like Friar Servando Teresa de Mier and Father Melchor de Talamantes, and many more.

The revolution for independence lasted a little more than a decade. It began in 1809 with the Valladolid Conspiracy, which attempted to save the kingdom of New Spain for Ferdinand VII. It ended in 1821 when Agustín de Iturbide, representing the Mexican side, and Juan O'Donojú, the last viceroy of New Spain, signed the Act of Independence.

During this time, the insurgent forces suffered triumphs and defeats. The country experienced fundamental change, and there were some serious economic crises, political persecutions and jailings, and many people were killed.

Once the Act of Independence was signed in 1821, there were new tasks to accomplish: how to establish an independent rule after so many years of political and social dependence in Spain, how to rally the people behind a new nation, and last but not least, how to end the internal struggles that ensued after so many crisis, adjustments, and readjustments. The colonial era had ended, and Mexicans were embarking upon an unknown but hopeful new epoch.

Rulers of War of Independence and First Empire, 1810–1824

Population of Mexico 1810: 5,910,005 Inhabitants

MIGUEL HIDALGO Y COSTILLA (1753–1811). "Father of the Nation." *Place of birth*: Corralejo Hacienda, Pénjamo, Guanajuato; *Place of death*: Chihuahua, Chihuahua; *Parents*: Cristóbal Hidalgo y Costilla and Ana María Gallaga; *Position*: General Captain, Supreme Commander, and Initiator of the Independence; *Term*: 1810–1811.

Hidalgo studied and became a professor of philosophy and theology at the college of San Nicolás in Valladolid (now Morelia) and later became its chancellor. He was a cultured man, mild mannered, gentle, kind, an attentive listener, and a man given to fancy uniforms and titles. He was considered so clever that his nickname was *El Zorro* (The Fox).

He was an avid reader of scientific books and closely followed the liberal ideas of the day, in vogue in France and the United States, through books, magazines, and newspapers. His taste for these books, which were forbidden at the time in Mexico, did not sit well with his superiors and held back his career in the ecclesiastical hierarchy.

The fact that he was sent to the parish of Dolores, an irrelevant little town, was a clear sign that his liberal views were disapproved of by his superiors. In the parish he found his churchly duties of little interest, and dedicated himself to the study of literature, grape cultivation, and the planting of mulberry trees as food for silkworms (eighty-four of the trees he planted still survive).

He also established factories to make bricks and earthenware pottery, and instructed the natives in the tanning of hides, as well as the principles of music. At first he had little interest in becoming involved in the movement for independence, but little by little he was influenced by his friend Captain Ignacio Allende. Eventually, Hidalgo became an unexpected leader of the movement for independence and later the commander in chief of the insurgent hordes.

The uncovering of the Conspiracy of Querétaro in 1810 propelled Hidalgo and his co-conspirators—Allende, the mayor of Querétaro Miguel Domínguez, and his wife, Josefa Ortiz de Domínguez, and many more—into beginning the movement of independence before they were militarily prepared.

Hidalgo's commitment to the War of Independence was sealed on the dawn of September 16, 1810, in the atrium of the Dolores parish church when, according to one version of the famous *Grito*, he voiced the feelings of the people, crying out "*¡Viva América!*," "*¡Viva Fernando VII!*," and "*¡Muera el mal gobierno!*" (Let bad government die).

He called for the people to leave the parish of Dolores in the struggle for independence. A banner with the Virgin of Guadalupe was picked up en route, and the people followed their leader with a good deal of enthusiasm, but little military discipline or equipment! Soon, many poor people joined the rebel force, along with many intellectuals and liberal priests who favored independence. To organize large numbers of people who had no military training and who felt confused and angered by so many years of oppression and hunger was not an easy task.

More because of the sheer number of combatants than military tactics or discipline, Hidalgo's army scored some important victories. San Miguel and Celaya were the first two important cities that the insurgents captured with little resistance. Then they marched toward Guanajuato, where the royalist army presented an unexpected challenge. The insurgents, however, prevailed and took the city.

In a transcendental political act, Hidalgo declared slavery abolished in Mexico. He also took the initial steps to establish diplomatic relations with the United States, and he even named Pascacio Ortiz de Letona as the representative of the insurgent government to the United States on August 13, 1810. The ambassador, however, was apprehended by the Spanish army and killed while en route to Philadelphia. Unfortunately for their cause, Hidalgo and Allende commanded not a true army but an unruly mob busy robbing, looting, and ransacking entire towns, and executing prisoners.

It was perhaps the fear of his army's behavior that made Hidalgo decide not to advance into Mexico City on October 30, 1810. Hidalgo had about 100,000 combatants in the best position to attack the city when he decided to retreat instead of attacking. Hidalgo hesitated, and his indecision marked the beginning of his eventual defeat. Beaten in Querétaro, Hidalgo sought refuge in Guadalajara, but the royalist army engaged him in battle and defeated his army at the Puente de Calderón, in January 1811. Hidalgo tried to retreat toward the north of the country, but failed in the attempt.

He, along with Allende, Juan Aldama, and José Mariano Jiménez, were betrayed, ambushed, and made prisoners at a place called Acatita de Baján, Chihuahua. The group of leaders was brought to Chihuahua where they were tried and shot. Later, the heads of Hidalgo, Allende, Aldama, and Jiménez were all put into cages and displayed on the four corners of the *Alhóndiga de Granaditas* in Guanajuato. This way the Spanish thought they might discourage others from joining the insurgents. Before his cruel death, Hidalgo was also defrocked and excommunicated by the church.

IGNACIO MARÍA DE ALLENDE Y UNZAGA (1769 OR 1779–1811).
"Insurgent Hero." *Place of birth*: San Miguel el Grande (today San Miguel de Allende), Guanajuato; *Place of death*: Chihuahua, Chihuahua; *Position*: Supreme Commander of the Insurgent Army (named by the most important insurgent army chief); *Term*: January–March 1811.

Allende was a *criollo*. The son of a Spaniard, he was raised in a wealthy environment. He was trained to be a military officer, and fought in Texas under the command of Félix María Calleja. Head of the Queen's regiment, he managed to turn its men to fight for Mexico's independence. Together with Miguel Hidalgo, he was one of the first leaders of the Mexican independence movement. Always a dignified and brave leader, he fought until the bitter end of his life for that cause.

He saw his own son die in one of the battles he participated in. After the insurgent army was defeated at the Calderón Bridge, he reached the rank of *generalísimo*. However, he lasted only a few months in this position. His fortune changed and he was imprisoned, tried, and executed. He is buried at the Independence Column in Mexico City.

IGNACIO LÓPEZ RAYÓN (1773–1832). "Insurgent Hero." *Place of birth*: Tlalpujahua, Michoacán; *Place of death*: Mexico City; *Position*: Chief of the Insurgent Revolution (named by the *Junta* of Zitácuaro); *Term*: 1811.

López Rayón studied at the College of San Nicolás in Valladolid (today Morelia). Then he went on to study law at the College of San Ildefonso in Mexico City. He dedicated himself to the mining and agricultural professions. He was one of the first men to join the struggle for independence, along with Miguel Hidalgo and Ignacio Allende. He became Hidalgo's secretary in Guanajuato, and later was a cabinet minister. He promoted the publication of the revolutionary newspaper *El Despertador Americano*.

Militarily, López Rayón won many battles, but he was chased by Félix María Calleja and Agustín de Iturbide and was betrayed by Nicolás Bravo, who turned him over to the royalist army. He was captured, tried, and sentenced to death, but his sentence was revoked and instead he remained in prison until 1820.

JOSÉ MARÍA MORELOS Y PAVÓN (1765–1815). *"Insurgent Hero and Caudillo of the Independence." Place of birth*: Valladolid (today Morelia), Michoacán; *Place of death*: San Cristóbal Ecatepec, State of Mexico; *Parents*: Manuel Morelos and Juana María Guadalupe Pavón; *Position*: Supreme Commander of the American Government and Depository (trustee of the executive power, named by Congress); *Term*: 1813–1815.

As a child, Morelos had very little schooling. As a young man, he worked in the agricultural fields and as a mule driver. As a young adult, he studied at the College of San Nicolás in Valladolid, and there he met Miguel Hidalgo. He graduated in ecclesiastical studies and later held chairs in grammar and rhetoric. He corresponded regularly with Hidalgo, and when the insurgents took up arms, he joined the revolutionary army under Hidalgo's orders.

His military career began in 1811, heading the uprising in southern Mexico. He won important battles in Michoacán, Oaxaca, and Puebla while en route toward Mexico City. His military triumphs tilted the balance of power in favor of the insurgents. His reputation as a military strategist got a big boost after the famous *Sitio de Cuautla*.

In February 1812, Viceroy Francisco Javier Venegas ordered Félix María Calleja to attack Morelos. Morelos decided to wait for him in Cuautla, and on February 18, Calleja and his army finally arrived and surrounded the city. The royalists attacked from various fronts, besieging Morelos and his troops. The insurgents resisted for months under very harsh conditions, without sufficient food or water. Finally, on May 2, the insurgents managed to leave Cuautla without being discovered by the Spanish army until the evacuation was almost complete.

After Cuautla, Morelos continued his military leadership with extraordinary success, and by the end of 1813, he was beginning his fourth military campaign. That same year, on Christmas Eve, Agustín de Iturbide surprised the insurgents in an audacious move. He defeated them in battle and captured Mariano Matamoros, another priest turned soldier, whom Morelos had called as reenforcement for the crucial combat. Encouraged by this victory, the royalists chased Morelos through the south of the country. Virtually on the run, Morelos was somehow able to participate in the drafting of the Constitution of Apatzingán in 1814. But severely weakened militarily, that same year, on October 3, Morelos lost his horse en route to Tehuacán and was finally apprehended in a place called Tezmalaca. On December 22, he was executed in San Cristóbal Ecatepec, in today's state of Mexico.

His achievements were many, and his memory is highly revered in Mexico. Before his death, he was defrocked and excommunicated by the Catholic Church, but after his death he was considered a patriot and a hero by the Mexican people. Maximilian of Austria erected a statue to his memory in the city of Valladolid on November 30, 1865. Later, Valladolid was renamed Morelia in his honor. He is considered a founder of the democratic principles of government and a military genius.

VICENTE GUERRERO (1783–1831) (1ST TERM). "Insurgent Hero." *Place of birth*: Tixtla, Guerrero; *Place of death*: Cuilapan, Oaxaca; *Wife*: Guadalupe Hernández; *Position*: Chief of the Army of the south (named by the *Junta* of Jaujilla in Michoacán); *Term*: 1817–1821.

Guerrero was born poor and had a very limited education. He spent his childhood and youth working the agricultural fields and as mule driver. In 1810, he joined the insurgent army and served under the command of Hermenegildo Galeana. Later on, José María Morelos made him a captain and commissioned him to battle in southern Mexico. He fought with mixed fortune, winning and losing some battles, but wherever he fought, he showed extraordinary courage.

After the death of Morelos, Guerrero was charged with protecting the Congress of Chilpancingo, the first Mexican political assembly, during its move from Chilpancingo to Uruapan, Tiripitío, Apatzingán, and Tehuacán where it was finally dissolved. By the beginning of 1816, the struggle for independence was going through a dark period, and many insurgent chiefs were seeking amnesty from the authorities. Concerned about Guerrero, Viceroy Apodaca tried to induce him into surrendering by sending Pedro Guerrero, Vicente's father, to convince him to stop aiding the Mexican insurgents and to join the royal army. Guerrero is said to have addressed the soldiers under his command with tears in his eyes saying, "My brothers, this old man who happens to be my father has offered me employment and compensations if I quit the struggle and join the Spanish army. I have always respected my father's wishes, but he should know that the fate of the fatherland comes first."

At the beginning of 1821, Agustín de Iturbide called Guerrero to a meeting to discuss Mexico's independence. Guerrero accepted, knowing quite well that his forces were not strong enough to battle Iturbide's. At this meeting, the famous *Abrazo de Acatempan* took place. The accord recognized Iturbide as the supreme commander of the newly created army of the three guarantees: independence, racial equality, and (Catholic) religion.

Shortly thereafter, Guerrero reinitiated his struggle against Iturbide, who had become emperor of Mexico.

AGUSTÍN DE ITURBIDE (1783–1824). *Place of birth*: Valladolid (today Morelia), Michoacán; *Place of death*: Padilla, Tamaulipas; *Wife*: Ana María Huarte y Muñiz; *Parents*: José Joaquín de Iturbide and Josefa Arámburu; *Position*: The Regency: President of the *Junta Provisional Gubernativa* (Tacubaya); *Term*: 1821; *Position*: Emperor; *Term*: 1822–1823.

Iturbide was a *mestizo*. His father was Spanish and his mother Mexican, from Michoacán. He studied at the Catholic Seminary in the city of Valladolid, and for a short time he worked at a *hacienda* owned by his family. He began his military career at a very early age and was enlisted in the royalist army, combatting the uprising headed by Gabriel Yermo. He rejected Miguel Hidalgo's proposal to make him a general of the insurgent forces. Some historians believe he was involved in the proindependence Valladolid Conspiracy, headed by Mariano Michelena, and actually betrayed them when he was not chosen their leader.

Iturbide served in the Spanish armed forces and was in charge of pursuing two important insurgent generals, José María Morelos and Vicente Guerrero. Later on, he persuaded Guerrero to meet with him and declare Mexico's independence. Their meeting henceforth was referred to as the *Abrazo de Acatempan*, because the two former rivals sealed their deal with an embrace.

In 1821, Iturbide entered Mexico City, heading the *Ejército Trigarante* (meaning the three guarantees that were the heart of the agreement that resulted from the meeting with Guerrero: independence, racial equality, and [Catholic] religion).

He appointed himself Emperor Agustín I, and a Congress confirmed him and his title by a vast majority. He was crowned emperor in 1822, but soon the honeymoon with Congress was over. Iturbide ordered the arrest of twenty-six deputies, and when Congress protested, he ordered the dissolution of the Chamber of Deputies.

The activities of the Masonic sects, originally introduced to Mexico in the 1780s, got a renewed impulse when Manuel Codorniu founded the newspaper *El Sol*. This newspaper served as the in-house publication for the Scottish Rite lodge in their struggle against Iturbide. General Antonio López de Santa Anna then launched the Plan de Casa Mata to reinstate Congress and create a republic. As the insurgents approached Mexico City, winning small victories on their way, Iturbide abdicated and left the country for Italy. He lived for a while in London. One day he decided to return to Mexico, was recognized upon landing in Soto la Marina, Tamaulipas, and was apprehended and shot.

His body rests in the Chapel of San Felipe de Jesús, in the cathedral of Mexico City.

SUPREME EXECUTIVE POWER OF PEDRO CELESTINO NEGRETE, NICHOLÁS BRAVO, GUADALUPE VICTORIA, MARIANO MICHE-LENA, AND MIGUEL DOMÍNQUEZ (MARCH 30, 1823–OCTOBER 10, 1824).

Pedro Celestino Negrete (1777–1846)—*Place of birth*: San Esteban, Viz-caya, Spain; *Place of death*: Burdeos, France; *Position*: Member of the Ex-ecutive Power, named by Congress. Negrete came to New Spain as the commander of the royalist army to fight the insurgents. When Mexico gained its independence, he retained his post, but this time in the new Mexican army.

He adhered to the Plan de Iguala, and served under the command of Agustín de Iturbide. Then he joined Antonio López de Santa Anna and his Plan de Casa Mata to unseat Iturbide. He played an important role in the emperor's downfall.

After Iturbide abdicated, Negrete was appointed to form a provisional government along with Nicolás Bravo and Guadalupe Victoria. The latter two never showed up, and José Mariano Michelena, Miguel Domínguez, and Vicente Guerrero were named to replace them.

Negrete was in charge for a few months and handed the government over to Victoria, who would become the first president of the Mexican Republic. Negrete tried once more to regain power, and conspired with another Spanish general against Victoria. Caught in the act, he was exiled to Spain where he was marked as a traitor for his participation in the Mexican independence. Exiled again, he lived the rest of his life in France.

Nicolás Bravo—*Position*: Member of the Executive Office. (See p. 73.)

Guadalupe Victoria—*Position*: Member of the Executive Office. (See p. 64.)

Mariano Michelena (1772–1852)—*Place of birth*: Valladolid (today Mo-relia), Michoacán; *Place of death*: Morelia, Michoacán. Michelena was a lawyer. He was one of the originators of Mexican independence, and also served in the Spanish military. He participated in the Valladolid Conspir-acy, and was imprisoned in San Juan de Ulúa in 1809. He was later exiled to Spain.

At the triumph of independence, he returned to Mexico and became a deputy in Congress.

Michelena fought against Agustín de Iturbide and was later named am-bassador to Great Britain in 1831. He brought Mocha coffee to Mexico, and labored assiduously with this crop. He was a member of the federalist party, and was appointed governor of Michoacán.

Miguel Domínguez (1756–1830)—*Place of birth*: Mexico City; *Place of death*: Mexico City; *Wife*: Josefa Ortiz; *Position*: Substitute Member of the Executive Office, named by Congress. Domínguez studied law. Viceroy Félix Berenguer de Marquina appointed him mayor of Querétaro. He is remembered for battling against police abuse in Mexico and for being a key participant in the country's political emancipation. He and his wife held secret meetings at their house in Querétaro with many insurgents. It was his wife who warned Miguel Hidalgo and Ignacio Allende that the conspiracy had been uncovered by the royalists. When she was captured, her husband acted as her lawyer. Later on, he was named president of the Supreme Justice Court of Mexico.

Vicente Guerrero—*Position*: Substitute Member of the Executive Office, named by Congress. (See p. 60.)

NEWLY INDEPENDENT MEXICO, 1824–1864

When Mexico won its independence in 1821, the country was in shambles and in a precarious state of political, economic, and social turbulence.

The territory of independent Mexico was the largest in Latin America at this time. Just one year after independence was accomplished, the country's boundaries were extended even further when the Central American area opted to become an incorporated part of Mexico.

The country's problems seemed unsolvable. Isolated internationally and internally convulsed, Mexico was ravaged by war and dangerously underpopulated for its size. There were approximately 6.5 million inhabitants in an area that was 2.890 million square miles. North and south, the problems of the young nation were overwhelming, and Great Britain posed a particularly ominous danger in the southern border country of Belize.

Nor was the economic panorama encouraging. The three basic industries that flourished before the War of Independence had declined considerably. Mining had decreased greatly; production was one-fifth of what it had been before. Agricultural production had been cut in half, and industrial production went down to one-third of what it once was. The country's deficit had grown beyond control.

On the political front there was also tremendous instability. The first political parties representing different ideologies were formed, including a split movement within the politically powerful Masonic sects. A group that favored a federalist system of government split from the Scottish lodge and formed another sect under the auspices of the New York lodge. Vicente Guerrero headed the *yorkinos*, while Nicolás Bravo led the *escoceses* in their pursuit of power. The presidential election took place through local legislatures and was "perfected in the Federal Congress." Except for one president, Guadalupe Victoria, none of the other presidents elected during this time managed to complete their terms of office. Political instability created weak and disorganized nascent political institutions. The republicans, who now had control, were seriously divided between federalists and centralists, or unitarists.

The weakness of governmental institutions was clearly evident from the very beginning of independence and was a clear sign of the many problems in store for the Mexicans. Dictatorship and anarchy dominated a people overwhelmed by misery, hunger, and ignorance. There were riots, uprisings, and many coups d'état. Mexico succumbed to internal factionalism and personalism and external invasions. At the final count, Mexico lost half of its territory because the country was broken both economically and spiritually.

At this juncture in its history, Mexico lacked a strong national identity. Up until the presidency of Benito Juárez in the 1850s, Mexico lacked a sense of *mexicanidad*, and its leader's allegiances were closer to their places of birth than to a national territory. Later on, the Porfirio Díaz' long tenure added support to the foundations of nationalism. Finally, the revolution of 1910 greatly furthered the national conscience.

Rulers of Independent Mexico, 1824–1864

Population of Mexico 1824: 6,500,000 Inhabitants

JOSÉ MIGUEL RAMÓN AUDAUCTO FERNÁNDEZ Y FÉLIX (1786–1843). " 'Guadalupe Victoria' Glorious Son of the Motherland." *Place of birth*: Tamazula, Reino de la Nueva Galicia (today Durango); *Place of death*: Perote, Veracruz; *Wives*: María Antonieta Bretón and Felipa Meza; *Position*: First Constitutional President (Vice president: Nicolás Bravo); *Term*: October 10, 1824–April 1, 1829.

Fernández adopted the name Guadalupe Victoria to honor the virgin of Guadalupe and the victory of the insurgent's cause. Victoria was born into a wealthy *criollo* family. He studied at a Catholic seminary in Durango and later at the College of San Ildefonso in Mexico City.

He fought alongside José María Morelos, and was famous for his courage in battle. He disappeared into the mountains for quite some time and resurfaced when the Plan de Iguala was announced. He traveled to Veracruz and joined the army of Antonio López de Santa Anna to overthrow the imperial regime of Agustín de Iturbide. Victoria was in charge of the attack against the San Juan de Ulúa fortress where the last Spanish forces remained.

Victoria was the first president of the Mexican republic. Elected with Nicolás Bravo as vice president in 1824, he faced severe economic problems from the very beginning of his administration. The struggle for power was ruthless. There were many uprisings, and Victoria sent several generals who were seeking to oust him to exile. Santa Anna led a revolt in Jalapa, and simultaneously, there was another uprising at the barracks of La Acordada.

The internal struggle took its toll, and the government suffered a severe monetary deficit. Two-thirds of the national budget went to the army alone, and Victoria thought the only way to solve the deficit was by contracting foreign loans. An English bank lent Mexico more than 3 million pounds at an exorbitant interest rate.

During his presidency, the liberation of slaves, championed earlier by Miguel Hidalgo, went into legal effect. He placed great importance on education and founded the National Museum. In his administration, the border with the United States was set.

Before the election of 1828, the Liberal Party split in two. The *puros*, led by Lorenzo de Zavala, favored a radical type of liberalism; the *moderados*, led by Vicente Gómez Farías, sought a milder kind of liberalism. Then there were the conservatives, mostly the landowners and the clergy, who favored a monarchy or a military dictatorship, and were led by Lucas Alamán.

To complicate matters even further, freemasonry was becoming immensely popular among politicians from both groups. This led to serious rifts among them, especially between the lodges of the Scottish and the New York rites. The fact that the U.S. ambassador to Mexico, Joel R. Poinsett, was deeply involved in recruiting politicians for his lodge did not help the situation. As a matter of fact, Poinsett got so involved in Mexican politics that president Victoria ordered him expelled from the country after finding out he was involved in a conspiracy to oust him.

The election of 1828 pitted two liberal candidates against each other. A radical anti-Spanish faction had Vicente Guerrero as its candidate, and Manuel Gómez Pedraza was the candidate of the moderates. The elections were marred by fraud, and the country became even more politically divided.

By the time Victoria's presidency came to an end, he was so frustrated that he retired into absolute seclusion. He died of complications resulting from his ongoing problems with epilepsy on March 21, 1843.

MANUEL GÓMEZ PEDRAZA (1789–1851) (1ST TERM).

Place of birth: Querétaro, Querétaro; *Place of death*: Mexico City; *Wife*: María Juliana Azcárate; *Position*: Constitutional President, but he never served his term; *Term*: His election was annulled by Congress.

Gómez Pedraza was both a military man and a politician. Very conservative, he fought against the insurgent army and helped in the capture of José María Morelos. He was governor of Puebla and later minister of War and the Navy during the Guadalupe Victoria presidency.

Before the election of 1828, he was the leader of the Moderate Party. His election was marred by fraud, and Antonio López de Santa Anna led a revolt against Gómez Pedraza. While government troops were fighting against Santa Anna, the popular movement in favor of Vicente Guerrero gained strength. A revolt begun at the jail of La Acordada soon spread into the city, and the troops stationed at the jail followed Lorenzo de Zavala in an assault on the National Palace. A riot ensued and a mob burned the Parián market.

Gómez Pedraza went into exile in France. Some time later he tried to return to Mexico, but was denied entry. He settled in New Orleans where he waited for the opportunity to return to Mexico, which took place in 1832.

VICENTE GUERRERO. *Position*: Constitutional President (Vice President: Anastasio Bustamante); *Term*: April 1, 1829–December 19, 1829. Guerrero was president of Mexico twice, in 1817–1821 and again in 1829. He played an important role in the War of Independence (see p. 60 for details).

In 1828 Guerrero was a presidential candidate, but lost the close election to Manuel Gómez Pedraza. However, when Gómez Pedraza went into exile after the riots during the Motín de la Acordada, Guerrero was named president of the republic. He was inaugurated on April 1, 1829.

During his presidency, Spain tried to reconquer Mexico, but was unsuccessful. The expeditionary force led by Spanish brigadier Isidro Barradas was not powerful enough to fight Guerrero's army.

When his own vice president, Anastasio Bustamante, headed a new rebellion under the Plan de Jalapa, Guerrero left Mexico City to fight him. As soon as he left, a military garrison headed by General Luis Quintanar adhered to the Plan de Jalapa, rebelled against the government, removed the president from office, and named Pedro Vélez as president. But Guerrero would not give up. Instead, he headed south and was joined by General Juan Alvarez in his struggle.

In 1831 Congress disqualified Guerrero and declared Anastasio Bustamante president. Bustamante's priority became capturing Guerrero. To that end, he ordered one of his cabinet ministers to hire an Italian ship captain named Francisco Picaluga, who was a friend of Guerrero, to betray him, under the pretense of a meeting between the government and the rebel to discuss peace. Guerrero agreed to meet at Picaluga's ship, named *El Colombo*, and once on board he was taken prisoner and sent ashore in Oaxaca. Captain Miguel González sentenced him to death and had him shot by a firing squad in Cuilapan. Picaluga was said to have been paid 50,000 pesos in gold for his services.

After his death, Guerrero's home state was named after him.

JOSÉ MARÍA BOCANEGRA (1787–1862). *Place of birth*: Labor de la Troje, Aguascalientes; *Place of death*: Villa de San Angel, Mexico, D.F.;

Position: Interim President, named by Vicente Guerrero; his election was rendered void; *Term*: December 18, 1829–December 23, 1829.

Bocanegra studied law at the College of San Ildefonso. He joined the Plan de Iguala and was a deputy in the *Congreso Constituyente* of 1824. This Congress ratified the Constitution of 1824, which adopted an extreme federalist system for Mexico, giving autonomy to the thirteen states that formed the republic.

During the administration of Guadalupe Victoria, Bocanegra was secretary of the treasury, then minister of foreign affairs, and later president of the supreme court. This post automatically made him president when Guerrero left the presidency to fight Anastasio Bustamante.

His interim presidency, however, lasted only a short while. General Luis Quintanar, who directed the coup against Guerrero, declared Bocanegra's ascension to president unconstitutional, and Bocanegra was relieved of his office.

He returned to the ministry of foreign affairs for a little while in 1844, but mostly devoted himself to his law practice. He also wrote a history book that is still greatly appreciated.

PROVISIONAL GOVERNMENT OF PEDRO VÉLEZ, LUCAS ALAMÁN, AND LUIS QUINTANAR (DECEMBER 23, 1829–DECEMBER 31, 1829).

Pedro Vélez (1787–1848)—*Place of birth*: Zacatecas, Zacatecas; *Place of death*: Mexico City; *Position*: Member of the Triumvirate in the Provisional Government (Vice President: Anastasio Bustamante). Vélez was considered a fine lawyer. He was the president of the Supreme Court of Justice, and this position enabled him to become Bocanegra's successor. He lasted only eight days in office. He returned to his original profession, and died on August 5, 1848.

Lucas Alamán (1792–1853)—*Place of birth*: Guanajuato, Guanajuato; *Place of death*: Mexico City; *Wife*: Narcisa Castrillo; *Position*: Member of the Triumvirate in the Provisional Government. Alamán, the premier conservative leader, was renowned for his intelligence. He was an historian and a politician. A staunch conservative, he was a defender of the colonial regime. He was well traveled and studied at the Seminario de Minería. He was the secretary for the *Junta de Sanidad* during the tenure of Viceroy Juan Ruiz de Apodaca. He organized the nation's archives and founded the Museum of Natural History. He was also the administrator for the property owned by the Marquis of the Oaxaca Valley, heir of the conqueror Hernán Cortés.

Luis Quintanar (1780–1837)—*Place of birth*: San Juan del Río, Querétaro; *Place of death*: Mexico City; *Position*: Member of the Triumvirate of the Provisional Government. Quintanar was both a military man and a politician. He fought in the insurgent army and became a general. He sided with Anastasio Bustamante when the latter launched his Plan de Jalapa, and led the coup d'état against Vicente Guerrero. He declared null and void the election of José María Bocanegra as president, was a member of the triumvirate that governed Mexico for a few days, and handed the government over to Bustamante.

ANASTASIO BUSTAMANTE (1780–1853) (1ST TERM). *Place of birth*: Jiquilpan, Michoacán; *Place of death*: San Miguel de Allende, Guanajuato; *Position*: Vice President of Mexico in charge of the government, ratified by Congress; *Term*: January 1, 1830–August 14, 1832.

Bustamante was the son of Spanish immigrant parents. He studied medicine and practiced without title in San Luis Potosí. He later became a military man who fought in many important battles of the rebellion. He destroyed the Spanish army at Celaya and Guanajuato, occupying both cities militarily. He was put in charge of a division within the *Ejército Trigarante* by Agustín de Iturbide. He supported the Plan de Iguala and came to the presidency by way of the Plan de Jalapa.

A conservative, he filled his cabinet with prominent men from his political party. He organized a strong secret service and ended freedom of the press. He faced several uprisings in San Luis Potosí, Yucatan, and the state of Mexico. He fought Vicente Guerrero's army in the south, and had to deal with the *Yorkino* rebellions.

An uprising at the garrison of Veracruz (Plan of Veracruz) in January 1831 contributed to his fall, and he was forced to flee to Europe.

MELCHOR MÚZQUIZ (1790–1844). *Place of birth*: Santa Rosa, District of Monclova, Coahuila; *Place of death*: Mexico City; *Wife*: Joaquina Bezares; *Position*: Interim President, named by the Chamber of Deputies; *Term*: August 14, 1832–December 24, 1832.

Múzquiz was a young man studying at the College of San Ildefonso when he decided to join the movement for independence alongside Ignacio López Rayón. Even though he initially supported Agustín de Iturbide and his Plan de Iguala, as a young congressman he opposed the crowning of Iturbide as emperor. He also strongly rejected absolutism and the monarchic system, and labeled himself a republican. He supported the Plan de Casa Mata against Agustín de Iturbide.

Múzquiz was Anastasio Bustamante's main assistant in military matters. When President Bustamante went to battle, Múzquiz was placed in the presidential office for a period of three months. He relinquished the position and placed Manuel Gómez Pedraza in the presidency. In 1837, he was named first deputy and later president of the Supreme Conservative Power, as Congress was called then. He was also governor of the state of Mexico.

He was an honest public servant, and he died in poverty on December 14.

MANUEL GÓMEZ PEDRAZA (2ND TERM). *Position*: President, elected by a *Junta* in Puebla (Vice President: Valentín Gómez Farías); *Term*: December 24, 1832–April 1, 1833.

When the government of Anastasio Bustamante ended abruptly in 1831, Gómez Pedraza finished the presidential term. He was installed as president in Puebla at the request of the *Convenios de Zavaleta*. He was later named foreign minister and deputy to Congress. In 1850 he tried for a second term, but lost the presidential election to Mariano Arista. He later became the director of the *Monte de Piedad*.

ANTONIO LÓPEZ DE SANTA ANNA (1794–1876) (1ST TERM). *Place of birth*: Jalapa, Veracruz; *Place of death*: Mexico City; *Wives*: María Inés de la Paz García and Dolores Tosta; *Position*: Elected President (Vice President: Valentín Gómez Farías); *Term*: April 1, 1833–May 16, 1833.

Santa Anna was a military man. By 1812 he was already a cadet serving at the Veracruz Infantry Division, and by the time he was twenty-seven years old, he had the rank of general.

He fought against General Isidro Barradas in Tampico when the Spanish crown tried to reconquer Mexico. He fought against the rebels in Texas in 1835. The successful way he fought *guerrillas* and thieves in the roads of the state of Veracruz enhanced his military reputation. He also became famous for the large debts he owed as a result of his passion for gambling.

He supported the Plan de Iguala, along with José Joaquín Herrera, and upon meeting Augustín de Iturbide, he began his political career. At first he was a protégé and supporter of Iturbide, but later Santa Anna changed his mind and became Iturbide's nemesis.

In February 1823, Santa Anna announced his Plan de Casa Mata against Iturbide, and for the next twenty-two years he engaged in small revolutions that allowed him to take or leave power according to his personal wishes. No one, it seemed, could stop him.

In 1827 the local legislature of Veracruz first made him vice governor and then governor of his home state. After less than a year in office Santa Anna was deposed by the military, but within a few months, he made a comeback and retrieved the governorship. From here he marched toward Mexico City, capturing Puebla.

Then, in an election held in March of 1833, Santa Anna won the presidency. He lasted only a few weeks as president because an alleged illness forced his retirement to his Jalapa *hacienda*, Manga de Clavo. His illnesses, real or fancied, were excellent excuses for evading difficult political decisions.

He repeatedly returned to political life, later denouncing the liberal ideas of President Gómez Farías as the cause of the ills of the country.

VALENTÍN GÓMEZ FARÍAS (1781–1858) (1ST TERM). "Father of the Reformist Movement." *Place of birth*: Guadalajara, Jalisco; *Place of death*: Mexico City; *Wife*: Isabel López; *Position*: Vice President in charge of the government; *Term*: June 2, 1833–April 24, 1834.

Gómez Farías studied medicine in Aguascalientes. He was considered an extreme liberal, and was mayor of the city of Aguascalientes. He was elected deputy to the Spanish court, but did not fill the position because of his loyalty to Mexican independence.

Gómez Farías' provisional presidency was interrupted several times due to the periodic return of Antonio López de Santa Anna to the presidency. He was known as a man of radical progressive ideas, and whenever he headed the government, he brought about many reform programs. He ended censorship laws in Mexico and permitted a free press. He abolished religious and military privilege in Mexico, and tried to improve the education of the poor.

The Mexican people were not ready for his ideas. He was both feared and loved by the Mexican people. He was exiled several times, and lived in New York and New Orleans.

Due to his liberal ideas, he was repeatedly attacked by his conservative and moderate political enemies, and his terms in office were shorter than the norm. He always tried to institute radical changes in the political and social structure of the country. For many critics, he was a doctrinaire radical who was unwilling to compromise to achieve his goals. He tried to move too far too fast.

ANTONIO LÓPEZ DE SANTA ANNA (2ND TERM). *Position*: President, proclaimed by the Plan de Cuernavaca (Vice President: Valentín Gómez Farías); *Term*: April 24, 1834–January 28, 1835.

Weary of the liberal ideas championed by Valentín Gómez Farías, Santa Anna, a former liberal turned conservative, decided to return to Mexico City and regain the presidency. Supported by the Plan de Cuernavaca, which called for religion, law, and Santa Anna, the general became president for a second time.

While president he ruled without a congress, without state legislatures, without a program, without cabinet ministers, and without funds. Like most countries at the time, Mexico depended largely on import duties for operating funds.

But not everyone was happy with Santa Anna's centrism. The opposition came from many quarters, not only from the liberal party. The people of Zacatecas, in the north of the republic, rose up in arms to defend the federalist system. Shortly after he was elected, Santa Anna stepped down from the presidency to fight against the rebels.

When he relinquished the presidency, he named Miguel Barragán as his successor.

Population of Mexico 1834: 7,734,292 Inhabitants

MIGUEL BARRAGÁN (1789–1836). *Place of birth*: Valle del Maíz, San Luis Potosí; *Place of death*: Mexico City (in the Government Palace while still president); *Wife*: Manuela Trebuesto y Casasola; *Position*: Interim President, named by Antonio López de Santa Anna and ratified by the Chamber of Deputies; *Term*: January 28, 1835–February 27, 1836.

Barragán was a military man. In 1821 he had assisted Augustín de Iturbide in the overthrow of the viceroyalty. He was named the military commander in Veracruz, and in 1825 was assigned the task of capturing the fortress of San Juan de Ulúa, which was still occupied by Spanish troops.

Soon he broke with Iturbide, and was apprehended and incarcerated. When Iturbide's government fell, he was freed. Then he supported the Plan de Montaño, with its demand for the expulsion of U.S. Ambassador Joel R. Poinsett, accusing him of meddling in the internal affairs of Mexico. Barragán was incarcerated for a second time and then exiled to South America.

Upon Barragán's return to Mexico, Santa Anna named him Minister of War and eventually made him interim president. Meanwhile, Santa Anna commanded an expedition to subdue Texas rebels in 1835. By that time, Texas was part of the Mexican state of Coahuila, although the vast majority of its inhabitants were American colonists and frontiersmen.

Back in 1832, the colonists had asked Santa Anna's government to abolish customs houses and patrols along the border with the United States. Santa Anna's response was to send an army to collect the duties. The Texans' response was also military. They intercepted the Mexican army at San Antonio, and made it retire to the Rio Grande. Santa Anna strengthened his army to punish the Texans. In February 1836, Santa Anna arrived at San Antonio, and the siege of the former mission, the Alamo, began. Two weeks later, Santa Anna, despite great losses, had overcome resistance at the Alamo, killing all defenders of the mission-turned-fortress, including some Tejanos.

Barragán did not live long enough to see the final chapter of Santa Anna's adventure in Texas. He died in March 1836. Even though he ruled for a very short time, Barragán won the affection of the Mexican people.

JOSÉ JUSTO CORRO (1794–1864). *Place of birth*: Guadalajara, Jalisco; *Place of death*: Guadalajara, Jalisco; *Position*: Interim President, named by the Chamber of Deputies; *Term*: February 27, 1836–April 19, 1837.

Corro was named president when the preceding president (Miguel Barragán) became too ill to govern. By this time, Antonio López de Santa Anna, misjudging the Texans, went searching for the rebel leaders. Meanwhile, the Texans had already declared their independence from Mexico and had named Sam Houston commander of the army to fight Santa Anna.

On April 21, 1836, Santa Anna and Houston faced each other near the San Jacinto River. Houston attacked the Mexican army, killing, wounding, and capturing hundreds of Mexican troops. Santa Anna was apprehended while trying to escape.

Corro's first political task was to retrieve Santa Anna from prison. At the same time, he attempted to subdue the Texan rebels, but failed in his attempts. Houston offered Santa Anna a deal—his freedom in exchange for the independence of Texas. Santa Anna accepted and signed the Agreement of Velasco. Later on, Santa Anna was brought to Washington D.C., and then went back to Mexico.

Corro refused to honor Santa Anna's agreement with Houston since it was made under duress, and sent more troops, commanded by General Blas Urrea, to Texas. In the meantime, Corro attempted to change the system of government in Mexico, adopting a centralist constitution.

He managed to have the Vatican recognize Mexico's independence. During his term, the United States acknowledged Texas's independence. He resigned and retired in Guadalajara.

ANASTASIO BUSTAMANTE (2ND TERM). *Position*: President, named by Congress; *Term*: April 19, 1837–March 20, 1839.

Bustamante came back from exile during the war against the Texas colonists to suppress their rebellion. Congress named him president by decree. Instantly, he was forced to fight uprisings throughout the country.

His problems, however, were not only internal but international. In 1838, the French government presented Bustamante with a claim for 600,000 pesos, a reimbursement for all the suffering the French people endured in Mexico during the riots of the Parián market in 1828. The French claimed that some businesses owned by French citizens had been damaged and gave as an example a bakery located in Tacubaya. Thus the name given by the Mexican people to the dispute was the *Guerra de los Pasteles* (the Pastry War). This claim would have repercussions later.

In a show of force designed to intimidate Mexico, the French government sent a warship into the Gulf of Mexico, close to the Veracruz coast. The French opened fire on the fortress of San Juan de Ulúa, and the fortress surrendered, as did the Veracruz garrison. Antonio López de Santa Anna went to Veracruz to fight the invaders as commander in chief of the Mexican army, and lost a leg in the ensuing battle. Santa Anna's loss brought him recognition as a Mexican hero.

While the French were occupying Veracruz, Bustamante left the capital to suppress other uprisings in the countryside, leaving Santa Anna as interim president.

ANTONIO LÓPEZ DE SANTA ANNA (3RD TERM). *Position*: Interim President, named by the Supreme Conservative Power; *Term*: March 20, 1839–August 10, 1839.

Pardoned for the loss of Texas and considered a hero for losing a leg when fighting against the French, Santa Anna was propelled back into the presidency. His first act as president was to agree that Mexico would pay the 600,000 pesos claimed by the French in three installments. In return, the French relinquished the fort of San Juan de Ulúa, and then left the country, stealing more than sixty cannons from the fortress.

Not everyone was happy with Santa Anna in the presidency again. There were uprisings in the isolated territory of Yucatan which was threatening to secede from the country; Valentín Gómez Farías returned from exile in the United States to lead a revolt against Santa Anna. More revolts, rebellions, and counterrevolts followed. Santa Anna tried to subdue all the revolts. He banned several newspapers and issued an order to arrest any individual judged to be disturbing the prevailing order. He went to Puebla on a stretcher because his wounds had not healed and issued a death sentence against rebel federalist General J. Antonio Mejía.

When Santa Anna returned to the capital, the Mexican public received him as a hero once again, and Congress honored him. He resigned and took time to heal.

Since Anastasio Bustamante was not present at the time of elections, the interim government passed into the hands of General Nicolás Bravo.

NICOLÁS BRAVO (1786–1854) (1ST TERM). *Place of birth*: Chilpancingo, Guerrero; *Place of death*: Hacienda de Chichihualco; *Wife*: Antonina Guevara; *Position*: Named by Antonio López de Santa Anna, Interim President; *Term*: July 10, 1839–July 19, 1839.

Bravo was one of the leaders in the group of insurgents who fought for Mexican independence alongside José María Morelos. When Morelos was executed, Bravo was named as his military successor in the southeast of Mexico. He was considered a strong and fair leader, and many times he was the head of the Supreme Power. He called a congress to elaborate a new constitution. In this, his first term as president, Bravo lasted only nine days because Anastasio Bustamante returned and took back his power.

ANASTASIO BUSTAMANTE (3RD TERM). *Position*: President, Military Dictator; *Term*: July 19, 1839–October 22, 1841.

By the time Bustamante returned to power, Mexico was going through even more difficult times than before. There were rebellions and liberal uprisings, famines and epidemics. Many states were threatening to follow

Texas' example and become independent. In Yucatan, a man named José María Gutiérrez de Estrada became very popular when he suggested Mexico needed a foreign prince to become head of state. Many Yucatecans concurred with his idea. Furthermore, in a bold move Yucatan set up diplomatic relations with the recent rebels of the Republic of Texas.

Bustamante's strategy to achieve stability called for two key agreements: one, with the security forces of the state, to reestablish law and order; the other, an accommodation with other political forces that would allow him some room to govern.

The negotiations with Spain to recognize Mexico's independence succeeded, and Spain sent its first ambassador, Angel Calderón de la Barca. He was married to Frances Erskine Inglis, better known as Madame Calderón de la Barca, a writer whose book of memoirs, *Life in Mexico*, became a classic chronicle of life in Mexico during that time.

Bustamante reformed the Seven Laws Constitution. He sent an army to reconquer Texas, while Yucatan and Tabasco rose up in rebellion. Meanwhile, in Mexico City Valentín Gómez Farías and General Blas Urrea led a rebellion against Bustamante in 1840. In Guadalajara, General Mariano Paredes rose up in arms and called for a new congress and a new constitution. Antonio López de Santa Anna joined forces with the rebels and negotiated Bustamante's resignation. On September 28, 1841, the Plan de Tacubaya was signed by the president and the rebels; it declared the suspension of all traditional powers and named a *Junta de Notables* that would call for a new congress. Bustamante resigned the presidency and went into exile in Europe.

FRANCISCO JAVIER ECHEVERRÍA (1797–1852).

Place of birth: Jalapa, Veracruz; *Place of death*: Mexico City; *Wife*: Refugio Almanza; *Position*: Interim President, named by Congress by reason of seniority as he was the oldest councilman; *Term*: September 22, 1841–October 10, 1841.

Echeverría's term was so short-lived that he hardly managed to do anything at all. The country remained in constant turmoil, and the groups allied to Antonio López de Santa Anna were creating political instability in the capital by calling for Santa Anna's return to power. Even though Echeverría lasted less than a month in power, he managed well for his personal benefit and left the presidency an extremely rich man.

ANTONIO LÓPEZ DE SANTA ANNA (4TH TERM).

Position: President, named by the *Junta de Notables; Term*: October 10, 1841–October 26, 1842.

Santa Anna marched into the capital with his troops. In what many historians consider an electoral farce, he was invested as president by the *Junta de Notables*, an assembly of prominent leaders.

To pay back the Mexican military that had strongly supported him, he raised the government's allowance to the military and supported a recruitment program that drafted unwilling men.

The election of a congress with a liberal majority in the Chamber of Deputies portended ill, and their attempt to write a liberal constitution angered Santa Anna. He dissolved Congress by the middle of 1842.

Santa Anna's support of fraudulent businesses and hiking taxes in order to raise funds to pay for his compulsive gambling habit did not make him a popular figure. Santa Anna furiously persecuted those who dared to criticize him. One day, perhaps sensing which way the political winds were blowing, Santa Anna decided to retire to Manga de Clavo. Nicolás Bravo was named as his successor.

NICOLÁS BRAVO (2ND TERM). *Position*: Substitute President, named by Antonio López de Santa Anna; *Term*: October 26, 1842–March 5, 1843.

During this, his second term, Bravo faced opposition from all parts of the political spectrum. The church, the army, and the Congress all confronted him, and Santa Anna kept interfering constantly in Bravo's handling of the government. Tired of so much pressure, Bravo resigned the presidency and reenlisted in the army.

ANTONIO LÓPEZ DE SANTA ANNA (5TH TERM). *Position*: Dictator, named by his own people; *Term*: March 4, 1843–October 4, 1843.

The squandering that had characterized Santa Anna's past presidencies was nothing when compared to what happened in this new term. He not only stole money from the treasury, but tried to gain access to the Catholic Church's wealth. He forced upon clergy and wealthy citizens a loan in the amount of 2 million pesos.

Mexico remained in a troubled situation with uprisings across the land. The common citizens grew increasingly tired of Santa Anna's way of governing. When he lost the support of his own party, Santa Anna was forced back to his hacienda, and Valentín Canalizo was named his successor.

VALENTÍN CANALIZO (1794–1850) (1ST TERM). *Place of birth*: Monterrey, Nuevo León; *Place of death*: Mexico City; *Wife*: Josefa Bocadillo; *Position*: Canalizo was sworn in as Substitute President before Antonio López de Santa Anna; later on, the senate named him Interim President; *Term*: October 4, 1843–June 4, 1844.

Canalizo was a cadet in Celaya's infantry in 1811. He became a major with the *Ejército Trigarante*, and allied himself with Agustín de Iturbide. He later supported the Plan de Casa Mata. He was also a commander in Oaxaca, as well as governor of the state of Mexico and a prefect in Cuernavaca. He was a close friend of Santa Anna, who left him with the post of president. A little later, Santa Anna reassumed the presidency.

ANTONIO LÓPEZ DE SANTA ANNA (6TH TERM). *Position*: Constitutional President; *Term*: June 4, 1844–September 12, 1844.

During this term, Santa Anna asked the Chamber of Deputies to give him 4 million pesos to cover his betting debts. U.S. President John Tyler had the port of Veracruz blockaded in an attempt to intimidate Santa Anna and the Mexicans, and force them to accept the annexation of Texas by the United States. In the meantime, the opposition party was able to unseat Santa Anna, supported by the Constitution of 1824. The dictator was apprehended in Veracruz, shipped away in the British vessel *Midway*, and forced into exile in Cuba.

JOSÉ JOAQUÍN HERRERA (1792–1854) (1ST TERM). *Place of birth*: Jalapa, Veracruz; *Place of death*: Mexico City; *Wife*: Dolores Alzugaray; *Position*: Council President, he governed in name only for a few days; *Term*: September 12, 1844–September 24, 1844.

Herrera was a humane and dignified president. A military man, he was considered a moderate liberal, an honest public servant, and a patriot. He served in both the royalist and the *Trigarante* armies, and supported the Plan de Iguala. He took part in the palace's independence festival on September 16, but did little else.

VALENTÍN CANALIZO (2ND TERM). *Position*: He took power from José Joaquín Herrera and was appointed by the senate; *Term*: September 24, 1844–December 6, 1844.

Canalizo rose to power at the time that Mariano Paredes y Arrillaga led a rebellion in Jalisco. Canalizo was another one of Antonio López de Santa Anna's puppets and was ordered by him to dissolve Congress. He did so one day when the deputies did not show up.

He had several confrontations with the deputies, and on December 6, General Manuel Céspedes's army began a revolution against Santa Anna's troops. The people took to the streets and tumbled down a statue of Santa Anna. The rebels arrested Canalizo, forced him out of office, and exiled him to Cadiz.

JOSÉ JOAQUÍN HERRERA (2ND TERM). *Position*: Substitute President, named by General Mariano Paredes and later on named Constitutional President by the senate; *Term*: December 6, 1844–December 30, 1845.

Herrera did not want the presidency at this time, but forced himself to undertake the job due to his patriotic nature. He attempted to reduce government spending. Mexico's biggest problem at this time was the United States and the question of Texas' independence. He tried to avoid war with the United States and to reach an agreement over Texas, but his own general, Mariano Paredes, unfairly accused him of fearing the United States. Herrera soon found himself politically isolated and was forced to resign.

MARIANO PAREDES Y ARRILLAGA (1797–1849). *Place of birth*: Mexico City; *Place of death*: Mexico City; *Wife*: Josefa Cortés; *Position:* Interim President, named by the *Junta de Notables*, later on he was elected by Congress (Vice President: Nicolás Bravo); *Term*: January 4, 1846–July 27, 1846.

Paredes was a military man who had served as a cadet in the *Ejército Trigarante*, but by 1823 he opposed Agustín de Iturbide. Paredes supported the Plan de Tacubaya, following the leadership of Antonio López de Santa Anna, but felt shortchanged when the leader reached power. He separated himself from Santa Anna, and continued his military career.

With the ongoing problems in Texas, Paredes was sent to fight the Texans. Judging José Joaquín Herrera a weak president, Paredes, who was a tough realist, revolted against the government and succeeded Herrera as president.

President James Polk asked the U.S. Congress to declare war on Mexico, and on April 25, 1846, General Zachary Taylor crossed into Mexican territory, chasing General Mariano Arista and catching up with him first in Matamoros and later in Monterrey. Colonel Stephen Kearny took Santa Fe, New Mexico, and then marched west to take San Diego and Los Angeles.

Mexico was in absolute disarray. When Paredes decided to suppress an uprising in Guadalajara, he left general Nicolás Bravo in charge of the government. Paredes went into exile. He came back a short time later and attempted to regain power militarily in 1849, but was defeated. He died that same year.

NICOLÁS BRAVO (3RD TERM). *Position*: He assumed power when President Mariano Paredes left the capitol; *Term*: July 28, 1846–August 4, 1846.

Mexico was in complete anarchy during the few days that Bravo was in power. Veracruz and San Juan de Ulúa adopted the Plan de Jalisco-Guadalajara, and José Mariano Salas ousted Bravo and took the presidency.

Bravo continued his military career and was the commander of the Mexican troops when the U.S. Army took Chapultepec Castle. Once the struggle against the U.S. invasion ended, Bravo retired to Chilpancingo, where he died in 1854.

JOSÉ MARIANO SALAS (1797–1867) (1ST TERM). *Place of birth*: Mexico City; *Place of death*: Villa de Guadalupe Hidalgo, D.F.; *Wife*: Josefa Cardeña; *Position*: *Caudillo* of the *Ciudadela* Revolution, he took power by force; *Term*: August 6, 1846–December 24, 1846.

Salas was a military man. He fought the revolutionary army, and later joined in Agustín de Iturbide's Plan de Iguala. When Antonio López de

Santa Anna became president, Salas was one of his most loyal supporters. When Mariano Paredes left the city to fight an insurrection in Guadalajara and left Nicolás Bravo in the presidency, Salas worked out a plan to restore Antonio López de Santa Anna to the presidency. The Salas-Bravo agreement was signed, and Nicolás Bravo handed over the National Palace to Salas without a fight. Santa Anna had just returned from exile in Cuba and was waiting in Veracruz for Salas's signal. Santa Anna moved to San Luis Potosí where he worked to organize an army to oppose the American invasion. By decree, Salas restored the Constitution of 1824 and installed Santa Anna in the presidency, with Valentín Gómez Farías as vice president. Santa Anna did not travel to Mexico City, but left Gómez Farías in charge of the government.

Salas ended up as governor of the state of Querétaro.

VALENTÍN GÓMEZ FARÍAS (2ND TERM). *Position*: Vice President of Antonio López de Santa Anna, he governed the republic when Santa Anna left the presidency to fight in the north; *Term*: December 24, 1846–March 21, 1847.

Before reaching the presidency, Gómez Farías was the treasury secretary in charge of raising money for the war effort. As president he found himself without funds to defend Mexico against the Yanqui invasion. He first went to the Catholic Church hierarchy and asked for a loan in the amount of 5 million pesos. The church refused to lend him the money, and Gómez Farías, who was a firm believer in the liberal anticlerical principles of his party, asked Congress to allow him to sell some of the land that belonged to the Catholic Church.

As a result, a tremendous struggle ensued between the church and the state. The people sided with the church, and the government proceeded to issue a decree that allowed it to confiscate the land owned by the church. He was able to collect about 15 million pesos from the transactions, as well as the eternal hatred of the church, which began an all-out attack against him that would eventually oust him from the presidency.

The whole country became a battlefield. The invading U.S. Army was in Veracruz and near San Luis Potosí. There were uprisings fueled by the church in Oaxaca and Durango. A regiment of the army known as the Polkos revolted against Gómez Farías, Congress, and Santa Anna. Another regiment, known as the Puros, clashed with the Polkos. Santa Anna returned to the capital to take charge of the government, albeit only for a few days.

ANTONIO LÓPEZ DE SANTA ANNA (7TH TERM). *Position*: Interim President (Vice President: Valentín Gómez Farías); *Term*: March 21, 1847– April 2, 1847.

Upon returning to Mexico City after thirteen days in the presidency,

Santa Anna petitioned Congress for massive loans and obtained about 20 million pesos to help fight the invading Americans at Veracruz. He left to fight them, and named General Pedro María Anaya as his temporary replacement.

PEDRO MARÍA ANAYA (1794–1854) (1ST TERM). *Place of birth*: Huichapan, Hidalgo; *Place of death*: Mexico City; *Position*: Substitute President. Antonio López de Santa Anna left him in office, and he was confirmed by Congress, which also abolished the vice presidency; *Term*: April 2, 1847–May 20, 1847.

Anaya was a capable military officer, secretary of War and the Navy. He played a big role in the defense of Mexico City during the U.S. invasion. He declared Mexico City under siege and warned that any person caught collaborating with the Americans would be considered a traitor.

Knowing his army was no match for the Americans, he decided to adopt guerrilla tactics against the intruder. Even though he was able to resist the American attack at the Churubusco Convent longer than expected, given the differences between the two armies, he lost the battle. Apprehended by the Americans, he was asked where he stored the ammunition. General Anaya answered, "If we had had ammunition in storage, you wouldn't be here."

From Churubusco, the U.S. Army marched toward Chapultepec Castle, which was defended by a handful of young cadets, the famed *Niños Héroes*, who fought courageously. The flag of the United States was raised over the National Palace of Mexico City on September 14, 1847. The Mexican government had fled and established itself in Querétaro, where Santa Anna was reinstated as president.

ANTONIO LÓPEZ DE SANTA ANNA (8TH TERM). *Position*: Interim President; *Term*: May 20, 1847–September 16, 1847.

Santa Anna was in power for a total of four months. During this, his eighth term, there was little Santa Anna could do. The U.S. Army had occupied Mexico City, the center of power in Mexico. Santa Anna resigned and fled the country.

MANUEL DE LA PEÑA Y PEÑA (1789–1850) (1ST TERM). *Place of birth*: Villa de Tacuba, D.F.; *Place of death*: Mexico City; *Wife*: [first name not known] Osta; *Position*: He was president of the Supreme Court when he was called to Querétaro to govern after Antonio López de Santa Anna's resignation; *Term*: September 26, 1847–November 13, 1847.

De la Peña studied law. He had strong Spanish links and was a City Hall Trustee, and in 1820 the king of Spain named him *oidor* of Quito. He did not, however, assume the post because he soon severed his ties with the Spanish Crown and joined the insurgent movement in Mexico. Agustín de

Iturbide appointed him as state counselor and, later on, ambassador to Colombia. He was a minister in the Supreme Court of Justice, secretary of the interior, and secretary of foreign affairs. He was also a senator and deputy to Congress several times. He was a member of the Medical Society and the San Carlos Academy. In 1841 he formulated a Civil Code. He was a member of the Conserving Power, as Congress was called then.

By the time he was installed in the presidency in Querétaro, the country was in complete chaos. Several states, such as Michoacán and Yucatan, were threatening to separate from the union. There were various uprisings in other states, and the Americans were still in Mexico City.

De la Peña attempted to hold peace talks with the Americans while trying to subdue Santa Anna militarily. He renounced the presidency.

PEDRO MARÍA ANAYA (2ND TERM). *Position*: Interim President; he took office in Querétaro; *Term*: November 13, 1847–January 8, 1848.

Anaya was named president by Congress and confirmed by a vote of the state governors. During these terrible times, Anaya asserted that the only way to rule was through the federal system of government. He suggested that the entire country adhere to the principles of the Constitution; thus, the country would be united and the republic could be saved. He designated the city of Aguascalientes as the site of the presidency, in case Querétaro was captured by the United States and the government was forced to move again.

As had been stipulated when he was named president, he resigned three months into his presidency and became the minister of war. He later became the director of the Mexican Post Office, the post he still held when he passed away.

MANUEL DE LA PEÑA Y PEÑA (2ND TERM). *Position*: President of the Republic, named by Congress; *Term*: January 8, 1848–May 30, 1848.

De la Peña presided over the signing of the peace agreements between Mexico and the United States. It was then that Mexico lost half of its territory—California, New Mexico, and Texas—for $15 million. This treaty, called Guadalupe Hidalgo, was signed on February 2, 1848, by Luis G. Cuevas, Bernardo Couto, and Miguel Atristáin, for Mexico, and by Nicholas Trist, for the United States. In May, in Querétaro, it was reluctantly ratified by the Mexican Congress. On March 16, the treaty was ratified, with amendments by the United States.

De la Peña resigned the presidency and went back to the Supreme Court of Justice.

JOSÉ JOAQUÍN HERRERA (3RD TERM). *Position*: Elected President, he took oath before Congress; *Term*: June 3, 1848–January 15, 1851.

Herrera became president as the American troops were leaving Mexico. The country was in shambles, and there were bands of thieves and bandits roaming throughout the nation. He tried to reestablish law and order and sought to organize government. He reduced public and military spending. He also attempted to put an end to corruption within the government. Rebellions began sprouting up everywhere. Some were inspired by nationalistic feelings, like the one begun in Aguascalientes and led by General Mariano Paredes who opposed the Treaty of Guadalupe with the United States. The *santanistas*, headed by Leonardo Márquez, also took up arms. The indigenous people revolted in the state of Veracruz as well. Herrera also survived the internecine War of *Castas* in Yucatan. Political parties were once again at each other's throats. Mexico seemed headed toward civil war.

Herrera, tired, sick, and impoverished, resigned the presidency and retired to his home in Tacubaya where he died.

MARIANO ARISTA (1802–1855). *Place of birth*: San Luis Potosí, San Luis Potosí; *Place of death*: On board the English ship *Tagus*, traveling from Lisbon to France; *Wife*: Guadalupe Martell; *Position*: Constitutional President, elected by Congress; *Term*: January 15, 1851–January 6, 1853.

At age fifteen, Arista enlisted in the Provincial Regiment of Puebla. In 1821 he aligned himself with Agustín de Iturbide. In 1833 when the liberals came to power, he was exiled to the United States.

He returned to Mexico when the Plan de Cuernavaca triumphed. He was a member of the *Tribunal de Guerra* of the *Junta del Código Militar* and a military inspector. He was also the secretary of war and the navy. Arista was a moderate who tried in vain to put an end to corruption in the military and the treasury.

With the country almost in bankruptcy, Arista attempted to energize agriculture, mining, and the incipient Mexican industrial plant. In his administration, the initial plans for a railroad route to Veracruz were mapped. He set the tone for the relationship between the state and the church that later would inspire the *Leyes de Reforma*. He struggled against *santanistas*, conservatives, the reactionary press, and several military factions.

In the midst of ferocious opposition, Arista always defended the federal system, sought to reestablish order through legal means, and tried to make liberty and justice prevail in Mexico.

When Arista resigned the presidency, the president of the Supreme Court assumed power, and Arista retired to Seville, Spain. Later, during Ignacio Comonfort's term, Arista was declared "*Benemérito de la Patria*" ("Glorious Son of the Motherland").

Population of Mexico 1852: 7,661,919

JUAN BAUTISTA CEBALLOS (1811–1859). *Place of birth*: Durango, Durango; *Place of death*: Paris, France; *Position*: Interim President, named by Congress; *Term*: January 6, 1853–February 8, 1853.

Ceballos studied law at the College of San Nicolás in Morelia. He was a good friend of Melchor Ocampo and Santos Degollado. He was a member of Congress and general secretary of the Government. When Mariano Arista renounced the presidency, Ceballos, being next in the line of succession as president of the Supreme Court, assumed the position.

MANUEL MARÍA LOMBARDINI (1802–1853). *Place of birth*: Mexico City; *Place of death*: Mexico City; *Wife*: Refugio Alegría; *Position*: President, through a military coup; *Term*: February 8, 1853–March 20, 1853.

Lombardini was a military man. He served in the Patriot Company in Tacubaya in 1814. He later fought in the war against the United States. His presidency lasted only a few days, but he faced serious political problems in the states of Oaxaca and Puebla. There were also uprisings led by Juan Alvarez and by Antonio López de Santa Anna.

Lombardini retired prematurely to let Santa Anna return to power, and became chief of war operations in Mexico City. He died soon afterward.

ANTONIO LÓPEZ DE SANTA ANNA (9TH TERM). *Position*: President; he took oath before the president of the Supreme Court; Military Dictator; *Term*: April 20, 1853–August 12, 1855.

Santa Anna began his last term as president of Mexico by suppressing freedom of the press. Then he named a commission to search for a European prince to govern Mexico. He created a secret police force to harass members of the opposition. He instituted a nonvoluntary recruitment for the army called "leva," and to restore the power of the army he borrowed heavily from the treasury. Soon the country was back again in bankruptcy, so Santa Anna established new taxes on property, industry, and commerce. He even devised a tax on windows, doors, and pets.

Then, in December 1853, came an offer Santa Anna could not refuse. The United States offered to buy 62,138.81 square miles in the lower portion of New Mexico and Arizona for $10 million. While the United States made it clear it would not take no for an answer, Santa Anna was not too unhappy to get the money, and the Mesilla Treaty was signed. Santa Anna may have felt lucky, but that was not the case for a new generation of Mexicans who could not take more from the man that had forced Congress to name him *Alteza Serenísima* (His Most Serene Highness).

In the south of Mexico, General Juan Alvarez launched a revolt against Santa Anna and promoted the Plan de Ayutla, which repudiated the dictator. Ignacio Comonfort attacked the *santanistas* vigorously in Acapulco. Santa Anna went into exile one more time.

In 1857, both in Mexico and in the United States, there was fear Spain would try to invade Mexico again. From exile, Santa Anna, while blasting General Alvarez, offered his services to head the Mexican army. In spite of the support of the American ambassador John Forsyth, his offer was declined.

Santa Anna, however, kept in touch with Mexico. Four years later, he tried to convince the members of the Conservative Party, who were searching for a foreign prince to rule Mexico, to allow him to conduct the negotiations. As payment for his services, he asked for a noble title and a position in the new monarchy. The conservative hierarchy declined his offer.

Santa Anna returned to Mexico in 1864. The French army had occupied the country, waiting for the arrival of Maximilian of Hapsburg, and Mexico's legitimate government was headed by Benito Juárez. Santa Anna published a manifesto, written while living in exile on the Caribbean island of Saint Thomas, which created some political unrest. It also angered French military commander General Francoise Bazaine, who became so incensed with the publication that he expelled the former president from his own country.

Once again exiled in Havana, Santa Anna waited in vain for the stopover of Archduke Maximilian of Hapsburg en route to Mexico. Santa Anna returned to Saint Thomas, where he wrote Machiavelian letters and another manifesto (July 8, 1865) favoring the restoration of the Republic in Mexico. Neither the letters nor the manifesto were considered favorably by the Conservative Party.

Afterward, he made several attempts at returning to his homeland, but they never materialized. Controversy followed him all his life. To conservatives, he was the great politician destined to save Mexico; liberals thought he was a traitor. Sometimes his movements were closely watched by the intelligence services of big powers like France. Once, French warships kept watch while he was in Saint Thomas.

His life was surrounded by judiciary problems, intrigues, lies, slander, and swindling, whether he was in Mexico City, Manga de Clavo, Havana, Saint Thomas, or Elizabethport, New Jersey.

Nothing ever killed the will of this old man to return to Mexico and grab power once again. On June 27, 1874, Santa Anna returned for the last time to Mexico, thanks to the efforts of his wife Dolores Tosta and his friend Joaquín Alcalde, who were able to obtain a special presidential permit. Only his brother-in-law awaited his arrival in Veracruz. The old dictator took offense at the indifference of his compatriots to his return. In Mexico City, he received a cold but courteous audience from President Sebastián Lerdo de Tejada. In the early hours of June 21, 1876, he died in his sleep. He is buried in a humble grave in Mexico City.

MARTÍN CARRERA (1806–1871). *Place of birth*: Puebla, Puebla; *Place of death*: Mexico City; *Wife*: María de los Angeles Lardizábal; *Position*: Interim President, named by the *Junta de Representantes de los Departa-*

mentos in the Chamber of Deputies; *Term*: August 15, 1855–September 12, 1855.

Carrera was a military man. As a child he accompanied his father in the military exercises of the viceroy's army. He became an officer at the age of twelve and was a member of the *Ejército Trigarante*.

In a gesture of loyalty toward President Vicente Guerrero, Carrera helped the president fend off an attempted coup during the time of the Acordada uprising in the capital. He took command of the garrison at San Luis Potosí and later fought in Mexico City, Guanajuato, and elsewhere.

He was granted the promotion to major general by Antonio López de Santa Anna. He was a senator and a consultant to the Minister of War. When the Plan de Ayutla was launched by Juan Alvarez to unseat Santa Anna, Carrera was elected president. He failed to obtain approval from the majority of those involved in the plan and resigned the presidency after a very short stay.

RÓMULO DÍAZ DE LA VEGA (1804–1877). *Place of birth*: Mexico City; *Place of death*: Puebla, Puebla; *Position*: Interim President; Martín Carrera left him in charge of the office, the city, and the district; *Term*: September 12, 1855–October 4, 1855.

Díaz studied for a military career, specializing in military engineering. In 1821 he supported the Plan de Iguala, launched by Agustín de Iturbide. He then joined the *Ejército Trigarante*. In 1830 he fought alongside Nicolás Bravo against General Juan Alvarez. In 1833 he was ousted from the army on charges of insubordination, but was reinstated in 1835.

Díaz fought in the war against the United States. In one battle, he was apprehended and taken to New Orleans. He was later released in a prisoner exchange. Unluckily, at the battle of Cerro Gordo he was again captured and held prisoner in San Juan de Ulúa by the Americans.

Once freed, Díaz was recognized as a military hero and was sent to Yucatan to suppress the indigenous rebellion there called the War of *Castas*. This campaign earned him the rank of general and command of the Mexico City garrison.

He participated in a conspiracy against President Ignacio Comonfort and was later apprehended and exiled. When he returned to Mexico City, he served in several positions in the federal government and was instrumental in bringing Maximilian of Hapsburg to Mexico. He held a government position during the Empire. When the Republic was restored, he was confined to Puebla where he died a very poor man.

JUAN N. ALVAREZ (1790–1867). *Place of birth*: Atoyac, Guerrero; *Place of death*: Hacienda de La Providencia, Guerrero; *Wife*: Faustina Benítez; *Position*: President, elected in Cuernavaca by the states' representatives; *Term*: October 4, 1855–December 11, 1855.

Alvarez was born into a wealthy family, but spent many years in his youth working as a cowboy. In 1810 he became a soldier in the independence movement, and during the war of independence, he was under the command of José María Morelos and fought in several battles with him. Injured in both legs during a battle in Acapulco, he was saved from death by a young soldier named Eugenio Salas.

In 1821 Alvarez supported the Plan de Iguala and fought alongside Agustín de Iturbide.

Alvarez was a liberal, a federalist, and a republican. He was devoted, physically and spiritually, to the causes he believed in, even to the point of putting his personal fortune at their service.

He battled against Agustín de Iturbide in 1828. In 1831 Alvarez attempted to save Vicente Guerrero, who was being betrayed. He was opposed to centralism, and for several years he fought Anastasio Bustamante. He was also active in fighting against the French and American interventions. He opposed Antonio López de Santa Anna as well, and launched his Plan de Ayutla to unseat him.

He was inaugurated president in 1855, and he swore he would respect and protect the Plan de Ayutla. He surrounded himself with the best and the brightest of the emerging liberal politicians—people like Benito Juárez, Melchor Ocampo, Guillermo Prieto, and Ignacio Comonfort. During his presidency, he always fought for the rights of the peasants in Mexico, but his term lasted only a short while. He resigned the presidency two months into his term, but continued fighting for his liberal principles until the end of his life. He fought in the War of Reform, and later, during the French intervention, he was in charge of the military campaign. President Juárez instructed all military commands and his cabinet that whenever circumstances of war prevented them from consulting with him, General Alvarez was to be consulted and had the authority to decide the course of action.

Once he retired, Alvarez wrote a book analyzing the peons' situation in Mexico at the time. When he passed away, the Mexican government named him *"Benemérito de la Patria"* ("Glorious Son of the Motherland").

IGNACIO COMONFORT (1812–1863). *Place of birth*: South of Puebla; *Place of death*: Molino de Soria, on the road to Celaya; *Position*: Substitute President and later on Constitutional President (Vice President: Benito Juárez); *Term*: December 11, 1855–January 21, 1858.

Comonfort studied in Puebla. He abandoned his studies when his father died, and as a very young man went to work in agriculture. In 1832 he enlisted in the army to fight against the government of Anastasio Bustamante. Once his cause won, he left the army and tried his luck in the private sector. Afterward, he entered the public sector, in what currently is the state of Guerrero, distinguishing himself with his administrative abilities.

In 1842 he was elected a federal deputy, but was never sworn in because

Antonio López de Santa Anna dissolved Congress. Elected deputy for a second time in 1846, he had the same fate. This time, however, it was President Mariano Paredes y Arrillaga who dissolved the Chamber of Deputies. One year later, he reenlisted in the army to fight against the American invasion. He finally was able to serve in Congress as a federal deputy in 1848, and as senator in 1851. In 1854 he became the customs administrator in Acapulco, but then Santa Anna fired him.

Comonfort supported the Plan de Ayutla, launched by General Juan Alvarez, and fought against Santa Anna in Acapulco. Alvarez sent Comonfort on a mission to raise funds in the United States. He was able to borrow 60,000 pesos at an exorbitant interest rate, bought some weapons and ammunition, and returned to Mexico to fight Santa Anna. Soon the revolutionaries were attacking the dictator on several fronts, and Santa Anna decided to leave the country in August 1855.

Alvarez became president, and Comonfort was appointed minister of war. Two months later, Alvarez resigned, and Comonfort became interim president.

During Comonfort's presidency, he dissolved the Congress and crushed the Zacapoaxtla Revolution that had been engineered by the Conservative Party as a maneuver against Comonfort's liberal-minded government. He also had to combat many other uprisings sprouting up all over Mexico.

During his administration, the *Ley Tejada* (Tejada's law) was promulgated. This law, elaborated by the minister of the treasury, Sebastián Lerdo de Tejada, allowed the government to confiscate the properties of the church, except the land on which the churches were built.

The move had a heavy political cost. Supported by a few liberals, Comonfort suffered an all-out military attack by the conservative armies. Generals Miguel Miramón and Francisco Orihuela took Puebla, Tomás Mejía secured Querétaro, Santiago Vidaurri controlled Coahuila and Nuevo León, and Luis G. Osollo attacked San Luis Potosí.

Meanwhile in Mexico City, Congress issued the Constitution of 1857. Elections were held, and Comonfort ascended to the presidency. He named Benito Juárez as Supreme Court head justice, and conservative General Félix Zuloaga proclaimed the Plan de Tacubaya, the goal of which was to invalidate the new constitution.

Comonfort made a mistake. He believed the conspirators had legal grounds to nullify the Constitution, and he even jailed Juárez. Encouraged by Comonfort's error, the conservatives demanded the presidency for their leader, Zuloaga. Comonfort appealed to his liberal constituency, but found no support. Realizing he had made a mistake, he freed Juárez and the other jailed legislators.

Then, Comonfort exiled himself in the United States, and Juárez, who as president of the Supreme Court was next in line for the presidency, became president.

Comonfort returned to Mexico after some years in exile. He volunteered his services during the French invasion of 1863. In November of that same year, he was attacked by a band of bandits near Celaya and was mortally wounded. He died while seeking medical assistance.

Once Comonfort quit the presidency, Mexico entered into a period of extreme political turbulence. It is perhaps best characterized as a time during which Mexico had two parallel governments running from 1858 to 1872. One government was headed by Benito Juárez; the other had a series of conservative leaders as head of state.

The conservative governments during these difficult times began with President Félix Zuloaga.

Liberals	Conservatives
Benito Juárez: January 19, 1858–March 1, 1861	Félix Zuloaga: January 23, 1858–December 23, 1858
	M. Robles Pezuela: December 23, 1858–January 21, 1859
	Miguel Miramón: February 2, 1859–August 13, 1860
	José Ignacio Pavón: August 14, 1860–August 15, 1860
Benito Juárez: March 1, 1861–November 8, 1865	Miguel Miramón: August 15. 1860–December 24, 1861
	French Occupation: 1862–1864
	Junta de Regencia: June 1863–April 1864
Benito Juárez: November 8, 1865–December 1, 1867	Maximilian of Hapsburg: January 10, 1864–May 15, 1867

FÉLIX ZULOAGA (1813–1898). *Place of birth*: Alamos, Sonora; *Place of death*: Mexico City; *Wife*: Guadalupe Palafox; *Position*: Interim President, elected by the majority of votes of the *Junta de Representantes de los Departamentos*; *Term*: January 23, 1858–December 23, 1858.

Zuloaga was a military officer and a conservative politician. He studied in Chihuahua and Mexico City. In 1834 he began his military career. In 1840 he was on President Anastasio Bustamante's side, but later, in 1841, he turned and aligned himself with Antonio López de Santa Anna.

Even though Zuloaga was very outspoken against the liberal Plan de Ayutla, he was very close to Ignacio Comonfort, so close that he was able to convince Comonfort, a liberal, that the Constitution of 1857 was too radical and could never be implemented. When Zuloaga issued the Plan de Tacubaya, Comonfort supported him, not realizing, perhaps, that his support was, in a way, a self-inflicted coup d'état. Comonfort was denying himself the legitimacy of his government as stated in the very same constitution he had just rejected.

As soon as Comonfort was ousted from office, the conservatives placed Zuloaga in the presidency. He started his government under two strict conservative principles, religion and patriotism. He upheld Catholicism as the official religion. He also declared himself to be in favor of upholding Mexico's independence. Zuloaga's government was short-lived. A conservative military uprising led by generals Miguel María de Echegaray and Manuel Robles Pezuela called for Zuloaga's ouster, and offered the presidency to Miguel Miramón. Zuloaga was indeed ousted, but Robles Pezuela became interim president.

MANUEL ROBLES PEZUELA (1817–1862). *Place of birth*: Guanajuato, Guanajuato; *Place of death*: San Andrés Chalchicomula, Puebla; *Wife*: Paula Rocha; *Position*: He took office by force, following the Plan de Navidad; *Term*: December 23, 1858–January 21, 1859.

Robles Pezuela was a conservative military man. He took part in many revolutions, and he fought tirelessly against the liberals of Mexico. He served as the minister of war and the navy in the Mariano Arista administration. He seconded the Plan de Navidad, which opposed General Félix Zuloaga.

Very little can be said about his term. It lasted about a month, and he did nothing to merit mention.

When the French army invaded Mexico in 1862, Robles Pezuela sided with the French and attempted to join the invaders in Veracruz. He was, however, spotted and militarily engaged by a Republican army. Taken prisoner, he was declared a traitor and shot by the forces of General Ignacio Zaragoza.

MIGUEL MIRAMÓN (1831–1867) (1ST TERM). *Place of birth*: Mexico City; *Place of death*: Cerro de las Campanas, Querétaro; *Wife*: Concepción Lombardo; *Position*: Substitute President, named by Félix Zuloaga; later on he was elected by the representatives of the *Departamentos* as Interim President; *Term*: February 2, 1859–August 13, 1860.

Miramón was a conservative leader. He had an impressive reputation as a military man. He was courageous, energetic, intelligent, and extremely skillful in commanding troops. He took part in the war against the United States as a very young man. He was imprisoned during the U.S. occupation and detested Mexico's northern neighbor.

He supported Antonio López de Santa Anna and fought against the liberal Plan de Ayutla. He also fought against Ignacio Comonfort. It was Miramón who reinstated Zuloaga as president when the Manuel Robles

Pezuela's uprising occurred, and in return Zuloaga named Miramón substitute president on February 2, 1859.

As president, Miramón negotiated a loan from a Swiss-French banker for approximately 1 million pesos. Once the interest was added, the amount owed grew to 15 million pesos! Later on, the French army would use this "loan" as a pretext for the invasion of 1862.

When the substitute presidency expired on August 13, 1860, Miramón transferred power to Supreme Court President José Ignacio Pavón. Pavón lasted only two days, as Miramón was elected interim president by a majority of votes by the states' representatives.

JOSÉ IGNACIO PAVÓN (1791–1866). *Place of birth*: Veracruz, Veracruz; *Place of death*: Mexico City; *Wife*: Felipa González del Castillo; *Position*: As president of the Supreme Court, he was left in charge of the executive office when Miguel Miramón had to leave office; *Term*: August 13, 1860–August 15, 1860.

Pavón belonged to the Conservative Party of Mexico. As president of the Supreme Court, he became president when Miguel Miramón's period as substitute president ended. His designation, however, lasted only two days because Miramón was immediately elected interim president.

MIGUEL MIRAMÓN (2ND TERM). *Position*: Elected by the majority vote of the states' representatives; *Term*: August 15, 1860–December 24, 1861.

Miramón started his second term following the same pursuits he had cherished during his first presidency—to defeat the liberals militarily and politically. He was especially focused on Benito Juárez, who had moved his government to Veracruz. To that end, Miramón attempted a combined land-sea attack against Juárez in Veracruz, but the boats purchased in Cuba for that sole purpose were taken away from the conservative forces by the U.S. fleet anchored at Veracruz. Frustrated, Miramón, who was in command of the land forces, returned to Mexico City empty-handed.

During Miramón's administration, the Mexican government was bankrupt. Regardless, he continued to sink more money into the crusade against the liberal party of Mexico. His battles had mixed outcomes. Sometimes he won, sometimes he did not, but in 1860 he was defeated at Silao. A few months later, he was defeated again in Guadalajara. Finally, after the battle of Calpulalpan (in the State of Mexico) on December 22, 1861, the War of Reform was over, and the conservatives had lost it.

Miramón returned to Mexico City, and after a cabinet meeting decided to resign and flee the country. He traveled to Havana, and while he was there, the Conservative Party asked him to go to Europe in search of a prince who would agree to govern Mexico. Miramón held meetings with Napoleon III of France and Queen Isabel II of Spain.

Some years later, when Maximilian of Hapsburg became the emperor of Mexico, Miramón returned to Mexico and put himself at the emperor's service. Maximilian sent Miramón to Berlin to study military tactics.

By 1866, as Maximilian was about to abdicate, Miramón returned from Europe and convinced the emperor to remain. Miramón was placed in charge of the imperial army.

When the definitive encounter between the conservatives and liberals took place in the city of Querétaro, Miramón was badly injured and was taken prisoner. He, Maximilian, and Tomás Mejía were executed by a firing squad on a hill called the Cerro de las Campanas. In a generous token of chivalry, Emperor Maximilian offered Miramón the center position before the firing squad.

Population of Mexico 1862: 8,396,524 Inhabitants

BENITO PABLO JUÁREZ GARCÍA (1806–1872). "Glorious Son of the Americas." *Place of birth*: San Pablo Guelatao, Oaxaca; *Place of death*: National Palace in Mexico City; *Wife*: Margarita Maza; *Parents*: Marcelino Juárez and Brígida García; *Position*: Constitutional President (Vice President: Jesús González Ortega); *Terms*: Juárez was president for five consecutive terms that ran from 1858 to 1872. When Ignacio Comonfort resigned in 1858, Juárez was the president of the Supreme Court and, given the rules for succession, became president from January 19, 1858, to March 1, 1861. He was reelected for a second term from March 1, 1861, to November 8, 1865. The third term came as a result of a decree he issued that extended his presidential functions and those of the president of the Supreme Court from November 8, 1865, to December 1, 1867, for reasons of national security. The fourth period began with the restoration of the republic in 1867 and ended in 1871. His last term began in that same year and ended with his death in 1872. Throughout his first three terms there was a parallel government headed by various members of the Conservative Party.

Juárez was the son of two Zapotec Indians dedicated to agriculture. As a child, he was a shepherd, and at the age of thirteen, he was illiterate and spoke only Zapotec. He learned to read when he moved to the city of Oaxaca and went to work as a servant for Antonio Salanueva, an educated priest who also taught him bookbinding and mathematics, and sent him to school.

At the Santa Cruz Seminary in Oaxaca, Juárez studied high school subjects and excelled in Latin and philosophy. At the Institute of Sciences and Arts, he graduated as a lawyer. Later on, he became a teacher and an administrator.

In 1831 he became the mayor of the city of Oaxaca and, two years later, a deputy to the state legislature. As a lawyer he defended the indigenous communities. In 1841 he was a civil judge, and in 1843 he married Margarita Maza, the daughter of one of his former employers.

Juárez became a federal deputy in 1847. It was Juárez's job to approve the loan that the church was to give to Valentín Gómez Farías. Later he became the governor of Oaxaca. Throughout his time in Oaxaca, he furthered many charitable works. He also became the director of the Institute of Sciences and Arts.

When Antonio López de Santa Anna returned to the presidency in 1853, many liberals were exiled from Mexico. While living in New Orleans, Juárez met Melchor Ocampo and other exiled liberals who were trying to organize a revolutionary council.

When the Plan de Ayutla triumphed, Juárez returned to Mexico and went to work under General Juan Alvarez. Once in the presidency, Alvarez appointed Juárez as the minister of justice. On November 23, 1855, Juárez, as chief justice, promulgated the *Ley sobre la Administración de Justicia de los Tribunales de la Nación*, better known as the Juárez Law, that ended all ecclesiastical and military privileges.

He returned to Oaxaca and held the governorship for a second time when a constitutional congress was meeting in Mexico City to articulate the 1857 constitution. Ignacio Comonfort appointed Juárez as minister of government and later on, president of the Supreme Court of Justice, making him the de facto vice president of the Republic, given the rules for succession.

At the end of December 1857, Félix Zuloaga issued the Plan de Tacubaya, which demanded nullification of the 1857 Constitution. President Comonfort supported the plan, but Juárez opposed it. Zuloaga issued an order for his arrest, and Juárez was imprisoned. The reaction of the liberals against Comonfort made him free Juárez, and forced his resignation and subsequent exile in the United States.

Juárez assumed the presidency on January 19, 1858, in Guanajuato. Five days later Zuloaga also became president and, supported by the conservative armies, began a chase of President Juárez throughout the territory. From Guanajuato, Juárez moved to Guadalajara, then to Colima and Manzanillo. From the west coast, he went to Veracruz, via Panama, on the Gulf of Mexico.

In 1859, while in Veracruz, Juárez issued the Reform Laws that established the separation between church and state. He ordered the expropriation of the properties of the church, suppressed the establishment of religious communities, and forbade the building of any new convents. He also established a law for civil marriage, the Civil Registry office, and the secularization of graveyards. He instituted freedom of religion and reduced the number of officially sanctioned religious holidays. He advocated widespread education, encouraged the development of industries, promoted trade and agriculture, and defended freedom of the press.

In January 1861 the constitutionalist troops entered Mexico City. Juárez returned to the capital, where he established his office and named a cabinet. The Constitution and the Reform movements were his inspiration.

Juárez was reelected president for a second term, and Jesús González Ortega became president of the Supreme Court on March 1, 1861. The country was in absolute disarray. There was no money in the treasury, and the army, which had been disbanded, turned to looting. Meanwhile, the conservative armies kept on the attack against the liberal government. Forced by circumstances, on July 17, 1861, Juárez suspended payments on the foreign debt.

Six months later, English, French, and Spanish ships anchored in Veracruz to enforce collection of the debt that Mexico owed them. Juárez began negotiations with the three powers, but was interrupted when new French ships arrived in Veracruz, this time carrying Mexican nationals—members of the Conservative Party who had traveled to Europe searching for a foreign prince to govern Mexico. A few years later, Maximilian of Hapsburg became emperor of Mexico.

The English and the Spaniards settled their negotiations with Juárez and left. The French remained, thus beginning their military occupation of Mexico.

The country was divided into two irreconcilable sides, with the liberals seeking support and funds in the United States and the conservatives doing the same in Europe. Juárez sent Melchor Ocampo to deal with the United States, and the latter negotiated the so-called McLane-Ocampo Treaty. The treaty was never approved by the U.S. Senate, but if it had been, it would have granted everlasting free transit to the United States in three parts of Mexico in exchange for diplomatic recognition.

By the beginning of 1862, the French army began its march from Veracruz to Mexico City. On May 5 of that year, the Mexican army, commanded by General Ignacio Zaragoza, heroically defended the city of Puebla and defeated the armies of Napoleon III. However, in less than a year, the French soldiers captured Mexico City, and Juárez had to abandon the capital and establish his government in San Luis Potosí. The occupation army named a *Junta Superior de Gobierno* composed of thirty-five people. The *junta* declared the formation of the monarchy and offered the crown to Maximilian.

The conservatives had gained the upper hand in the war and continued chasing Juárez unmercifully throughout the country. Juárez, running from one place to another, figured out a maneuver that would allow him to uphold his position and freeze the functions of the president of the Supreme Court, thus saving the presidency for himself. The move dismayed many liberals; however, there were many others who understood why Juárez had proceeded that way.

Juárez's third term took place while Maximilian was emperor of Mexico.

Juárez kept moving the site of the government from one place to another—from Chihuahua to Zacatecas to Jerez and to San Luis Potosí. The balance of military power finally began to tilt in Juárez' favor by 1865 when arms and ammunition coming from the United States reached Juárez' forces, and Napoleon III had second thoughts about keeping his armies in Mexico while Prussia's power was rising in Europe.

The liberal armies gained momentum and captured Guadalajara, Oaxaca, Monterrey, and Tampico while the French troops marched to Veracruz to sail back to France.

Several skirmishes took place between the liberal and conservative forces, and finally, on May 15, 1867, Maximilian surrendered after a series of battles near Querétaro. Maximilian, Miguel Miramón, and Tomás Mejía were sentenced to death and shot in the Cerro de las Campanas.

Juárez returned to Mexico City on July 15, and the republic was restored.

JUNTA DE REGENCIA (OF THE CONSERVATIVE PARTY) OF JUAN N. ALMONTE, JOSE MARIANO SALAS, PELAGIO ANTONIO DE LABASTIDA, AND JUAN B. ORMACHEA (JUNE 1863–APRIL 1864).

Juan N. Almonte (1803–1869)—*Place of birth*: Nocupétaro or in Carácuaro, Michoacán; *Place of death*: Paris, France; *Wife*: Dolores Quesada; *Position*: President. Almonte was the illegitimate son of José María Morelos y Pavón. He learned the secrets of warfare by following his father in battle, and he was wounded in battle. He was sent to study in the United States as a teenager. He came back to Mexico when the Plan de Iguala was proclaimed, only to return to the United States when Agustín de Iturbide named himself emperor.

After Iturbide's fall, Almonte returned to Mexico and then followed a diplomatic career in the Mexican embassies in London and Rio de Janeiro. In 1834, he worked on the tracing of the boundary between Mexico and the United States. He fought the Texans in the battle of San Jacinto, and was imprisoned in 1836. Later, he was released and returned to Mexico. In 1842, Almonte was named Mexican ambassador to Washington, D.C., and later played a key role in defending Mexico during the U.S. invasion of Veracruz.

Politically, he flipped-flopped from republican to liberal to conservative to clerical and monarchical, as did many other Mexicans of his time. Once he became a member of the conservative party, he fought against the liberals and the Constitution of 1857. Almonte traveled to Europe as part of a group searching for a monarch to govern Mexico. Upon his return to Mexico, he went back into politics. In 1862, while in Veracruz, and with the support of the French army, he appointed himself chief of the nation, denying recognition to the government of Benito Juárez.

Once the French occupied Mexico City, Marshall Elias Frederick Forey appointed a *Junta Superior de Gobierno*, which adopted a monarchical type of government and declared that the crown was reserved for Maximilian of Hapsburg. Almonte was appointed second in command. He was also in charge of the welcoming celebrations for Maximilian and Carlotta's arrival in Mexico.

Among the few actions he took as acting head of the government was his persecution of Supreme Court judges that were involved in the expropriation of the properties of the church.

Maximilian named Almonte a marshall and sent him to France to try to persuade Napoleon III to keep the French army in Mexico to support the empire. Almonte failed in this mission. He remained in Paris until his death.

José Mariano Salas (2nd term)—*Position*: Member of the *Junta de Regencia*.

Pelagio Antonio de Labastida (1816–1891)—*Place of birth*: Zamora, Michoacán; *Place of death*: Oacalco, Morelos; *Position*: Member of the *Junta de Regencia*. Labastida was the bishop of Puebla and the archbishop of Mexico. He was an alumnus, teacher, and president of the Seminary of Michoacán. He was also a lawyer and a judge. In 1856 he was exiled for his support of the revolt of Zacapoaxtla and the threats he issued against the government of Ignacio Comonfort.

He returned to Mexico after the French occupation and formed part of the *Junta de Regencia*. He was dismissed from the *Junta* and traveled to Europe where he remained for a few years. When he finally returned to Mexico, under a political amnesty program in 1871, he devoted himself to the church until his death.

Juan B. Ormachea (1812–1884)—*Place of birth*: Mexico City; *Place of death*: Tulancingo, Hidalgo; *Position: Suplente de la Junta de Regencia*. Ormachea was the bishop in Tulancingo and a member of the *Junta de Regencia*. He was an alumnus of the Archdiocesan Seminary and had a Ph.D. in civil law. He participated in the *Concilio Vaticano* where he made two eloquent speeches, one in Latin and the other in Spanish. He protected schools and hospitals. He wrote many books, and his funeral orations are considered outstanding.

SECOND EMPIRE, 1864–1867

Mexico continued to be in extreme economic ruin at midcentury. Divided into two irreconcilable factions due to the War of Reform, it was heavily in debt and occupied militarily by a foreign power. The legitimate government, headed by Benito Juárez, was constantly on the run.

England, Spain, and France had sent expeditionary forces to Mexico. France, which had an interest in creating a new colonial empire in America, aligned itself with the anti-Juárez Conservative Party and stayed in Mexico for a few years. This allowed the French to maintain a military, political, and economic presence next to the United States. Napoleon III, the Conservative Party of Mexico, and the *Junta de Notables* recruited Maximilian of Hapsburg as the "liberal" prince who could unite public opinion favorably in a short period of time. However, Maximilian did not accomplish his goal, and his attempts to consolidate his empire were futile.

At first, Maximilian was closely allied with the Conservative Party and supported by the French troops. As his situation evolved, he became more liberal and tried to distance himself from the church. When he refused to nullify the Reform Laws, his alliance with the Conservative Party began to erode.

Unfortunately for Maximilian, Napoleon III realized there was little to gain from the occupation. Thus, in less than three years, he ordered the French army to abandon Maximilian, to leave Mexico, and return to Europe. At the same time in France, the liberals were fighting against him; and Germany, which was rising as a military power, was casting a shadow over France.

To make matters worse for Maximilian, his liberal ideals were not supported by the Liberal Party of Mexico, which Juárez dominated. The United States was busy fighting the Civil War and did not pay too much attention to Juárez' problems. The French intervention in Mexico and the Civil War in the United States took place during the same years. When the Union won the war in the United States, the American government immediately expressed its displeasure at having the French army in Mexico, and made surplus military supplies available to the *juaristas*.

Ruler of the Second Empire, 1864–1867

FERDINAND MAXIMILIAN OF HAPSBURG (1832–1867). "Archduke of Austria, Emperor of Mexico." *Place of birth*: Palace of Schönbrunn in Vienna, Austria; *Place of death*: Cerro de las Campanas, Querétaro, Mexico; *Wife*: Empress Carlotta Amalia of Belgium, daughter of King Leopold; *Position*: Emperor; the *Junta de Notables* offered him the imperial throne of Mexico; he accepted the crown and signed the Miramar Treaty with Napoleon III; *Term*: April 10, 1864–May 15, 1867.

Maximilian was the son of Archduke Francis Charles and Duchess Sophie and brother of the Austro-Hungarian Emperor, Francis Joseph. In 1854 he was appointed chief of the Imperial Fleet. In 1856 his brother sent him to France to be an apprentice to Napoleon III, and to learn the trends of nineteenth-century international politics. In 1857 he traveled to Brussels, met Carlotta, and married her. He was the governor of the Lombard-

Venetian Provinces and the viceroy of Milan. In 1859 he established residence in the Miramar Castle, in Trieste.

At about this time, Mexico was coming out of the War of Reform, destitute and bankrupt. President Benito Juárez refused to honor the country's external debt to France, Spain, and England, giving an excellent pretext for an invasion by these three big European powers.

When Napoleon III and the Mexican conservatives asked Maximilian to become emperor of Mexico, he gave a conditional acceptance. He demanded confirmation of the wish of the Mexican people to have him as their sovereign. In 1863 he assumed the crown, believing a Mexican vote had asked for him. He signed the Treaty of Miramar and relinquished any rights to the Austrian crown.

In 1864 Maximilian entered Mexican territory. His reception in liberal Veracruz was cold, but in conservative Puebla and Mexico City, his reception was warm and gracious. His rule had three stages:

1. From June 1865 to February 1866, Maximilian governed under the influence of Napoleon III

2. From February to November 1866, Maximilian went through a transitional stage, trying to free himself from external and internal influences

3. From November 1866 to May 1867, Maximilian was able to establish a more liberal ideology although he was still heavily influenced by the Mexican conservatives.

During his time in office, Maximilian established diplomatic relations with many foreign countries—but not the United States. He traveled extensively throughout Mexico and managed to spend much time in Cuernavaca, near Mexico City, at the Borda Gardens, or at his residence in Acapatzingo.

Maximilian supported liberty, a free press, religious tolerance, civil matrimony laws, and civil rights in opposition to the conservatives of Mexico. He supported the Reform Laws. These liberal inclinations were not appreciated by members of the Conservative Party, which had brought him to Mexico. General Francisco Achilles Bazaine, the French commander, also was not very pleased with his political behavior.

Losing ground on every quarter, Maximilian sent his wife Carlotta to Paris and Rome to seek help that did not materialize. Meanwhile, Juárez and the republican troops kept fighting with determination and moving closer to Mexico City.

In 1866, the emperor left the capital for Orizaba where he had planned to abdicate and return to Europe. At the last minute he changed his mind and decided to stay in Mexico and face the consequences.

On its way to Querétaro, Juárez's army captured him. He was placed in prison in Querétaro and, along with some of his closest collaborators, was sentenced to death. Until his last breath Maximilian remained truly dignified. He was shot at the Cerro de las Campanas, along with Miguel Mira-món and Tomás Mejía. Three months later, his mother, the Archduchess Sophie, sent for Maximilian's body. In November 1867, his corpse was sent home on the ship *Novara*. He is buried in the imperial graveyard of the Capuchins in Vienna.

RESTORATION OF THE REPUBLIC, 1867–1876

After Maximilian's death, there was finally just one government in Mex-ico. Benito Juárez was reinstated as the legitimate president of Mexico. Juárez reestablished the Constitution of 1857 as the supreme law of the land. However, Mexico was in extremely dire straits, economically, so-cially, and morally.

Juárez attempted to move the country into a new era of social, industrial, and spiritual transformation. Yet he knew quite well there were no real possibilities of quickly solving the severe existing social and economic in-equalities. He lacked the economic resources to pull the country from its precarious condition. Public health was endangered by unsanitary living conditions. There was no viable infrastructure of roads or other means of communication. There was rampant corruption in the private and public sectors. Mexico was a country hopelessly behind technologically, and was working with antiquated irrigation systems in agriculture. This was the desolate panorama that Juárez faced.

Freedom and equality, two principles firmly embedded in the Constitu-tion and in Juárez's mind, did not seem to fit in with the sad reality of a country torn apart by a prolonged state of disorder. However, these were the two main principles under which Juárez returned to govern.

Rulers of the Restoration of the Republic, 1867–1876

Population of Mexico 1872: 9,097,056 Inhabitants

BENITO PABLO JUÁREZ GARCÍA. *Position*: Constitutional President, elected twice by Congress; *Terms*: December 1, 1867–July 18, 1871 and August 1871–July 18, 1872.

Juárez continued the political program of the Reform to bring about the separation of church and state that was stated in the Constitution of 1857. He also disbanded the army to save money. This measure, however, created two problems. Without work, many soldiers became bandits; without sol-diers, many generals grew upset and began plotting against the government.

Elections were held, and Congress declared Juárez president for a fourth term. Then, Juárez tried to implement new regulations regarding the separation of power, some presidential attributions, and restrictions to the jurisdiction of the Permanent Commission in Congress. Many of these changes demanded constitutional amendments that were not universally popular. Revolts sprang up everywhere in Mexico, especially in the states of Mexico, Yucatan, Sinaloa, Puebla, Tamaulipas, and Jalisco.

In spite of this climate of discontent, Juárez managed to carry on with his program of government. He founded the *Escuela Nacional Preparatoria* (upper high school), began the construction of the railroad to Veracruz, and worked indefatigably to make Mexico a country of laws rather than leaders.

In 1871 Juárez prepared to run for a fifth term. This time, even some of his friends opposed the idea. Juárez ran against his former protégé, Porfirio Díaz, and also against fellow liberal, Sebastián Lerdo de Tejada.

None of the three candidates won a majority of votes, and Congress named Juárez president. Díaz and many other generals rose up in arms against the government.

Seven months later, President Juárez died at his desk of angina pectoris.

SEBASTIÁN LERDO DE TEJADA (1823 OR 1827–1889). *Place of birth*: Jalapa, Veracruz; *Place of death*: New York, United States; *Wife*: None; Position: Interim President; later Congress named him Constitutional President in an election; *Term*: July 19, 1872–November 20, 1876.

Lerdo was the son of a Spaniard and a *criolla*. He studied at the Seminario Palafoxiano at Puebla. After being ordained to the priesthood, he changed his mind and abandoned ecclesiastical life for a career in jurisprudence at the College of San Ildefonso in Mexico City. He became the fiscal advisor of the Supreme Court and minister of Foreign Affairs during Ignacio Comonfort's presidency in 1857.

At one point, he was appointed president of the College of San Ildefonso, but later returned to political life as a deputy in Congress. He was famous for his gifts in the art of oratory. He was a liberal and a staunch nationalist. In 1863 he became the minister of justice and later of foreign affairs in the government of Benito Juárez.

As president, he incorporated the Reform Laws into the Constitution. He tried to do away with the local bosses and to integrate the whole national territory into one nation. He favored foreign and national investment to build a communication infrastructure that would facilitate commerce within Mexico and between Mexico and other nations. During his term, some scientific institutes were begun and, together with the development of the mining and railroad industries, a slight progress in Mexico's economy began to take place.

When Lerdo sought reelection, a group of generals rose up in arms under the Plan of Tuxtepec, opposing Lerdo's reelection and naming Porfirio Díaz head of the revolt. Lerdo was reelected, and the political and military situation of the country worsened.

Díaz traveled north and launched a revised version of the Plan de Tuxtepec, which not only opposed the principle of reelection but supported the Constitution of 1857 and the Reform Laws. This new plan suppressed the senate, denied recognition to the government of Lerdo, and called for elections.

Angered by what he considered an election marred with fraud, José María Iglesias, who was president of the Supreme Court of Justice, declared himself president and established his government in Guanajuato. In the meantime, Díaz was fighting his way to Mexico City. The revolutionary forces won a decisive battle near Puebla, and in January 1877, Lerdo fled Mexico City.

From the port of Acapulco, he sailed to San Francisco, California, where he lived for nearly a decade. He died in New York City, and his body was brought back to Mexico. He was buried with military honors at the Circle of Distinguished Citizens in the Dolores graveyard.

JOSÉ MARÍA IGLESIAS (1823–1891). *Place of birth*: Mexico City; *Place of death*: Villa de Tacubaya, D.F.; *Wife*: Juana Calderón; *Position*: Iglesias declared himself Interim President when Sebastián Lerdo de Tejada left the country; his government was recognized by the governors of Querétaro, Guanajuato, Aguascalientes, Jalisco, and San Luis Potosí; *Term*: October 31, 1876–January 23, 1877.

Iglesias was a jurist and a politician. He studied at the College of San Gregorio. He then became a professor in physics and law. He was a lawyer for the *Ayuntamiento* in Mexico City. He was also a member of the Liberal Party, a writer for a newspaper called *Siglo 19*, and an author. Iglesias held three important posts in Ignacio Comonfort's administration. He was minister of ecclesiastical affairs, justice, and public instruction. He was a journalist during the Reform War, and covered the struggle from a liberal standpoint.

When Benito Juárez became president, Iglesias traveled with him throughout the country. He became a member of the Supreme Court and was minister of the treasury in Juárez's cabinet.

In 1876 Lerdo was reelected in an election that Iglesias, as president of the Supreme Court, judged fraudulent. Being next in the line of succession, he assumed the presidency.

When Porfirio Díaz began his march toward Mexico City, Iglesias understood he was no match for a consummate military leader like Díaz. He tried to reach an agreement with General Díaz without success and finally decided to flee the country. He lived in New York for a few months and published a book called *La Cuestión Presidencial en 1876*, which dealt with his short-lived government.

DÍAZ DICTATORSHIP, 1876–1911

Four years after the restoration of the Republic, Porfirio Díaz assumed the presidency of Mexico, a position he held for the next thirty-four years with only two interruptions. The first was at the beginning of Díaz's first term, during a two month interim presidency of Juan N. Méndez. Méndez was president while Díaz chased José María Iglesias out of the country. The second one lasted four years, during which his *compadre*, Manuel González, occupied the presidency.

To this day, Mexicans have not come to grips with the legacy of the Díaz presidency. Considered a ruthless dictator by some and a statesman of unparalleled vision by others, Díaz's place in Mexican history is yet to be objectively and definitively established.

This dilemma is no accident. His long presidency was known for its contradictory nature. For example, even though Díaz wasted no effort in raising the academic standards for higher education, illiteracy among children and the poor went up in Mexico. By the end of his term, more than 76.9 percent of the population was illiterate, perhaps in part a result of the rapid increase in population in times of peace. The agricultural production of the hacienda system was recognized by Díaz as highly efficient, but the livelihood of laborers decreased significantly when they were reduced to virtual slavery with the complicity and police support of the regime. This military man, who at the beginning of his political career was a mason, both liberal and anticlerical, suffered a profound transformation after he reached the presidency. As president he advocated better relations between church and state, and promoted business deals with the rich.

During his terms, he worked intensely in an effort to improve Mexico's infrastructure. He ordered the construction of magnificent public buildings, created an impressive national railroad network, and mandated important works in the sewage system of Mexico City.

The upper classes and many people from the small middle classes recognized Díaz as the man who brought peace, order, and stability to a land where chaos had been the rule. But under the peace, order, and progress of Díaz's dictatorship, the rich got richer and the poor got poorer.

State governments were modeled after Díaz's national government. Governors remained in office as long as Díaz wanted. The governors protected their relatives and friends and pampered the foreign investor, just as Díaz did.

Although Mexico improved in many ways, the poverty of the majority of the population deepened. Political acts and opposing ideas were forbidden. The life of intellectuals, and many other responsible citizens who wanted democracy, took a turn for the worse; in the end, many people resented the Díaz dictatorship.

When the first decade of the new century began, Mexico revolted against the dictatorship and put an end to it.

Rulers of the Porfiriato, 1876–1910

PORFIRIO DÍAZ (1830–1915). *Place of birth*: Oaxaca, Oaxaca; *Place of death*: Paris, France; *Wives*: Delfina Ortega and Carmen Romero Rubio y Castelló; *Parents*: José de la Cruz Díaz and Petrona Mori; *Position*: Declared Constitutional President by the Chamber of Deputies, and Commander in Chief of the Army, in charge of the Executive Office; *Terms*: November 23, 1876–December 11, 1876 and February 17, 1877–November 30, 1880.

Díaz began to work at a very early age to help support his mother after his father's death. He went to elementary school in Oaxaca. While studying at a Catholic seminary, he considered the priesthood, but dropped out and continued his education at the Institute of Sciences and Arts. He enrolled in the School of Law, but dropped out to join the National Guard and fight against the United States' invading forces. Ironically, the teenager did not see action at this time.

He supported the liberal Plan de Ayutla. During the Three Years War, he fought alongside the liberals. Afterward he fought against the French invaders. His outstanding performance during the Battle of Puebla on May 5, 1862, earned him the rank of general. One year later, while defending Puebla, he was made a prisoner. His spectacular escape from prison greatly enhanced his reputation; he settled in Mexico City.

Díaz's enterprising spirit took him back to Oaxaca where he once again was made a prisoner, only to escape one more time. By 1865 he was the commander of the Mexican troops that defeated the Imperial French Army in Tehuitzingo, Puebla. He won many battles, and his military reputation was very much on the rise. His friendship with President Benito Juárez became strained mainly due to a conflict of their strong personalities. Díaz was forced to retire from the military.

The Mexican state presented him with the Hacienda of the Noria, and it was there that he formulated the Plan de la Noria, the goal of which was to overthrow the Juárez administration. At that time Díaz said he was opposed to the principle of reelection. The Plan de la Noria did not prosper, and it was not until President Juárez died that Díaz saw an opportunity to achieve his political ambitions.

He continued his political campaign, now against President Miguel Lerdo de Tejada. While living in Tlacotalpan, Veracruz, he was apparently dedicated to agriculture and the manufacturing of furniture, but obviously was thinking seriously about politics.

In 1876 a group of military men in Oaxaca issued the Plan de Tuxtepec, which aimed to overthrow Lerdo and appoint Díaz as their military leader. Meanwhile Díaz, pretending to be on a business trip, traveled from Veracruz to New Orleans and then to Mexico's northern border. His strategy was to recruit an army to attack Lerdo from the north, while his followers attacked from the south.

José María Iglesias, who was the president of the Supreme Court, also refused to accept Lerdo's reelection and proclaimed himself interim president. Díaz took advantage of this situation and launched an attack against both *Lerdistas* and *Iglesistas*.

Díaz was defeated in combat and escaped to the United States. He returned to Veracruz, traveled to Oaxaca, reorganized his army, and marched toward Mexico City. He entered the capital in triumph and called for elections. The Chamber of Deputies elected him Constitutional President in November 1876. A month later, he left the government in the hands of Juan N. Méndez while he went to fight Iglesias. Díaz and Iglesias met in Querétaro, but Iglesias refused to negotiate with him. In January 1877, after being defeated in a battle at Unión de los Adobes, in Jalisco, Iglesias fled to the United States. Díaz came back to Mexico City and took over the government of Mexico, albeit provisionally, while Congress called for new elections. Díaz won the election.

During his first administration Díaz worked hard to centralize all political, economic, and military power. He restored order in the streets and roads that had been taken over by bandits. He also reformed the government financial system in Mexico.

In 1879 there was a rebellion in Veracruz known as the *Rebelión de los Cañoneros* (a rebellion of the gunships *Libertad* and *Independencia*). Governor Luis Mier y Terán, acting under direct orders from Díaz, apprehended the rebels and ordered them shot.

In 1880, as Díaz was finishing his first term, he authorized two foreign railroad companies to build a railroad system in Mexico. After the election of 1880, won by his *compadre* and fellow general, Manuel González, Díaz was appointed governor of Oaxaca. His term as governor was highly praised for the number of public works he embarked upon. A few years later, he made a big comeback to the national political scene.

JUAN N. MÉNDEZ (1820–1894). *Place of birth*: Tetela de Ocampo, Puebla; *Place of death*: Mexico City; *Wife*: Trinidad González y Castruera; *Position*: General Porfirio Díaz left him in charge of the government; *Term*: December 11, 1876–February 17, 1877.

In 1847 Méndez joined the army to combat the American invaders. He supported the Plan de Ayutla. He also fought against the French at Puebla, and in 1862 was made a prisoner. He was exiled by the occupying French forces, but soon he came back to continue fighting.

When the Republic was restored with President Benito Juárez, he became governor of Puebla twice. He also supported both the Plan de la Noria and the Plan de Tuxtepec. He was a senator and president of the Supreme Court.

During his short stay as president, he was known for his attempts at strengthening the national guard. He died a very poor man while president of the military tribunal of the Mexican army.

MANUEL GONZÁLEZ (1833–1893). *Place of birth*: Ranch "El Moquete" in Matamoros, Tamaulipas; *Place of death*: Hacienda of Chapingo, in the State of Mexico; *Wife*: Laura Mantecón; *Position*: President of the Republic; *Term*: December 1, 1880–November 30, 1884.

González finished only elementary school, but worked hard in commercial activities as a young man. In 1847 he began his military career fighting against the American invaders. He sided with the Conservative Party during the War of Reform, until it joined the French invaders. He switched sides and joined Benito Juárez in his national struggle. He was assigned to assist General Porfirio Díaz as chairman of the Joint Chiefs of Staff. At the battle of Puebla, on May 5, 1862, he was wounded and lost his right arm. He was captured and imprisoned, but managed to escape. He accompanied Díaz in his endeavors and supported the Plan de la Noria and the Plan de Tuxtepec.

He became governor of Michoacán and was also deputy in Oaxaca. He was Díaz's most trusted officer and won the presidency because Díaz wanted to reward his loyalty. González was never able to shake off Díaz's tutelage.

During his presidency, González furthered the new railroad system. The *Banco Nacional de México* was founded, and Mexico's treasury issued new coins made of nickel and copper. He established the metric system in Mexico as well. Elementary education became mandatory and free for all children in Mexico. Communication with the rest of the world was greatly improved when a submarine cable was laid to link Mexico with the United States and Europe. The military school was reorganized. González ordered a modification in the Constitution that relieved the president of the Supreme Court from having to take control during the absence of a president; the power to act as president was passed on to the president of the Senate. He also refused Guatemala's territorial claim to the state of Chiapas.

In a curious attempt to populate the country, he sent for 1,500 Italian nationals and gave them land in the state of Puebla. There they worked on different industries and agriculture.

When González stepped down as president, he appointed himself governor of Guanajuato.

After his death, the people mourned him. He was a popular and well-liked man.

Population of Mexico 1888: 11,490,830 Inhabitants

PORFIRIO DÍAZ. *Position*: Reelected Constitutional President seven times, he did not finish his last term; *Terms*: 1884-1888—(December 1, 1884) First reelection; 1888-1892—Second reelection; 1892-1896—Third reelection; 1896-1900—Fourth reelection; 1900-1904—Fifth reelection; 1904-1910—Sixth reelection; 1910-1911—Seventh and last reelection.

When Díaz returned to the presidency after Manuel González' four-year interlude, his first task was to amend the Constitution to allow for immediate reelection. The anti-reelectionist spirit that had distanced him from Benito Juárez and inspired him to fight against Sebastián Lerdo de Tejada was forsaken.

He unified the political parties under his leadership, bringing many liberals and followers of Lerdo to his side. He formed a cabinet with extremely talented citizens who became collectively known as "*Los Científicos*" (the Scientists.)

For the next twenty-five years of Porfirismo, the country experienced solid economic progress. An extensive railroad system was developed, with 12,427.76 square miles of railways. Under the direction of his able treasury minister, José Ives Limantour, the bureaucracy got leaner and the government became more efficient. Together, Díaz and Limantour reorganized the banking system, balanced the budget, and gained the confidence of foreign investors in Europe and America. Mexico began exporting agricultural products such as cotton, tobacco, cocoa, and sugar. Industrial production was growing at an impressive annual rate of 6.4 percent, and by the turn of the century, the Mexicans were producing steel and iron, textiles, paper, soap, cement, shoes, glass, cigarettes, beer, and hats. They introduced new technologies in the mining industries that produced lead, zinc, nickel, silver, gold, copper, and developed new mines.

Labor conditions, however, were miserable. This led to labor unrest that culminated in strikes at Cananea, Sonora, in 1906, and Río Blanco, Veracruz, in 1907. This was a challenge Díaz's authoritarianism could not accept. The response to the striking workers was brutal in both cases.

In 1908 the government leased Magdalena Bay to the United States for a period of two years, and that same year, a reporter named James Creelman published an article in *Pearson's Magazine* of New York that labeled Díaz as the "Hero of the Americas." This piece brought on the beginning of a revolution when Mexicans read Díaz's statement that he would not seek reelection. Those who believed him were wrong. He did in fact seek reelection.

In 1909 two new political parties were formed, the Democratic Party and the National Anti-Reelection Party. Francisco I. Madero led the opposition against Díaz, and in 1910 his Anti-reelectionist Party convention selected him and Francisco Vázquez Gómez as their candidates for the presidency and vice presidency, respectively.

Vázquez Gómez, who was a personal friend of Díaz and his physician, tried to convince the president to implement various reforms and programs. He also suggested some changes in the cabinet. Vázquez Gómez was concerned with the precarious situation of the peasants working the land and suggested reforms in agriculture. He advised President Díaz to get rid of the nefarious Ramón Corral as vice president. A second and harder-to-follow suggestion was made: Fire Limantour, the belt-tightening treasury minister.

On June 24, 1910, the two friends met at the Chapultepec Castle, and Vázquez Gómez made a last attempt to convince Díaz to follow his suggestions. Díaz's answer was revealing. "And what," he asked, "am I going to do without Limantour?" Vázquez Gómez answered, "General, your dilemma is this: Either you sacrifice Limantour and prevent a revolution or you keep Limantour and let the country go up in flames." Díaz chose not to pay attention to the warning. Saddened, Vázquez Gómez severed his friendship with Díaz, and accepted the candidacy for the vice presidency offered to him by Madero and the Anti-Reelectionist Party.

In Mexico, 1910 was an eventful year. In September Díaz marked the 100th anniversary of the struggle for independence with a celebration that had no parallel in Mexican history. A few days later, Madero and several of his followers were imprisoned in San Luis Potosí. Madero soon escaped and fled to the United States to Saint Louis, Missouri. It was from this city that he launched the so-called Plan de San Luis, calling all Mexicans to an armed rebellion against the dictatorship on November 20, 1910.

The elections in 1910 were marred by massive fraud, but in spite of it, Díaz decided to remain in the presidency. The struggle against Díaz began as scheduled, and, after a faltering start, within six months the rebels had captured Ciudad Juárez. Suddenly and surprisingly, after one lost battle, Díaz realized he had lost the war. He resigned and left for Veracruz where the ship *Ipiranga* was waiting to take him to Europe.

Once in exile, Díaz traveled extensively. He was received with honors in Europe, and lived in France until his death. He is buried at Montparnasse in Paris.

4

REVOLUTION AND MODERN MEXICO, 1910–1997

During Porfirio Díaz' dictatorship, Mexico joined the global economy, exporting minerals and agricultural products. Reinvesting profits from the agricultural sector and with foreign investment, the Mexicans built a wide infrastructure of roads, railways, telegraphs, and telephones. For the first time in Mexico, there was a sizable and growing internal market. This market expansion, in turn, strengthened the power of the state. But there was one enormous problem. The *hacienda*, which was the economic motor of an export-oriented economy, took exploitation of the peasants to its ultimate limits. The poor, who were the vast majority of the population, rejected the old order and reclaimed the land through an armed struggle. The intellectuals within the incipient middle class sided with the underprivileged, and the country was engulfed in an upheaval that turned fratricidal quickly. The country exploded into a revolutionary movement in spite of the fact that the economy was expanding and the country was evidently prosperous.

The destitute thought that once the armed struggle was over, the workers would be able to organize themselves to protect their economic gains. The peasants thought the time had come to recover the land for those who worked it.

On November 20, 1910, the armed insurrection began after every other alternative to achieve political change at the top failed. Other leaders saw the armed revolution as the only chance to redress the existing economic inequalities among the Mexicans. Not all the leaders of the revolution had the same agenda or ideology, and not all of them were concerned with the same problems and issues.

Francisco I. Madero was a central figure of the early revolution. He was a rich and educated *hacendado* who was well acquainted with the ideas of the enlightenment. Having studied in Europe, Madero drew inspiration from the books of French philosopher Charles Louis de Secondat Montesquieu. Madero sincerely believed the way to modernize Mexico was simply to make every vote count and to forbid reelection.

Another key figure in the revolution was Emiliano Zapata, the chief of the liberationist "army" of the south. His motto was *"Tierra y Libertad"* (Land and Liberty). For this *caudillo* of the poor people, revolution was the only possibility the Indians had of recovering their lands—lands that the Spanish Crown had confirmed to them and that had been taken away by the owners of the *haciendas*, with the support of local authorities. Zapata fought for minimal personal freedom for his people.

There were, of course, many other *caudillos* who contributed to the revolutionary movement. Doroteo Arango, better known as Pancho Villa, and Pascual Orozco fought in the north for loot and against social injustice. Later on, leaders like Venustiano Carranza, Pablo González, Alvaro Obregón, and Plutarco Elías Calles would fight for their individual agendas and to restore the constitutional order, which was broken when President Madero was assassinated.

The revolution, with its successes and failures, caused a major social and political change in Mexico. It capped the development of a feeling of nationalism—of *mexicanidad*. The Mexico that emerged after 1910 aimed to reduce the great social and economic inequalities that existed in the country prior to the revolution. It called for better living conditions and access to education for everyone. It demanded better working conditions and paying jobs. To what extent these goals of the revolution were achieved is still the topic of debate in Mexico.

IMPORTANT REVOLUTIONARY LEADERS

Although neither of the two political figures that follow were ever president of Mexico, both were key figures in the Revolution and at some time in their lives held presidential power. That is why they are included in this chapter.

EMILIANO ZAPATA (1879–1919). *Place of birth*: San Miguel Anenecuilco, Morelos; *Place of death*: Hacienda de Chinameca, Morelos; *Wife*: Josefa Espejo; *Parents*: Gabriel Zapata and Cleófas Salazar; *Position*: Leader in the Revolution; *Term*: 1908–1919.

Zapata was born a peasant who rose up to hold prestigious positions in the *haciendas* of Mexico due to his knowledge of and abilities with horses. He dedicated his life to the plight of the *hacienda* workers in Mexico.

In 1908 he was forced to join the ninth Cavalry Regiment, which was stationed in Cuernavaca. When the Maderista revolution erupted, Zapata gathered arms at Villa de Ayala and fought against Porfirio Díaz. Among the many notable figures who joined Zapata's side during this battle were the professor Pablo Torres Burgos, Otilio Montaño, Margarito Ramírez, Emiliano Tepepa, and thousands of indigenous peoples who had been deprived of land and civil rights.

In 1911 Zapata began the armed struggle by taking Villa de Ayala with a small group of peasants. From there they continued toward Cuautla and then Chiautla, Puebla. They succeeded miraculously, but went on wild rampages, looting the towns they occupied militarily. Colonel Aureliano Blanquet gave them their first defeat three months after they rose up in arms. But in May of the same year, General Manuel Asúnsulo took Cuernavaca and handed it to Zapata. Winning and losing battles, on June 6 the Zapatista army, led by Emiliano Zapata and his brother Eufemio, entered Mexico City triumphantly to meet Francisco I. Madero.

When Zapata returned to Morelos, he established himself in Cuernavaca. Madero traveled to Cuernavaca to ask him to honor the Plan de San Luis, and to lay down arms and dissolve his army. At first, Zapata refused to do this. He argued, with some reason, that his people needed to take possession of the land they were granted before disarming the troops. Madero insisted on his demands, and Zapata refused again. In the meantime, Madero sent General Victoriano Huerta to protect the *haciendas* from Zapata's forces. On August 14 Madero returned to Cuernavaca in another attempt to persuade Zapata to change his mind. The two leaders conferred for a very long time without reaching an agreement. At the same time, Zapatistas and Huertistas continued engaging in skirmishes.

When Madero became president on November 6, 1911, Zapata launched his Plan de Ayala, in which he repudiated the Madero administration and vowed to continue the struggle for the underdog.

Concurrently General Bernardo Reyes began a rebellion in the state of Tamaulipas, and in Chihuahua, Francisco and Emilio Vázquez Gómez, frustrated with Madero, also took up arms. Pascual Orozco also joined the revolution on the side of Zapata. Félix Díaz, the nephew of Porfirio Díaz, led a revolt in Veracruz, and Pancho Villa fled the prison in Tlatelolco to reorganize his forces. It was just a matter of time before Madero and Vice President José María Pino Suárez would end up treacherously murdered by General Victoriano Huerta.

In 1913 Huerta became the new president. Zapata continued his rebellion against the established government, fighting in the south. In the north, Venustiano Carranza, who was then governor of Coahuila, rose up in arms against Huerta, promising he would restore the constitutional order broken by Madero's assassination. Carranza became the head of the "Constitutionalist Army" and organized it into three divisions. The North Division was commanded by Villa, Pablo González headed the Northeastern Division, and Alvaro Obregón became commander of the Northwestern Division.

Huerta did not resist their combined force and resigned in 1914. The triumphant revolutionary leader was Venustiano Carranza, and the Tratados de Teoloyucan, signed after the military defeat of Huerta's army, specified that the federal army surrendered without conditions.

Once again the Zapatistas repudiated a government that would not return their land to them, and kept on fighting for the next five years.

On April 10, 1919, Zapata agreed to meet Colonel Jesús Guajardo at the *hacienda* of Chinameca, where Guajardo said he would present him with weaponry to continue the struggle. Zapata went to the meeting, but it turned out to be a betrayal, and Zapata was ambushed and brutally murdered by Guajardo's men.

DOROTEO ARANGO (FRANCISCO "PANCHO" VILLA) (1878–1923).

Place of birth: Ranch "La Coyota," San Juan del Río, Durango; *Place of death*: Parral, Chihuahua; *Wives*: Petra Espinosa, Luz Corral, Soledad Seáñez, Austreberta Rentería; *Parents*: Agustín Arango, illegitimate child of Jesús Villa and Micaela Arámbula; *Position*: Leader in the Revolution; *Term*: 1910–1920.

Villa lived a very violent life. As a young man he was always trying to flee from justice. He worked as a peon, a miner, a brick layer, a merchant, a rancher, and a bandit. In 1910 Villa joined the anti-reelectionist movement of Francisco I. Madero. Madero appointed Villa as a colonel in his army. On May 10, 1911, Villa and Pascual Orozco attacked and captured Ciudad Juárez. The next day, Madero established his headquarters there.

Porfirio Díaz resigned and sailed to France. Madero seemingly had won the revolution, and Mexico had a new interim president, Francisco León de la Barra, who was Díaz's foreign affairs minister and next in the line of succession. Not everyone agreed with this chain of events, and the military garrison at Ciudad Juárez named Emilio Vázquez Gómez as president of the Republic.

In 1912 Villa returned to Chihuahua to work as a merchant. Later, Villa joined Madero's federal army and was placed under the command of Victoriano Huerta, a former *porfirista* general who hated him. A silly incident in which Villa was involved gave Huerta a good pretext to jail him and sentence him to death. Madero saved his life, but Villa remained in jail.

On January 8, 1913, Villa managed to escape from prison and fled to El Paso, Texas. After Madero was assassinated, Villa returned to Mexico to fight against Huerta under the command of Venustiano Carranza, heading the legendary *División del Norte*. On his way to Mexico City with an army of approximately 16,000 men, he seized Ciudad Juárez, San Pedro de la Colonias, and Torreón. Ordered by Carranza not to participate in the attack of Zacatecas, Villa disobeyed him, and the two leaders had a falling out. Villa resigned his military post, and Carranza accepted his resignation, naming him governor of Chihuahua. Villa's victory in Zacatecas, however, convinced Huerta he had lost the war and caused him to flee the country.

Francisco Carvajal became interim president. On August 20, 1914, Carranza arrived in Mexico City to implement his Plan de Guadalupe. In October 1914 Carranza organized the Convention of Aguascalientes with all the revolutionary forces. Emiliano Zapata, Carranza, Villa, and Alvaro Obregón, however, could not reach an agreement.

Eulalio Gutiérrez was elected acting president. Villa was reelected as chief of the north division. Carranza rejected the agreements of the convention and moved his government to Veracruz. On December 6, 1914, Villa and Zapata entered Mexico City and had their picture taken lolling in the presidential palace. Beginning in 1915, however, Villa was defeated by Obregón in three consecutive key battles at Celaya, León, and Aguascalientes.

The United States recognized Carranza's presidency on October 19, 1915. Feeling betrayed by the United States, Villa entered Columbus, New Mexico, burned buildings, and killed American soldiers. The U.S. government sent troops, under John Pershing, to capture Villa in a "punitive expedition," but Villa could not be found.

In 1920, after Carranza was assassinated, Villa promised President Adolfo de la Huerta that he would never rise up in arms again. He retired to tend his *hacienda* in Canutillo. On July 20, 1923, Villa was shot to death. The names of the killers were made public, but nobody knows who ordered the assassination of Villa. He had legions of enemies.

Rulers of the Revolution and Modern Mexico, 1910–1997

Population of Mexico 1910: 15,160,369 Inhabitants

FRANCISCO LEÓN DE LA BARRA QUIJANO (1863–1939). *Place of birth*: Querétaro, Querétaro; *Place of death*: Biarritz, France; *Wife*: Refugio Barneque; *Parents*: Bernabé León de la Barra y De Maria and Luisa Quijano y Pérez Palacios; *Position*: Interim President; *Term*: May 25, 1911–November 6, 1911.

León de la Barra was a follower of Porfirio Díaz. He was also Mexico's ambassador in Washington and Díaz's minister of foreign affairs. Next in the line of succession, León de la Barra formed the transitional presidency between the old order—represented by Díaz—and the new order—represented by Francisco I. Madero.

During the Victoriano Huerta regime, León de la Barra was appointed ambassador to France. Following the fall of Huerta, he remained in Europe.

He was a highly respected lawyer, specializing in international law. At the request of the French government, he acted as a mediator in some European conflicts.

FRANCISCO I. MADERO (1873–1913). *Place of birth*: Hacienda El Rosario in Parras, Coahuila; *Place of death*: Mexico City; *Wife*: Sara Pérez; *Parents*: Francisco Madero Hernández and Mercedes González Treviño; *Position*: Constitutional President of the *Partido Nacional Antireeleccionista*—Votes: 19,997 (Vice President: José María Pino Suárez); *Contenders*: Francisco León de la Barra—Votes: 87 and Emilio Vázquez-Gómez—Votes: 16; *Term*: November 6, 1911–February 22, 1913.

Madero was born into a prominent family in the Mexican state of Coahuila. He studied abroad and graduated with a degree in the field of commerce. He then studied to become an agriculturist. His knowledge of and dedication to new systems of cultivation were outstanding. He also studied philosophy, sociology, spirituality, and homeopathic medicine. With his own money he funded the Commerce School in San Pedro for the disadvantaged youths of Mexico, and engaged in defense of and assistance to peasants.

In 1904 he launched his political career in Coahuila. He wrote political essays for the journal *El Demócrata*, and published a hugely successful book, *La sucesión presidencial en 1910*.

He ran against Porfirio Díaz in 1910, but was defeated in an election marred by the usual fraud. He was incarcerated before the election, but managed to flee to the United States. After Díaz's reelection, Madero launched the Plan de San Luis to unseat the dictator. While in the United States, he began the revolution against Díaz. Back in Mexico, Madero fought in several battles and the minor injuries he suffered did not stop him in his pursuits. Injured, he showed up in Ciudad Juárez when the revolutionary forces took the city.

Madero became immensely popular, and his election to the presidency became inevitable and anticipated, but he did not dare take power without elections.

On November 6, 1911, Madero was elected president of Mexico. In an attempt to bring back law and order to the revolutionary country, convincing Emiliano Zapata to end his revolt was one of his first priorities. Zapata would not agree to do so without in turn receiving the land for which he and his followers had fought so hard. Later Zapata launched "his" Plan de Ayala, which confirmed his will to keep on fighting until his demands for land were met. In 1912 Madero created a special force to fight Zapata.

Madero was never able to consolidate his presidency. He had enemies on all sides. Zapata, Pascual Orozco, Félix Díaz, and Bernardo Reyes were all opposed to his moderate stance. U.S. Ambassador Henry Lane Wilson and Victoriano Huerta also aligned themselves to plot against Madero.

Huerta betrayed the trust of the president, and an insurrection ensued in Mexico City. It lasted ten days and was known as *La Decena Trágica*, or the Tragic Ten Days. Madero and Pino Suárez were incarcerated, and when the revolt ended on February 22, 1913, both men were executed.

Thus ended tragically one of the very few democratic experiments in Mexico's history.

PEDRO LASCURÁIN PAREDES (1856–1952). *Place of birth*: Mexico City; *Place of death*: Mexico City; *Wife*: María Flores; *Position*: Temporary President; *Term*: February 19, 1913. He lasted forty-five minutes in office (another version said that it was only twenty-five minutes, from 10:35 P.M. to 11:00 P.M.).

Lascuráin was a lawyer. He was also a trustee and president of Mexico's City Hall and a professor and director of the *Escuela Libre de Derecho*. He served as secretary of foreign affairs in the cabinet of President Francisco I. Madero. Deceived by General Victoriano Huerta, he convinced President Madero to resign, believing that would save the lives of both President Madero and Vice President José María Pino Suárez.

Lascuráin was the secretary of foreign affairs, and in the absence of the president and the vice president, he was next in line for the presidency, according to the Constitution.

Lascuráin did become president. His only act of government was to appoint Huerta as secretary of foreign affairs, which put him next in line for the presidency. He then resigned the presidency. This allowed Huerta to become president within the law. Lascuráin refused to serve in Huerta's cabinet.

Lascuráin was a respected lawyer, a member of the Mexican Bar Association, and the author of famous essays on civil rights.

VICTORIANO HUERTA (1845–1916). *Place of birth*: Colotlán, Jalisco; *Place of death*: El Paso, Texas; *Wife*: Emilia Aguila; *Position*: President of the Republic; *Term*: February 19, 1913–July 15, 1914.

Huerta studied at the Military College of Mexico, where he excelled in mathematics and astronomy. In 1903 he fought against the Maya Indians in Quintana Roo. Seven years later, he fought the Zapatistas in Morelos. When Porfirio Díaz resigned and headed for Veracruz, it was Huerta who escorted the retired president. In 1912 he fought Pascual Orozco, and tried to execute Pancho Villa. In 1913 Francisco I. Madero appointed Huerta as military commander of government forces in Mexico City.

Huerta conspired with generals Bernando Reyes and Félix Díaz and with U.S. Ambassador Henry Lane Wilson against Madero and his presidency.

He imprisoned both President Madero and Vice President José María Pino Suárez, had both resign, and then ordered their deaths.

Pedro Lascuráin, who was the foreign affairs secretary in the Madero cabinet, was appointed president when Madero died. Lascuráin's only act of government was to appoint Huerta secretary of foreign affairs. When Lascuráin resigned, Huerta automatically became his successor.

It is believed by many that Huerta's extremely corrupt cabinet was approved of in the halls of the American Embassy in Mexico City. When Congress opposed Huerta's appointment, he ordered an especially brutal murder of a leading deputy named Belisario Dominguez. When Congress reacted against this act of sadism, Huerta responded by incarcerating many deputies and dissolving Congress.

One month into his administration, Huerta was accused by Governor Venustiano Carranza of breaking the Constitution. Supported by many revolutionary leaders like Alvaro Obregón, Pancho Villa, and Pablo González, Carranza organized the so-called "Constitutionalist Army" and launched a ferocious offensive against Huerta.

Meanwhile, Emiliano Zapata continued his opposition to Huerta in the south.

In 1914 there was an incident with the U.S. ship *Dolphin*, and later on, the Marines landed in Veracruz, an event that seriously weakened Huerta. It wasn't long before the Constitutionalist Army descended upon Mexico City. The battle of Zacatecas, in which Villa destroyed the Huertistas, convinced Huerta it was time to resign and leave Mexico.

Huerta fled to Europe and later to the United States. He was incarcerated in Fort Bliss in 1915 by the U.S. government, and shortly before his death, he was released to his home in El Paso, Texas, where he soon died.

FRANCISCO S. CARVAJAL (1870–1932). *Place of birth*: Campeche, Campeche; *Place of death*: Mexico City; *Wife*: Single (while in exile he may have married an American woman); *Position*: Provisional President, named by Congress; *Term*: July 15, 1914–August 13, 1914.

Carvajal studied to be a lawyer. In 1911 Porfirio Díaz appointed him as a negotiator between himself and Francisco I. Madero. He became the president of the Supreme Court and minister of foreign affairs. His imprint was not felt on Mexican politics due to his short presidency.

EULALIO GUTIÉRREZ ORTIZ (1881–1939). *Place of birth*: Hacienda Santo Domingo, Ramos Arizpe, Coahuila; *Place of death*: Saltillo, Coahuila; *Wife*: Petra Treviño; *Parents*: Jesús Gutiérez and Ciriaca Ortiz; *Position*: Provisional President, named by the Aguascalientes Convention (Vice Presidents: Francisco Murguía and Francisco P. de Mariel); *Term*: November 3, 1914–January 6, 1915.

As a child, Gutiérrez was a miner in Concepción del Oro, Zacatecas. He later became the mayor of that town. He was a moderate liberal, a Maderista, a Carrancista, and an anti-reelectionist. In 1914 he became provisional governor of San Luis Potosí. On November 1, 1914, he became the provisional president of the Convention of Aguascalientes. All three of the main political forces—Zapatista, Villista, and Obregonista—endorsed Gutiérrez as the compromise candidate. Thus, when his presidency began, he had members of all three groups in his cabinet and the strong support of none.

The coalition did not last long, and Gutiérrez broke with Venustiano Carranza, Francisco "Pancho" Villa, and Emiliano Zapata. Shortly thereafter, he was ousted and forced into exile in the United States.

After Carranza's death in 1920, Gutiérrez returned to Mexico to support Alvaro Obregón. He was appointed a state senator and later governor of Coahuila, but he had problems with Obregón. He tried unsuccessfully to start a rebellion and then fled the country. When he was granted amnesty in 1935, he returned to Mexico.

ROQUE GONZÁLEZ GARZA (1885–1962). *Place of birth*: Saltillo, Coahuila; *Place of death*: Mexico City; *Wife*: Concepción Garay; *Parents:* Agustín González and Prisciliana Garza; *Position*: Provisional President of the Aguascalientes Convention and Francisco "Pancho" Villa's representative there; *Term*: January 16, 1915–June 10, 1915.

González Garza studied commerce in Saltillo, Coahuila. In 1908 he began his political career in a crusade against Porfirio Díaz. He was a very close friend of Francisco I. Madero. He participated in the battle of Ciudad Juárez with Madero and Pancho Villa.

When Madero and José María Pino Suárez were murdered, González Garza joined forces with Villa to fight against Victoriano Huerta. He went to the Aguascalientes Convention as a representative of Villa. When Venustiano Carranza returned to Mexico City to head the government, González went into exile due to his relationship with Villa.

Many years later, he returned to Mexico and served in the cabinet of President Manuel Avila Camacho (1940–1946). In 1962 President Adolfo López Mateos brought him back into public service as head of a minor presidential commissn. He died that same year.

FRANCISCO LAGOS CHÁZARO (1878–1932). *Place of birth*: Tlacotalpan, Veracruz; *Place of death*: Mexico City; *Wife*: Single; *Parents*: Francisco Lagos Jiménez and Francisca Cházaro Montero; *Position*: Provisional President of the Aguascalientes Convention; *Term*: June 10, 1915–October 10, 1915.

Lagos Cházaro studied law. When the Aguascalientes Convention ousted Provisional President Roque González Garza, Lagos Cházaro was named his successor. During his presidency, the Carrancista northeastern army, headed by General Pablo González, attacked the government of the convention, forcing it to move to Toluca.

When Carranza returned to Mexico City, Lagos Cházaro left the presidency. He tried unsuccessfully to join Villa in the north and ended up living in Central America until Carranza's death. He then returned to Mexico and pursued a career as a lawyer until his death.

VENUSTIANO CARRANZA (1859–1920). *Place of birth*: Cuatro Ciénegas, Coahuila; *Place of death*: Tlaxcalaltongo, Puebla; *Wife*: Virginia Salinas; *Parents*: Jesús Carranza and María de Jesús Garza; *Position*: First Commander in Chief of the Constitutional Army, in charge of the Executive Office from 1914 to 1917; elected President of the Republic, May 1917—Votes: 797,305, *Contenders*: Pablo González—Votes: 11,615 and Alvaro Obregón—Votes: 4,008; *Term*: May 1, 1917–May 21, 1920.

Carranza studied at the Ateneo Fuente in Saltillo and at the Preparatory School of Mexico City. His family owned numerous *haciendas*. He was mayor of Cuatro Ciénegas, Coahuila, twice, and was also a state deputy, a substitute federal deputy, and a senator. In 1908 he became governor of Coahuila. Francisco I. Madero appointed him minister of war and the navy. He battled valiantly for the anti-reelectionist principles.

When Francisco I. Madero was killed, Carranza formulated the Plan de Guadalupe (1913), which repudiated the presidency of Victoriano Huerta. Carranza fought for the restoration of the constitutional order that had been violated when Huerta assassinated the legitimate president of Mexico—Madero.

To this end, Carranza formed the Constitutionalist Army, to which he appointed himself first chief. After a short military resistance, Huerta gave up, resigned, and left the country. Carranza continued to have some difficulties with Pancho Villa, and relieved him of his position as commander of the *División del Norte*. The two leaders soon became irreconcilable enemies.

Carranza entered Mexico City in 1914 and tried to reach an agreement (agreeable to him) between the three main revolutionary forces through a convention in Aguascalientes. Carranza offered to resign the presidency, but demanded assurances from Villa and Zapata that they would not rise up in arms. No agreement between them was possible, and Eulalio Gutiérrez was chosen to head the convention, and then to head the government.

Once Gutiérrez was recognized as president of Mexico, Carranza moved his government to Veracruz, and fighting between the revolutionary forces burst once again. After Alvaro Obregón defeated Villa in the battle of Celaya, Carranza returned to Mexico City. Carranza knew quite well the problem regarding the tenure of the land in Mexico, and ordered one of his brightest and most trusted assistants, Luis Cabrera, to formulate the Agrarian Law of January 6, 1915. The law mandated the restitution of *ejidos* that had been appropriated by *hacendados* and also ordered a new distribution of communal lands.

Carranza called an extraordinary congress to formulate a new constitution, which became known as the Constitution of 1917. That same year he called for elections in the two houses of Congress. Carranza had to deal with many uprisings. In 1919 he ordered the assassination of Emiliano Zapata.

When the time came to decide who would succeed him, Carranza chose a nonentity, Ignacio Bonilla, ignoring the two leading military *caudillos*, Pablo González and Alvaro Obregón, who had remained loyal to him.

Adolfo de la Huerta, Plutarco Elías Calles, and Obregón, the three generals from Sonora, were angered by his choice of successor and turned against him. While fleeing to Veracruz by railroad, Carranza was betrayed and murdered by a local *cacique*, General Rodolfo Herrero, in Puebla's high sierra.

ADOLFO DE LA HUERTA MARCOR (1881–1955). *Place of birth*: Guaymas, Sonora; *Place of death*: Mexico City; *Wife*: Clara Oriol; *Parents*: Torcuato de la Huerta and Carmen Marcor; *Position*: Provisional President; *Term*: June 10, 1920–November 30, 1920.

De la Huerta studied music and accounting in Guaymas and in Mexico City. He worked as an accountant at the Bank of Mexico. Beginning in 1908, de la Huerta formed a group of some of his friends with political ambitions—General Miguel Alemán, José María Pino Suárez, and Francisco S. Carvajal, among others. He fought with these men against Porfirio Díaz's presidency.

In 1913 Venustiano Carranza gave De la Huerta a post in the Secretariat of Government. He later became provisional governor and senator in Sonora. He was consul general of Mexico in New York, and later constitutional governor of Sonora.

De la Huerta supported Alvaro Obregón's Plan de Agua Prieta, opposing Carranza. After the death of Carranza, Congress named De la Huerta interim president. He lasted only a few months on the job. He tried unsuccessfully to reorganize the country's finances. When he began to have problems with Obregón, his future in Mexico became clouded.

Obregón became president in December 1920, and three years later, De la Huerta plotted against Obregón and ended up an exile in Los Angeles, California. After Obregón's death, De la Huerta later returned to Mexico and held several positions in the government bureaucracy.

Population of Mexico 1921: 14,234,780

ALVARO OBREGÓN (1880–1928). *Place of birth*: Hacienda de Siquisiva, Alamos, Sonora; *Place of death*: La Bombilla restaurant, Mexico City;

Wives: Refugio Urrea and María Tapia; *Parents*: Francisco Obregón and Cenobia Salido; *Position*: Constitutional President; *Term*: December 1, 1920–November 30, 1924.

Obregón studied in the tiny towns of Huatabampo and Alamos, Sonora. He became an elementary school teacher and then an agriculturist. He worked assiduously on a farm he owned named "Quinta Chilla." In 1911 he was appointed mayor of Huatabampo. At this time he fought against Pascual Orozco.

When Francisco I. Madero was assassinated, Obregón was named as the military commander of Hermosillo, the capital of Sonora. To fight Victoriano Huerta, he joined the Constitutionalist Army created by Venustiano Carranza, and was made commander of the Northwestern Division. From Sonora to Coahuila, Sinaloa, Nayarit, and Jalisco, Obregón advanced victoriously toward Mexico City.

Huerta resigned on July 14, 1914, but Obregón continued his march to Mexico. Finally, on August 13, Francisco Carvajal, the new interim president of the republic, negotiated a peace treaty with Obregón in Teoloyucan, state of Mexico. Two days later Obregón's army entered Mexico City.

As soon as Carranza took charge of the government, he ordered Obregón to travel north to negotiate a settlement with Pancho Villa, who was disillusioned with Carranza. Twice, Villa nearly executed Obregón, but the latter managed to escape and return to Mexico City.

Obregón was a delegate to the Aguascalientes Convention, which was originally called by Carranza, and there he displayed his enormous political talent. However, when the convention tilted to the side of Villa and Emiliano Zapata and against Carranza, Obregón reorganized his army and began to fight against Villa.

His military talents grew larger during this campaign. First he defeated Villa in Celaya (1915), then in Salamanca, Irapuato, and Silao. In one of these memorable battles, on the plains of La Trinidad, near León, Guanajuato, Obregón lost his right arm to a piece of shrapnel.

Villa was on the run, and at Agua Prieta, Sonora, he was defeated once again. This time he lost to a young general named Plutarco Elías Calles.

Obregón announced his retirement in 1917, and for a short while he went back to agribusiness. In 1919 he accepted the nomination for the presidency. But Carranza had other plans, and the two former allies became enemies. Carranza tried to have him arrested, charging him with vague irregularities. Obregón returned to Mexico City to defend himself, but realizing he would be jailed, he fled the city disguised as a railroad worker.

Obregón launched his Plan de Agua Prieta, calling for the ousting of Carranza; once again the country was up in arms. Carranza sensed he would be safer in Veracruz, where his son-in-law was governor, but he was murdered while trying to get there.

In 1920 Adolfo de la Huerta became interim president and called for elections. In November, Obregón was elected president by an over-whelming majority.

Throughout his term, Obregón was supported by the *Confederación Regional Obrera Mexicana* (CROM), a labor union he encouraged. He worked diligently to promote agriculture, and cultivated good working relations with the United States. The Bucareli Treaties were drafted during his administration.

When the time came to choose a successor, Obregón chose Plutarco Elías Calles. De la Huerta, who had presidential ambitions, took issue with this selection and rose up in arms in 1923. That same year, Villa was assassinated in Parral, Chihuahua.

After the election of Elías Calles in 1924, Obregón went into political retirement and back to agriculture. But the retirement did not last long, and he soon returned to politics.

In 1928 Obregón was reelected president with 1,670,453 votes, but was assassinated by a religious fanatic named José de León Toral before he could take office.

PLUTARCO ELÍAS CALLES (1877–1945). *Place of birth*: Guaymas, Sonora; *Place of death*: Cuernavaca, Morelos; *Wives*: Francisca Bernal, Natalia Chacón, and Leonor Llorente; *Parents*: Plutarco Elías and Jesusa Campuzano; *Position*: Constitutional President—Votes: 1,340,634; *Contender*: Angel Flores—Votes: 252,599; *Term*: December 1, 1924–November 30, 1928.

Orphaned at the age of four, Plutarco Elías later adopted the name of his stepfather, Juan B. Calles. He studied in Hermosillo, and subsequently worked as a school inspector. He became widely known for his columns in a newspaper called *Siglo XX*.

In 1911 Calles became police commissioner of Agua Prieta. He fought against Pascual Orozco and, alongside Alvaro Obregón, against Victoriano Huerta in Venustiano Carranza's Constitutionalist Army. He defeated Pancho Villa in the famous battle of Agua Prieta, in Sonora, and was named governor of that state.

In 1919 he became the secretary of industry, commerce, and public works for the Carranza administration, but by 1920 he had split with Carranza. He joined Obregón's rebellion against Carranza, and supported the Plan de Agua Prieta.

Calles was named the secretary of war and the navy during Adolfo de la Huerta's presidency, and secretary of government during Obregón's presidency.

In 1924 Elías Calles, as Obregón's choice, was elected president of Mexico. During his administration, several roads and water systems were developed. The Bank of Mexico, the *Banco de Crédito Agrícola y Ejidal*, and the National Banking Commission were founded. Divorce was legalized in

Mexico, and he promulgated a law to create a retirement fund for civil servants. In an attempt to avoid new bloodshed, rebellions, revolts, and revolutions in Mexico and to ensure his continued control, he founded the National Revolutionary Party (PNR), which ultimately evolved into the *Partido Revolucionario Institucional* (PRI). Under this scheme, all political positions were to be filled by the revolutionary leaders from within the party. It was one party rule. Democracy was not a priority, and opposition to the legacy of the revolution was not an option.

Calles vigorously promoted education, especially in rural Mexico, and ordered the creation of high schools nationally. He was furiously anticlerical, and on January 27, 1926, when the Archbishop of Mexico José Mora y Del Río announced the church would demand the reformation of the Constitution of 1917 regarding religious freedom, Calles' reaction was strong and swift. He ousted most foreign Catholic priests, including the papal nuncio, and shut down all Catholic schools and convents. Calles also reformed several provisions in the penal code that dealt with religious sects. The Catholic Church answered by suspending all religious rites throughout the nation. This was not all: On August 15, 1926, a new armed revolt broke out in several states of the republic. It was known as the Cristero Revolt, and soon it spread across the land.

When Calles's government ended in 1928, Obregón was elected president, but was assassinated before taking office. That same year, Congress named Emilio Portes Gil as his successor, but Calles remained the power behind the throne until 1936 when his nominee, President Lázaro Cárdenas, expelled him from Mexico.

After the Cárdenas administration ended, Calles was allowed to return to his homeland.

EMILIO PORTES GIL (1891–1978). *Place of birth*: Ciudad Victoria, Tamaulipas; *Place of death*: Mexico City; *Wife*: Carmen García; *Parents:* Domingo Portes and Adela Gil; *Position*: Interim President, named by Congress; *Term*: December 1, 1928–February 5, 1930.

Portes Gil's grandfather was Simón de Portes, one of the independence heroes of the Dominican Republic. Portes Gil studied law in Mexico, and in 1909 he joined the revolution. He became legal counsel in the Ministry of War and the Navy in 1915, and then acted as judge and as a magistrate in the Supreme Tribunal of Justice of Sonora. He later became a federal deputy and then interim governor of Tamaulipas.

Plutarco Elías Calles appointed him minister of the Secretariat of Government, and when Alvaro Oregón was assassinated, Portes Gil, being next in the line of succession, was named president.

During his administration, he mended relations with the Catholic Church, thus ending the Cristero Revolt that had lasted for almost three years. On June 1, 1929, Portes Gil declared an amnesty, but let the anticlerical laws stay. The Catholic Church accepted the terms, and the churches opened their doors once again.

Also in 1929, Portes Gil faced another rebellion, headed by General José Gonzalo Escobar. Escobar's rebellion did not last long, and all the rebel generals ended up exiled to the United States.

During Portes Gil's presidency, the National University of Mexico was declared an autonomous institution. He created the National Institute for the Protection of Infants (INPI), and introduced a strong national campaign against alcoholism.

In 1929 he called for presidential elections. José Vasconcelos, a well known Mexican intellectual and conservative politician, headed a political party that opposed the "official" party, the *Partido Nacional Revolucionario* (PNR). Vasconcelos had a very successful campaign and, as he gained more popularity, pressure on the government grew dramatically. The election results were less than clear and disturbances, riots, and assassinations ensued. Vasconcelos fled to safety in the United States.

In 1930 Portes Gil severed all relations with the Union of Soviet Socialist Republics, and ousted all foreign communists who were living in Mexican exile.

He became a consultant to several later presidents, and wrote many books on politics and history before his death.

PASCUAL ORTIZ RUBIO (1877–1963). *Place of birth*: Morelia, Michoacán; *Place of death*: Mexico City; *Wife*: Josefina Ortiz; *Parents*: Pascual Ortiz Ayala and María Rubio; *Position*: Constitutional President, PNR—Votes: 1,947,848; *Contenders*: José Vasconcelos, *Partido Nacional Anti-Reeleccionista*—Votes: 110,979 and Pedro Rodríguez Triana, *Partido Comunista Mexicano*—Votes: 32,279; *Term*: February 5, 1930–September 2, 1932.

Ortiz Rubio studied at the College of San Nicolás, in Morelia, and at the National Institute of Engineering in Mexico City. He graduated in Topographical Engineering in 1902, and practiced his profession in Michoacán.

In 1913, when Victoriano Huerta dissolved Congress, Ortiz Rubio was one of the many deputies incarcerated. Upon his release from jail, he fought for constitutionalism in Mexico and became the governor of Michoacán in 1917.

He supported the Plan de Agua Prieta. In return, Alvaro Obregón named him secretary of communications and public works. Due to serious political infighting within the cabinet, Ortiz Rubio did not finish his tenure and left Mexico to live in Barcelona, Spain.

When Plutarco Elías Calles became president, Ortiz Rubio was appointed the Mexican ambassador to Germany and then Brazil. He also served as secretary of the Secretariat of Government for a short while. He was then chosen by Calles to be the presidential candidate for the *Partido Nacional*

Revolucionario (PNR). His election was marred by what many historians consider the first massive fraud by the PNR, the antecedent of the *Partido Revolucionario Institucional* (PRI). How he managed to beat out an extremely popular candidate like José Vasconcelos is still debated.

On the day of his inauguration, Ortiz Rubio received a bullet wound in the face in an attempt on his life. The gunman was caught and died mysteriously while in prison. Oddly enough, two brothers of the gunmen were also assassinated.

During his presidency, Ortiz Rubio inaugurated the National Board of Tourism in Mexico. Baja California was split into two territories, and as a part of the Pan-American Highway that would connect the two continents, a leg of road between Mexico D.F. and Nuevo Laredo was constructed. A new Federal Work Law was established, and the nation's archives were reorganized. He initiated diplomatic relations with the new Spanish Republic.

Ortiz Rubio resigned in 1932, due to Plutarco Elías Calles' constant intrusion on his presidency.

ABELARDO L. RODRÍGUEZ (1889–1967). *Place of birth*: San José de Guaymas, Sonora; *Place of death*: La Jolla, California, United States; *Wife*: Aída Sullivan; *Parents*: Nicolás Rodríguez and Petra Luján; *Position*: Substitute President of PNR, named by Congress; *Term*: September 3, 1932– November 30, 1934.

Rodríguez studied in Nogales, Arizona, and worked at the Cananea mines. He worked in several American cities before returning to his native land in 1913 to join the revolution. He aligned himself with the constitutionalists and supported the Plan de Agua Prieta. He became the governor and military chief of the territory of Baja California Norte. In 1931 he was appointed secretary of Commerce, Industry, and Labor.

After the resignation of President Pascual Ortiz Rubio, Congress appointed Rodríguez as a trusted assistant of Plutarco Elías Calles, who had made himself "The Supreme Chief of the Revolution."

During Rodríguez's presidency, the relationship between church and state, which was already tense, became severely strained when Rodríguez, under the influence of Calles, tightened regulations regarding the activities of the clergy. The response of the church came from the Vatican. Pope Pius XI published an encyclical that was very critical of Mexico. Infuriated, Rodríguez expelled the papal nuncio.

Also acting under Calles' influence, he ordered the amending of Article 3 of the Constitution to provide what was called socialist education in all elementary schools in Mexico. At the same time, he ordered harsh police action against a group of mothers who were demonstrating their opposition to the teaching of sex education in the schools.

Rodríguez founded the *Banco Hipotecario y de Obras Públicas*. He set new standards for a minimum wage, but at the same time, he opposed the participation of unions in national politics. He pushed for a law against monopolies in Mexico. In 1935 he founded an institution known as National Finance Bank, as well as many industrial and fishing enterprises.

In 1934 he handed the presidency to Lázaro Cárdenas, and went back to live in Sonora. He worked alternatively in the private and public sectors, from entrepreneur to governor and back again to the private sector.

He was buried on his ranch near Ensenada, Baja California Norte.

LÁZARO CÁRDENAS (1895–1970). *Place of birth*: Jiquilpan, Michoacán; *Place of death*: Mexico City; *Wife*: Amalia Solórzano; *Parents*: Dámaso Cárdenas and Felícitas del Río; *Position*: Constitutional President, PNR—Votes: 2,225,000; *Contenders*: General Antonio I. Villareal—Votes: 24,395, Adalberto Tejeda, PS—Votes: 16,037, and Hernán Laborde, *Partido Comunista Mexicano*—Votes: 539; *Term*: December 1, 1934–November 30, 1940.

As a young man, Cárdenas worked in his hometown of Jiquilpan, Michoacán. In 1913 he joined the revolution. He fought in the Constitutionalist Army, under the command of Alvaro Obregón. Once Victoriano Huerta was defeated, Cárdenas was sent to combat Emiliano Zapata. He also fought against Pancho Villa, under the command of Plutarco Elías Calles. Later he was sent to subdue the Yaqui Indians in Chihuahua.

Cárdenas supported the Plan de Agua Prieta. He served in various military posts in Michoacán, Isthmus of Tehuantepec, and the oil-rich region called *La Huasteca*, which includes parts of four states (Tamaulipas, Veracruz, Hidalgo, and San Luis Potosí). It was precisely during the time he spent in the Huasteca oil fields that Cárdenas learned about the politics of oil.

In 1928 he became the governor of Michoacán, and during Abelardo L. Rodríguez's government, he served as chief of military operations in Puebla and as the minister of war and navy.

Cárdenas was selected as the party candidate by Calles, and was elected president in 1934. He served for the full term of six years. He refused to live in the Chapultepec Castle, and instead chose to live in a simpler house where several pine trees had been planted—hence the name Los Pinos used to designate the Mexican presidential residence.

Somewhat of a puritan, as soon as he became president, Cárdenas abolished gambling in Mexico and made military service mandatory for young Mexican men. His preoccupation with issues regarding land ownership, education, agriculture, and labor organizations of peasants and workers became central to his political career.

At the beginning of 1934, the government of the revolution had created the first comprehensive Agrarian Code in Mexico. The code set a minimum size for an *ejido*, or community land. But it was only when Cárdenas became president that a thorough agrarian reform was truly enforced. The president ordered the expropriation of very large landed states and the enforcement of the agrarian laws.

Perhaps there is no better example of the scope of Cárdenas' agrarian reform than what he accomplished in the so-called Laguna community, in the north of Mexico. This was a rich, cotton producing region owned by a handful of people. Cárdenas expropriated the land and gave it to thousands of peasants. This was not all: Cárdenas also founded a small bank that gave loans at low interest rates to the small farmers. Later, he also dramatically changed the old patterns of land ownership in Yucatan.

During his term, the country went through a classic example of class struggle with the "have-nots" challenging the "haves." But it was much more than that; it was a political struggle for power within the revolutionary family.

Cárdenas' support for unions translated into a wave of strikes, demonstrations, and even riots across the country. These economic dislocations led to political confrontations, the largest of which came when Calles, in a newspaper interview, criticized the president and hinted that the army would have to intervene if the president could not maintain law and order in the country.

In his public answer, Cárdenas vowed he would continue his policies, which benefited the vast majority of the population: the workers, peasants, and public employees. He asked for the resignation of his entire cabinet in order to purge those who were staunch *callistas*. Then, on April 1, 1936, Calles was told he had to leave the country by order of the president. A presidential plane flew him to the United States.

Cárdenas founded the Confederation of Mexican Workers (CTM) in 1936, which would serve as his political base. But he needed much more than that. With Calles out of the way, Cárdenas thought the time had come to change the ideology, structure, and image of the PNR, the party created by Calles and his corrupt allied politicians to perpetuate their political power.

Cárdenas wanted to return to the ideals of the revolution, and transformed the structure of the party to include four basic sectors as its foundation.

Of the 393 members to the third National Ordinary Assembly of the PNR, 100 were workers, 96 belonged to peasants unions and leagues, 96 belonged to the "popular sector" (public employees and others), and 101 were military. What came out of that convention was the new PRM, the *Partido de la Revolución Mexicana.*

In 1937 Cárdenas accepted the Soviet revolutionary Leon Trotsky as a refugee in Mexico. He was also known for his strong support of the Spanish republic's government.

In 1938 Cárdenas made history by expropriating the petroleum industry in Mexico. The oil expropriation created serious problems between Mexico and the United States. It also created problems with Great Britain, which severed diplomatic relations with Mexico. Domestically, however, the expropriation won him widespread support. He also nationalized the railroad system and convoked the first Inter-American Indigenous Congress.

Cárdenas ended his presidency in 1940, leaving the country tremendously divided into two apparently irreconcilable sides, which were extremely polarized politically. He was greatly revered by the indigenous people of Mexico, who nicknamed him Tata Lázaro. He was despised and rejected by the upper class, who deemed him to be a communist. They also disapproved of the state of the national economy during his term in office—a time of worldwide depression and anticipation of World War II.

MANUEL AVILA CAMACHO (1897–1955). *Place of birth*: Teziutlán, Puebla; *Place of death*: Ranch La Herradura, State of Mexico; *Wife*: Soledad Orozco; *Parents*: Manuel Avila Castillo and Eufrosina Camacho; *Position*: Constitutional President, PRM—Votes: 2,476,641; *Contenders*: General Juan Andrew Almazán—Votes: 151,101 and Rafael Sánchez Tapia—Votes: 9,840; *Term*: December 1, 1940–December 1, 1946.

Avila Camacho studied accounting in college. In 1914 he affiliated himself with the constitutionalist movement. In 1920 he was named chief of the *Estado Mayor* of the First Brigade of Sonora. He served in the military and traveled extensively throughout Mexico. He fought against the *Cristero* movement in Mexico. In 1933 he was appointed undersecretary of war and navy.

President Lázaro Cárdenas selected Avila Camacho as the candidate of the party, the Partido de la Revolución Mexicana (PRM), for the election of 1940. His election as president was fraught with many irregularities and accusations of fraud. There were many people killed, and riots occurred throughout the country protesting the tainted election. The followers of opposition leader Juan Andrew Almazán alleged the election was fraudulent, but they were never able to prove it.

With the legitimacy of his election at issue, Avila Camacho began his presidency seeking national reconciliation. The country was deeply divided over issues such as socialist education. Another big concern was the precariousness of the overall economic condition of Mexico.

During his term, what was formerly the Department of War and Navy changed its name to the Secretariat of National Defense. Avila Camacho made a strong effort to eradicate illiteracy in Mexico. He ordered a freeze on rents for some specific housing tracts where poor people lived. In 1941 Fidel Velázquez became the leader of the Confederation of Mexican Workers (CTM), and established himself as the undisputed leader of the labor movement in Mexico, a position he held until his death in 1997.

On the eve of World War II's arrival in the Americas, there was a climate of uncertainty in Mexico. To smooth the path, Avila Camacho mended diplomatic relations with the Soviet Union and Great Britain. He also worked out an agreement with the United States government regarding the still-pending issue of payment to American citizens for the damage their properties suffered during the revolutionary period. He signed a second agreement with the United States providing compensation to the oil companies whose property had been expropriated by Cárdenas in 1938. In 1942 Mexico joined the Allied Forces to fight Germany. It was during his term that Joseph Stalin's hired assassins traveled to Mexico and assassinated Leon Trotsky.

Avila Camacho established a new social security law in 1943, and inaugurated the Cardiology Institute in Mexico. In 1944 Avila Camacho suffered an attempt on his life upon his arrival at the government's palace, but was unhurt. In 1945 he created the new Federal Electoral Laws. He was also known for the historic celebration in which he brought together the previous six presidents—Pascual Ortiz Rubio, Emilio Portes Gil, Abelardo L. Rodríguez, Plutarco Elías Calles, Adolfo de la Huerta, and Lázaro Cárdenas—in a ceremony called *Acercamiento Nacional*, which could be loosely translated as "National Reunification."

During Avila Camacho's term, a noticeable political shift to the right began. He abandoned some of Cárdenas' land reform programs and promoted Mexico's industrialization.

MIGUEL ALEMÁN VALDÉS (1900–1983). *Place of birth*: Sayula, Veracruz; *Place of death*: Mexico City; *Wife*: Beatriz Velasco y Mendoza; *Parents*: General Miguel Alemán González and Tomasa Valdés; *Position*: Constitutional President, PRM—Votes: 1,786,901; *Contenders*: Ezequiel Padilla—PDM—Votes: 443,357, Jesús Agustín Castro—Votes: 29,337, and Enrique Calderón Rodríguez—Votes: 33,952; *Term*: December 1, 1946–December 1, 1952.

Alemán first studied in Jalapa, Veracruz. His law degree was from the *Universidad Nacional Autónoma de México* (UNAM). He was a senator and later was governor of the state of Veracruz. He served as chairman of the presidential campaign of Manuel Avila Camacho, and when Avila Camacho was elected president, Alemán was named secretary of the Secretariat of Government.

Avila Camacho chose Alemán to be his successor, and in 1945 he ran for president and headed several round tables where Mexico's problems were discussed at length. Ezequiel Padilla, a former secretary of foreign affairs during the Avila Camacho administration, challenged the PRM and ran as an independent candidate. Padilla thought his close relationship with Washington could enable him to win the presidency, but that was not the case. Alemán won, and Padilla cried fraud.

Alemán was the first civilian president to be elected after the Mexican

Revolution. His national agenda was very focused and very anti–Lázaro Cárdenas. He organized a strong modernization program for Mexico, which relied on capitalism and foreign capital. He aligned Mexico economically with the United States, and tried to end the bitterness between the two countries. In 1947 he met twice with American President Harry S. Truman.

With Alemán, Mexico entered into an intense program of industrialization, the main priority of which was to develop a national industry through protectionism.

Dynamic and colorful, Alemán was a very charismatic president, and he used his charisma to expand the already enormous latitude within Mexican presidentialism. His cabinet was formed of extremely talented and prestigious people. The trend to the right was stepped up.

To erase the influence of Cárdenas in the official party, Alemán converted the Partido de la Revolución Mexicana (PRM) into the Partido Revolucionario Institucional (PRI), which dropped the military sector. For Alemán, the revolution had evolved into institutions, and Mexico was then a country of institutions created precisely by the revolution.

During Alemán's term, Mexico's infrastructure grew enormously. New roads, new dams, consolidated railroad lines, and new ports, as well as more schools, were built. Illiteracy decreased dramatically; he ordered the construction of the University City. Alemán was the impetus for the construction of multifamily dwellings that were sold at a low cost to people working in the government. Baja California Norte became a state. The country's electrification systems were also expanded and improved.

Unfortunately things didn't end well. The country suffered a serious epidemic of aphthous fever, a hoof-and-mouth disease, among its cattle. The Mexican currency was devalued substantially, going from 4.80 pesos to 8.65 pesos per dollar. The devaluation boosted the burgeoning tourist industry. Massive amounts of Mexican money were transferred out of the country.

Corruption ran rampant and the line between private and public business was considerably blurred during his administration.

Alemán remained in the government after his presidency ended, and served in an important position in the tourism industry. In 1961 President Adolfo López Mateos named him the director general of the National Tourism Commission, a position he held until his death.

Population of Mexico 1950: 25,791,017 Inhabitants

ADOLFO RUIZ CORTINES (1890–1973). *Place of birth*: Veracruz, Veracruz; *Place of death*: Veracruz, Veracruz; *Wives*: Lucía Carrillo and María Izaguirre; *Parents*: Domingo Ruiz and María Cortines; *Position*: Constitutional President, PRI—Votes: 2,713,419; *Contenders*: Miguel Hen-

ríquez Guzmán, FPP—Votes: 579,745, Efraín González Luna, PAN—
Votes: 285,555, and Vicente Lombardo Toledano, PP—Votes: 72,482;
Term: December 1, 1952–December 1, 1958.

Ruiz Cortines had just graduated from high school when economic needs
forced him to abandon his studies and begin working in a store. He was a
follower of Francisco I. Madero and a strong anti-Huertista (Victoriano).
For many years he was an assistant of Alfredo Robles Domínguez, who
was the governor of Mexico City during the Venustiano Carranza administration. He followed Robles when the latter became governor of Guerrero.
In 1937 he was a federal deputy representing Tuxpan, Veracruz.

Early on he served in the Manuel Avila Camacho administration in the
Secretariat of Government, and then became governor of Veracruz from
1944 to 1948. He returned to the Secretariat of Government as secretary
until Miguel Alemán picked him as the candidate of the PRI for the presidency.

His election to the presidency in 1952, like that of Avila Camacho in
1940, was also marred by fraud, violence, and bloodshed, especially against
the followers of General Henríquez.

Ruiz Cortines was widely considered to be honest, thrifty, and cautious.
His government was austere and marked a contrast with the expenditures
of Miguel Alemán. As a matter of fact, Ruiz Cortines had to pay a 300-
million-peso debt left by Alemán's presidency.

Another difference with the former administration was that there were
no public accusations of open corruption leveled against Ruiz Cortines.
During his administration, women were given the right to vote. The country's infrastructure was improved, and the El Cóbano hydroelectric plant
was built. Through increased irrigation, arable acreage was greatly expanded and agricultural production was increased. The army was modern-
ized, and the minimum wage was raised to 12 pesos in Mexico City and
10.5 pesos daily in the countryside. The Falcón Dam on the border between
Mexico and the United States was inaugurated, and there the meeting between Ruiz Cortines and President Dwight D. Eisenhower took place.

In 1954 the peso went through another devaluation, going from 8.65
pesos to 12.5 pesos per dollar. In 1954, the ousted Guatemalan president
Jacobo Arbenz, and, in 1955, a young revolutionary named Fidel Castro
were granted asylum in Mexico. A year later, however, Castro and revolutionary Ernesto "Che" Guevara were detained and jailed for a short
while.

In 1956 the students at the Instituto Politécnico Nacional (IPN) went on
strike. First the students were brutally repressed, and later their school was
occupied by the army. After the completion of his term, Ruiz Cortines
retired. He was brought back to serve as the commissioner for minerals
and mines during Adolfo López Mateos' presidency, which followed.

Population of Mexico 1960: 34,923,129 Inhabitants

ADOLFO LÓPEZ MATEOS (1910–1969). *Place of birth*: Aizapán de Zaragoza, State of Mexico; *Place of death*: Mexico City; *Wife*: Eva Sámano; *Parents*: Mariano Gerardo López y Sánchez Román and Elena Mateos Vega; *Position*: Constitutional President, PRI—Votes: 6,767,754; *Contender*: Luis H. Alvarez, PAN—Votes: 705,303; *Term*: December 1, 1958–December 1, 1964.

López Mateos studied at the French School in Mexico City. He studied law in Toluca, and then received his degree at UNAM in 1934. In 1928 he joined the Vasconcelos movement, and by the time Pascual Ortiz Rubio was installed in the presidency, he had moved to Guatemala. Later he returned to Tapachula, Chiapas, where he worked as a journalist. In 1929 he was the student leader of the Socialist Labor Party. He became a professor at the Literary Institute of Toluca, and later he worked in the presidential campaign of Miguel Alemán.

In 1942 he was elected federal senator of the state of Mexico, and in 1951 he became the general secretary of PRI. He was the campaign manager for presidential candidate Adolfo Ruiz Cortines; after the election López Mateos became secretary of labor. In 1957 Ruiz Cortines chose him as his successor. López Mateos' election was also marred by accusations of fraud, but this time there was no violence as had been the case in previous elections.

At the beginning of his term he faced a serious problem with Guatemala, as the result of an attack by the Guatemalan Air Force against five Mexican fishing ships. Mexico broke off diplomatic relations with Guatemala.

Throughout his term López Mateos had enormous problems with the labor movement, often led by leftists. The railroad, teachers, oil men, and telegraph unions all tested his will. There were also numerous confrontations with students from both the IPN and UNAM. Painter David Alfaro Siqueiros, journalist Filomeno Mata, professor Othón Salazar, and Communist leader Arnoldo Martínez were all charged with "antisocial behavior" and imprisoned. Agrarian leader Rubén Jaramillo and his entire family were brutally murdered by members of the Mexican Army.

But these were not the only jailings and killings during his term. There were many others, and there was also manipulation and political maneuvering to remove radical union leaders, as was the case with the oil workers' union. Being rid of the authentic leaders of the petroleum union, López Mateos installed a man called Joaquín "La Quina" Hernández Galicia, who would remain in that position for many decades.

López Mateos reformed the electoral laws to allow the opposition to the PRI a small share of power. He renewed the revolutionary emphasis on land distribution, greatly outstripping all of his predecessors, except Lázaro Cárdenas.

He placed a heavy emphasis on the electrification of the country and nationalized the electricity industry. He created the *Instituto de Seguridad y Servicio Social para los Trabajadores del Estado* (ISSSTE), with a retirement fund and a hospital system. He created the National Commission for Free Text Books and worked out the milestone denuclearization Pact of the American subcontinent by signing the Tlatelolco Treaty.

He was also widely known because he traveled all over the world, and in Mexico he received many foreign dignitaries such as Prime Minister Jawaharlal Nehru of India, U.S. president John F. Kennedy, French president Charles de Gaulle, Queen Julienne of the Netherlands, Field Marshall Joseph Broz "Tito" of Yugoslavia, and Osvaldo Dorticós, the Cuban president.

This very active foreign policy allowed López Mateos to negotiate with Kennedy for the return of the Chamizal, which had been claimed as American territory when the Rio Grande changed its course. López Mateos always upheld the traditional Mexican foreign policy principles of self-determination and nonintervention in the affairs of other nations. He refused to break diplomatic relations with Cuba and rejected the motion to expel Cuba from the Organization of American States when all the other nation members did so to please the United States.

To reduce domestic political intrigue by past presidents, he named all living former presidents to new posts. López Mateos was also responsible for bringing the XIX Olympics to Mexico, and later, once out of the presidency, he was named president of its organizing committee.

In 1967, he became very ill with a brain aneurysm and died two years later. He enjoyed great popularity in life and became even more popular when he died a somewhat premature death.

Population of Mexico 1970: 48,225,238 Inhabitants

GUSTAVO DÍAZ ORDAZ (1911–1979). *Place of birth*: San Andrés Chalchicomula (today Ciudad Serdán), Puebla; *Place of death*: Mexico City; *Wife*: Guadalupe Borja; *Parents*: Ramón Díaz Ordaz and Sabrina Bolaños Cacho; *Position*: Constitutional President, PRI—Votes: 8,368,446; *Contender*: José González Torres, PAN—Votes: 1,034,337; *Term*: December 1, 1964–December 1, 1970.

Díaz Ordaz studied in Oaxaca and Guadalajara. He studied law at UNAM, and his degree was issued by the University of Puebla. He became a professor and the vice chancellor of his alma mater.

He worked as president of the *Junta de Conciliación y Arbitraje* (a board that rules on labor disputes) in Puebla. He was prosecutor in the regional attorney's office in Tlatlahuqui, Puebla, and general secretary of the government of Puebla. He later became a federal deputy and then was a senator from Puebla. He was appointed secretary of the Secretariat of Government in the Adolfo López Mateos administration.

In 1963 his friend López Mateos chose him as the PRI candidate for the Mexican presidency. He won the election, and during his presidency he continued the economic programs of his predecessor, keeping Antonio Ortiz Mena in his post as treasury secretary. This was the last administration that was able to maintain an accelerated economic growth, 6 percent annually with low inflation rates.

Díaz Ordaz modified tax laws and consolidated and reduced public spending to allow better control and planning of domestic investment. The peso gained international recognition by being declared a hard currency. He made substantial improvements in Mexico's infrastructure, building dams in states like Coahuila, and the subway transportation system in Mexico City. He got back from the United States a small part of Mexican territory called the Chamizal, whose ownership had been in dispute for decades. He did, however, have several problems both in the city and in the countryside. He faced trouble in Sonora and in Guerrero with regional *caciques* and with the peasants.

Díaz Ordaz had a reputation as a hard, authoritarian president; he opposed the democratization of the PRI that Carlos A. Madrazo, its president, was trying to implement. During his term, several guerrilla organizations came out in Chihuahua and Mexico City. There were uprisings in Guerrero, like the one headed by Genaro Vázquez and later by Lucio Cabañas. The army was sent to the University of Morelia to put down leftist students' demonstrations.

In 1968 the army suppressed a demonstration by massacring a large number of students at Tlatelolco in Mexico City, and Díaz Ordaz was held responsible. Others blamed his secretary of government, Luis Echeverría, for unleashing the troops. Díaz Ordaz presided over the XIX Olympics, which Adolfo López Mateos had brought to Mexico; they were held with great critical acclaim.

After his retirement, Díaz Ordaz was named ambassador to Spain by President José López Portillo. Soon thereafter he resigned as a result of the enormous scandal his appointment caused in Mexico.

Disgusted with politics, he secluded himself in his home until his death.

LUIS ECHEVERRÍA ALVAREZ (1922–). *Place of birth*: Mexico City; *Wife*: María Esther Zuno; *Parents*: Rodolfo Echeverría Esparza and Catalina Alvarez Gayou; *Position*: Constitutional President, PRI—Votes: 11,970,893; *Contender*: Efraín González Morfín, PAN—Votes: 1,945,070; *Term*: December 1, 1970–December 1, 1976.

Echeverría studied law at the UNAM. In 1946 he joined the PRM party and worked alongside the PRM chief, General Rodolfo Sánchez Taboada. He worked in the Navy Secretariat and in the Education Secretariat. In

1958 he was named undersecretary of government. Later, being in charge of National Security during Gustavo Díaz Ordaz's term, he was also held responsible for the tragic massacre of students by the army in 1968 at the *Plaza de las Tres Culturas* in Tlatelolco.

In 1969 Díaz Ordaz chose him as his successor, and the PRI made him its presidential candidate. He won the election. Declaring himself a leftist president, he tried to distance himself from his predecessor and called into his cabinet many young people who had been part of the student movement of 1968. There were many young intellectuals, economists, and activists in his cabinet.

Only seven months after his inauguration, on June 10, 1971, a group of students took to the streets for an unauthorized demonstration in support of a cause in Monterrey, Mexico. They were savagely repressed by a paramilitary group called "The Hawks," which was on the payroll of the government. Echeverría claimed he had been set up by rival politicians, but many in Mexico believed he knew much more about the Hawks and their tasks than he admitted.

Echeverría began his administration by raising public spending substantially. Petroleum production increased and electricity output was also increased during his presidency. New airports, highways, and ports were also built at this time. Echeverría traveled widely and sought financial and technological autonomy from the United States. He turned the state into an entrepreneur. He bought many unproductive businesses in a vain attempt to keep jobs for the Mexican people. By the middle of his term, his policies divided the country and sent the nation into a severe economic crisis. Unemployment nearly doubled. Foreign debt increased radically, and the currency entered a flotation system that ended in a devaluation that lowered the peso from 12.50 pesos to 20 pesos per dollar.

He promoted worldwide a political manifesto called *La Carta de Deberes y Derechos Económicos de los Estados,* and many countries symbolically supported the prescribed program. His critics accused him of having ambitions to head the United Nations.

Echeverría developed a close relationship with the Chilean and Cuban socialist governments at this time. Paradoxically, he came down very hard against Mexican leftist groups. He fought adamantly against guerrillas, terrorists, and student activists in Monterrey, Chihuahua, Culiacán, Puebla, Tlaxcala, and Mexico City. Two important guerrilla leaders passed away during his term. Genaro Vázquez died in an accident while fleeing from the police, who were chasing him. Lucio Cabañas died in combat. There were many kidnappings of industrialists, politicians, prominent people, and even of Terence Leonhardy, the U.S. consul in Guadalajara, and of the president's father-in-law, a retired politician from the state of Jalisco. As one of his last actions as president, he expropriated nearly one-quarter million acres in the northwest and distributed the land in *ejidos.*

Even though he had said on several occasions that freedom of speech was sacred, he could not stand criticism in the editorial pages of one Mexican newspaper (*Excelsior*), and maneuvered to have the publisher of the newspaper fired.

When his presidency ended, Echeverría became the ambassador of UNESCO and later the Mexican ambassador in Australia. He founded the Third World University in Mexico City.

Population of Mexico 1978: 65,000,000 Inhabitants

JOSÉ LÓPEZ PORTILLO PACHECO (1920–). *Place of birth*: Mexico City; *Wives*: Carmen Romano and Sasha Montenegro; *Parents*: José López Portillo Weber and Refugio Pacheco; *Position*: Constitutional President, PRI—Votes: 16,727,993; No *contender* of importance; *Term*: December 1, 1976–December 1, 1982.

López Portillo attended elementary school at the Benito Juárez Public School in Mexico City. He also went to a public high school in the capital, and received his law degree from the University of Santiago de Chile and later from UNAM.

He was a professor of law at UNAM, and in 1958 he worked for the political campaign of Adolfo López Mateos. One year later he worked in the Secretariat of National Patrimony. He was undersecretary of the presidency from 1968 to 1970, director general of the Federal Electric Commission in 1972, and secretary of the treasury in 1973.

López Portillo's friend from early childhood, Luis Echeverría, chose him to be his successor for the 1976–1982 presidential period, and ran him for the presidency as the PRI candidate. He ran without opposition because every other political party boycotted the election. The official count of votes gave him almost 5 million more votes than his predecessor had received.

During the first year of his administration, the country seemed overwhelmed with political problems. There was also a high degree of uncertainty among the Mexicans as a result of the peso devaluation, which had taken place at the end of Echeverría's term. Thus in his inaugural speech, López Portillo promised "wealth and moral renovation" for the country.

His initial strategy was to seek a reconciliation with the private sector with which his predecessor, Echeverría, had clashed repeatedly. By 1978 the president announced the discovery of vast new oil reserves. López Portillo thought the price of oil in the world market would keep on rising and ordered an increase in production. He also increased public spending and doubled the number of privately owned enterprises bought and administered by the public sector. This move, of course, led to hiring double the number of bureaucrats. When the price of oil fell in 1981, López Portillo continued spending, now borrowing the money. From 1978 to 1981, the economy grew at an 8 percent rate. However, inflation, grew at a 50 percent annual rate. Mexico's external debt, which was already enormous, tripled. It should also be pointed out that his administration was tainted by allegations of widespread corruption.

In 1982 the country spiraled into a severe economic crisis. Capital flight reached new heights. The peso underwent two devaluations and went from 24.50 pesos per dollar to 69.50 pesos. Payment of interest on the huge external debt was suspended.

In the political realm, López Portillo promoted a political reform that led to the creation of new political parties. He also reorganized the federal bureaucracy.

In foreign affairs, López Portillo renewed diplomatic relations with Spain in 1977, and supported the Sandinista Revolution in Nicaragua politically, financially, and technologically. He tried, unsuccessfully, to position himself as the intermediary between the United States and the Central American guerrillas. In 1979 the United States withdrew the most preferred nation status from Mexico. One year later, a boycott against the sale of Mexican tuna in the United States was implemented. Also in 1980, López Portillo hosted a dialogue in Cancun between countries from the north and the south. In 1982, 10,000 Guatemalan refugees received asylum in Chiapas.

In his last State of the Union speech, the president announced the nationalization of the Mexican banking system. He ended his term as a widely unpopular president. Mexican public opinion judged his government as nepotistic and corrupt. One of his protégés, Arturo Durazo, who acted as police chief of his administration, was jailed by the next administration and was accused of "inexplicable enrichment." At the end of López Portillo's administration, the country fell into a widespread economic and moral crisis.

Population of Mexico 1982: 73,122,000 Inhabitants

MIGUEL DE LA MADRID HURTADO (1934–). *Place of birth*: Colima, Colima; *Wife*: Paloma Cordero Tapia; *Parents*: Miguel de la Madrid Castro and Alicia Hurtado Oldenbourg; *Position*: Constitutional President, PRI— Votes: 16,748,006; *Contenders*: Pablo Emilio Madero, PAN—Votes: 3,700,045, Arnoldo Martínez Verdugo, PSUM—Votes: 821,995, Ignacio González Gollaz, PDM—Votes: 433,886, Rosario Ibarra de Piedra, PRT— Votes: 416,448, Cándido Díaz Cerecedo, PST—Votes: 342,005, and Manuel Moreno Sánchez, PSD—Votes: 48,413; *Term*: December 1, 1982– December 1, 1988.

When De la Madrid was two, his father died, and his twenty-four-year-old mother became his sole provider. He went through school with grants, scholarships, and by working. He graduated with a degree in law from UNAM in 1957. He then went on to complete a masters program at Harvard, receiving a degree in public administration. Later on he became a professor at UNAM. He is the author of several books on law.

In 1960 he began his career in public administration. He worked at the National Bank of Foreign Commerce, Bank of Mexico, Mexican Petroleum Company, Treasury Department, and then Secretariat of Programming and Budget.

In 1981 he was chosen by President José López Portillo as the PRI candidate for the presidency. His election was considered a watershed moment in the history of Mexico because, for the first time since 1952, the Mexican public was able to choose from several different political parties to elect a president.

As soon as De la Madrid was elected, he went to work trying to redress the severe economic and moral crisis that was prevalent in Mexico. His first initiative was a moral renewal of society. To prove the point, his administration charged, prosecuted, and jailed two corrupt officials of the past administration: Jorge Díaz Serrano, former PEMEX director, and Arturo Durazo, former police chief.

His presidency was marred by natural and human disasters. A huge gas explosion in the suburbs of Mexico left many citizens dead, and then came the 1985 earthquake, which devastated Mexico City and left thousands of people dead or homeless. The southeastern part of the country was also hit hard by a tremendous hurricane in 1988.

To add to De la Madrid's problems, the chaotic state of the economy left him without options. There was no money to promote economic growth, and the country had an enormous and increasing internal debt. Mexico had no access to international markets, and there were no internal savings to fall back on.

During the third year of De la Madrid's administration, he began a program of privatization of government agencies in coordination with the World Bank and the International Monetary Fund. He also began a program of decentralization of the government and the industrial sector. Mexico joined the General Agreement on Tariffs and Trade (GATT), which was to make Mexico conform to worldwide standards in trade. The maquila industry in the border region with the United States grew tremendously and foreign investment began coming to Mexico. By 1986 inflation was over 100 percent, but two years later it was brought down to 51.7 percent. Mexico's external debt by the end of De la Madrid's administration was over $104 billion.

In foreign policy De la Madrid tried to diminish the excessive ideologization of his predecessor's policy in Central America, while presenting a principled position vis-à-vis the U.S. policy of the Reagan administration. His strategy was anchored on the collective force of the so-called *Grupo Contadora*, composed of Mexico, Colombia, Panama, and Venezuela. These countries convinced Argentina, Brazil, Peru, and Uruguay to form a support group for *Contadora*. Unfortunately for De la Madrid's cause, not even the collective strength of eight countries seeking peace in Central America was able to convince Reagan of the soundness of their position. During the De la Madrid administration, the relationship between Mexico and the United States went through one of its worst moments.

De la Madrid's term was characterized by its austerity. He was able to keep Mexico's social fabric intact in spite of so many crises, especially the rising opposition to PRI. As a soccer enthusiast, in 1986 he managed to bring the World Cup to Mexico for the second time.

When his term was over, De la Madrid was appointed general manager of the *Fondo de Cultura Económica*, one of the largest and most important publishing houses in Mexico.

Population of Mexico 1990: 81,249,649 Inhabitants

CARLOS SALINAS DE GORTARI (1948–). *Place of birth*: Mexico City; *Wives*: Cecilia Occelli and Paula Gerard; *Parents*: Raúl Salinas Lozano and Margarita de Gortari Carvajal; *Position*: Constitutional President, PRI— Votes: 9,687,926; *Contenders*: Cuauhtémoc Cárdenas, PARM, PPS, PMS, PFCRN—Votes: 5,929,585, Manuel J. Clouthier, PAN—Votes: 3,208,584, Gumersindo Magaña, PDM—Votes: 190,891, Rosario Ibarra de Piedra, UP—Votes: 74,857, and Heberto Castillo, PMS (he withdrew from the election and supported the candidate of the PFCRM); *Term*: December 1, 1988–December 1, 1994.

Salinas graduated with an economics degree from the UNAM in 1969. He earned two masters degrees and a Ph.D. from Harvard University. He began his career as a public official in the Treasury Department and held several positions there. In 1979 he went to the Secretariat of Programming and Budget. In 1982 he became the secretary of that office, and then in 1987, he was chosen by Miguel de la Madrid to become the PRI presidential candidate.

His election was one of the most disputed in the entire history of Mexico. Many observers believe an enormous fraud took place, a belief that cast a shadow on the legitimacy of his presidency.

At the very beginning of his term, Salinas stirred public opinion by jailing a series of influential people who were accused of corruption. Among them were the powerful leader of the oil union Joaquín "La Quina" Hernández Galicia, banker Eduardo Legorreta Chauvet, and government official José Antonio Zorrilla, accused of masterminding the killing of a journalist. From 1989 to 1993 he also jailed several important drug traffickers: Miguel Angel Félix Gallardo, Rodolfo Caro Quintero, and Joaquín "El Chapo" Guzmán Loera.

Yet it would be in the field of economics where Salinas attempted his daring revolution. From the 1940s until 1982, Mexico's economic policy was designed to protect the rising national industries against foreign competition through tariffs and other barriers to trade. The system collapsed and then-president Miguel de la Madrid had to pick up the pieces and start the process of *apertura*, or the opening of the economy, which Salinas accelerated during his term.

Salinas and his team of economists set a policy, the key elements of which were to eliminate the deficit in the public sector accounts, to reduce inflation dramatically, to privatize businesses owned by the government, to search for foreign investment and open the Mexican economy to import competition, and to diversify Mexican exports, substituting oil for manufactured goods.

There were some risks involved in the strategy, like relying too much on the influx of short-term speculative foreign capital to Mexico to keep the peso steady and to finance consumption. But the results, up to 1994, were good. Salinas dramatically reduced inflation from a high of 160 percent, in 1987, to 7 percent, in 1994. He sped up the pace of the reprivatization program, returning to the private sector the banking system, the telephone company, sugar mills, and the steel industry. Hundreds of inefficient businesses that were owned by the state in past administrations were either sold or abandoned. However, not enough of the new efficient industries were created to substitute for the old ones. Also, there were accusations of corruption against people close to Salinas in connection with the privatization effort, and most important, the people of Mexico never felt the benefits of his economic reform.

With the help of government-dominated unions, his administration was able to keep wages low. He reformed Article 27 of the Constitution and ended the agrarian system called *ejido*, allowing peasants to sell their parcels of land if they wanted to do so. He also favorably renegotiated the country's foreign debt. But his biggest accomplishment was to successfully negotiate the North American Free Trade Agreement, signed between Mexico, the United States, and Canada, which went into effect on January 1, 1994.

Apart from the economic revolution, there were also some changes in the political arena. Salinas opened political space, albeit in a very selective way, for the right wing opposition party and virtually closed it to the left wing, while placing the presidency in control of politics in the country. Salinas made himself the ultimate judge for each election.

It was during the administration of Salinas that, for the first time ever, the victories of an opposition party, the PAN, in gubernatorial races were acknowledged. The first one was that of Governor Ernesto Ruffo in Baja California. Later came PAN victories in Guanajuato and Chihuahua. At the same time, Salinas removed a record number of PRI governors from their posts.

The centerpiece of his social policy was the so-called National Solidarity

Program, which financially assisted the poorest people of Mexico. Using the money coming from the privatization of thousands of companies that the government was running, the Salinas administration devised a system to channel the funds to finance specific projects forged in the communities to attend their health, housing, education, or infrastructure needs. The project was successful, but it was also criticized from two different perspectives. Some people accused Salinas of using it as a tool for electoral purposes. Others believed it was a source of corruption.

Attending another area of concern of the people, Salinas created the National Commission of Human Rights as an independent office that would rule, without possibility of enforcement, on human rights violations. This was another innovative idea in Mexico that did much good, but was also criticized for not being independent and for lacking teeth.

Ending a century-long conflict between the state and the Catholic Church, Salinas reestablished diplomatic relations for Mexico with the Vatican. Also during his term, the El Salvador Peace Agreements were signed in Chapultepec Castle.

During the Salinas administration, several natural and man-made disasters occurred. In Guadalajara, for instance, a drainage system exploded and destroyed several houses and streets. Then, Cardinal Juan Jesús Posadas Ocampo was murdered by drug traffickers in the airport's parking lot. Later, an automobile exploded near the Hotel Camino Real in Guadalajara in an incident that was interpreted as drug traffic–related.

In 1993 Salinas designated Luis Donaldo Colosio as his successor. Another pre-candidate named Manuel Camacho Solís became vehemently opposed to his nomination, and the PRI became somewhat divided. Shortly thereafter there was an uprising in Chiapas led by a group called the *Ejército Zapatista de Liberación Nacional* (EZLN). Camacho Solís, who was named secretary of foreign relations as a consolation prize, was appointed commissioner for peace in Chiapas.

On March 23, 1994, during a campaign stop in Baja California, Colosio was assassinated in Tijuana. This development shocked and saddened the country profoundly. A few months later, José Francisco Ruiz Massieu, the secretary general of the PRI and former brother-in-law of Salinas, was also murdered.

The president named Ernesto Zedillo as the new PRI candidate for the presidency, and Mexico witnessed its first public campaign debate on May 12, 1994, between three candidates for the presidency: Zedillo for the PRI, Diego Fernández de Cevallos for the PAN, and Cuauhtémoc Cárdenas for the PRD.

The elections of August 21 were called by all observers the cleanest ever in Mexico. They were also marked by the largest number of voters participating in an election, with 77 percent of the eligible voters going to the polls. For the first time ever, there were foreign observers watching the elections. When the electoral process ended, it seemed that the country had rejected violence and opted for the old system, electing the PRI candidate.

Salinas' presidency was characterized by drastic political and economic reforms in Mexico, but also by the infiltration of narcotic traffickers into the political system. There were severe internal divisions within the PRI in these six years, and the PAN gained considerable political strength. Polls indicated that Salinas ended his term as one of the most popular presidents ever. However, after a new economic debacle in December 1994 and the arrest of his brother Raúl Salinas de Gortari, his popularity declined severely. Salinas went on a hunger strike in a vain attempt to clear his name, and a few days later, on March 10, 1995, he left the country in disgrace. He was blamed for every single problem facing the presidency of Zedillo.

Salinas' term ended on December 1, 1994. In mid-December there was a renewal of the Chiapas rebellion, and by December 19, foreign reserves in Mexico were down to $6 billion. The results of this liquidity crisis led to a devaluation that was improperly handled by the new administration and unleashed a financial turmoil that had global repercussions.

Population of Mexico 1995: 93,985,848 Inhabitants

ERNESTO ZEDILLO PONCE DE LEÓN (1951–). *Place of birth*: Mexico City; *Wife*: Nilda Patricia Velasco Núñez; *Parents*: Rodolfo Zedillo Castillo and Martha Alicia Ponce de León; *Position*: Constitutional President, PRI— Votes: 17,336,325; *Contenders*: Diego Fernández de Cevallos, PAN— Votes: 9,222,899, Cuauhtémoc Cárdenas, PRD—Votes: 5,901,557, and Cecilia Soto, PT—Votes: 975,356 *Term*: December 1, 1994–.

When Zedillo was three years old, he and his family went to Mexicali, Baja California, in search of a better life. When he was fourteen years old, he and his brother returned to study in Mexico City. He studied economics at the Escuela Superior de Economía, in the National Polytechnic Institute (IPN). In 1971 he joined the PRI and served in several positions. In 1973 he obtained a scholarship to study at Bradford University in Great Britain, and then another one for Yale in the United States. At Yale he obtained his Ph.D. in economics.

In 1978 Zedillo returned to Mexico and began working for the Bank of Mexico. In 1987 he was appointed undersecretary of the Secretariat of Programming and Budget. In 1988 President Carlos Salinas de Gortari named him secretary of the same office.

Zedillo led the National Institute of Geography, Statistics, and Information (INEGI) in designing the best and most accurate census of population in the history of Mexico. In 1992 he was appointed secretary of education, and in 1993 he was chosen to be campaign manager of Luis Donaldo Colosio's presidential campaign. In March 29, 1994, when Colosio was killed, Zedillo was chosen by Salinas as the new PRI candidate for the presidential election of 1994.

In August 1994 Zedillo won the presidency in the cleanest election ever and with the largest voter turn out in the history of Mexico. Out of 45.7 million registered voters, 77 percent voted.

Zedillo began his term under the best auspices. A few days after his inauguration he traveled to the Miami Summit of the Americas, along with thirty-two other heads of government in the continent. Then came the debacle of December 1994. Faced with a liquidity crisis, the recently installed administration improperly handled a peso devaluation, sending mixed signals to investors and failing to introduce needed adjustment measures. The crisis created enormous dislocation in Mexico and unleashed a financial turmoil that had global repercussions.

In early 1995, the Mexican crisis worsened when large amounts of *Tesobonos*, short term bonds payable in pesos for their equivalent in dollars, held by foreigners were due in the first eight months of 1995 and were not rolled over. The administration of U.S. president Bill Clinton came to the rescue and arranged a financial bailout for Mexico in the amount of $20 billion, and paved the way for another $20 billion financed by the International Monetary Fund, the World Bank, and other multilateral organizations. Up until February 1996, Mexico had used $13.5 billion. By the end of 1996, most of the debt had been paid, including the interest, and in January 1997 it was fully paid, three years in advance. This bailout package forced the Zedillo administration to rekindle an austerity program that translated into more economic duress for the Mexican people.

In a daring move, Zedillo appointed a member of an opposition party to his cabinet, and PAN's Antonio Lozano García became attorney general.

Lozano's biggest challenge was to solve the assassinations of Cardinal Juan Jesús Posadas Ocampo, presidential candidate Luis Donaldo Colosio, and PRI's secretary general, José Francisco Ruiz Massieu. Shocking public opinion, in 1995, Lozano accused Raúl Salinas of masterminding the killing of Ruiz Massieu, but in trying to prove his theory, he got entangled in a sloppy investigation. By the end of 1996, Lozano was fired, and Jorge Madrazo Cuellar, who was the president of the Human Rights Commission, got the job.

On February 28, 1995, the shocked country watched one of the most dramatic political feuds in Mexican history when Raúl Salinas, brother of former president Salinas, was captured and jailed. Alarmed by the arrest of his brother and frustrated with the popular perception that the economic crisis the country was experiencing was a byproduct of his administration, former president Salinas went on a hunger strike and, a few days later, left the country in disgrace.

In another scandal also related to the Salinas administration, Mario Ruiz Massieu, former deputy attorney general for narcotics and brother of the assassinated José Francisco Ruiz Massieu, left Mexico and was arrested in Newark, New Jersey. He was charged with U.S. currency law violations for allegedly failing to declare the amount of money he was carrying. The Mexican government asked for his deportation, accusing him of several crimes. Up until February 1996, Ruiz Massieu had successfully fought off five attempts to extradite him.

On February 9, 1995, some members of the Zapatista movement in Chiapas were arrested, and the identity of the masked guerrilla spokesperson, called Subcomandante Marcos, was revealed. He was Rafael Sebastián Guillén Vicente, a professor born and raised in a middle class family in the provincial port of Tampico. Simultaneously, the president ordered the Mexican army to attack the guerrillas, who retreated to their camps in the Chiapas ravines.

During 1995, urban violence, thefts, robberies, assaults, and so forth, increased dramatically in all major cities in Mexico. Drug trafficker Héctor Luis "Güero" Palma, of the Sinaloa cartel, was apprehended in June 1995. In January 1996, Juan García Abrego was apprehended and deported to the United States. He was one of the ten most wanted criminals on the FBI lists.

On October 10 Presidents Zedillo and Clinton met in Washington, D.C., for the third time. The topics on the agenda were NAFTA, economic reform, judiciary reform, and international cooperation in the struggle against drug trafficking. A very important goal for Zedillo was to show the American people that the financial bailout was working. He paid most of the principal and some interest on the debt.

In November, however, the economic prospects for the country were not good. The peso lost value and the exchange rate went from 3 to 7.80 per dollar; inflation was running at a 50 percent rate annually (seven times what it had been one year before); 1 million people recently rendered jobless added to the annual need for 1 million new jobs; 1 million people refused to honor the debts owed to their banks; and the economy suffered a negative growth of 6 percent. There was also some good news. Exports from Mexico reached a record high of $76 billion, an amount roughly equivalent to 25 percent of GDP. In August 1996, it was reported that the economy grew at 7.2 percent in the second trimester as compared to the same term in 1995, giving hopes that Mexico was overcoming its recession.

In June 1996 a new and highly suspicious new guerrilla group called Popular Revolutionary Army (EPR) surfaced in the state of Guerrero. On August 29 they attacked several police and army posts in the states of Mexico, Oaxaca, Guerrero, and Chiapas.

Kidnapping people for ransom became a very profitable business in Mexico during the first three years of the Zedillo administration.

All political parties have agreed to a sweeping political reform that was somehow watered down by the time Congress approved it with only PRI votes. The other parties voted against it. On the positive side, the reform limits private campaign financing, requiring detailed disclosure, and it names an independent national election commission.

The real test for the reform, however, will come when an important election, like the presidential election of the year 2000, takes place.

General José de Jesús Gutiérrez Rebollo, who served as Mexico's anti-narcotics czar, was jailed February 19, 1997, on drug corruption charges, of taking bribes, and fostering cocaine trafficking for the biggest drug-smuggling cartel headed by Amado Carrillo Fuentes. The news of the arrest created a furor in the United States. A group of congressmen and women, as well as the Drug Enforcement Agency, asked President Clinton to de-certify Mexico as an ally in the war against drugs. President Clinton pre-vailed and certified Mexico's conduct, but new tensions arose between the two countries. Then on July 5, Amado Carrillo Fuentes died during a plas-tic surgery operation in a hospital in Mexico City. A few days before, on June 21, 1997, the powerful union leader of the Confederación de Traba-jadores de México (CTM), Fidel Velázquez, who held the post for fifty-six years, died.

On July 6, Mexican voters elected, for the first time ever, a governor of Mexico City and changed the whole Chamber of Deputies and thirty-two seats in the Senate. Many congressional deputies, governors, senators, and mayors from the rulling PRI were unseated in a tidal wave that split the country's political power into roughly three equal parts—the PRI, the center-left PRD (the Democratic Revolutionary Party), and the conservative PAN (National Action Party).

The new governor of Mexico City is the PRD Cuauhtémoc Cárdenas, who becomes Mexico's second most powerful political figure after the pres-ident. In Congress the PRI lost its absolute majority. The new composition of Congress will bring about a real separation of powers between the ex-ecutive and the legislative branches.

"This election," wrote Mexican writer Octavio Paz in a Mexican news-paper, "represents, perhaps, a new era in the history of Mexico. . . . The true winner of the election is the people of Mexico. . . . The other winner is President Zedillo, who kept his promise to honor the results of the elec-tion and has demonstrated his commitment to a real and deep democratic reform."

GLOSSARY

NAHUATL NAMES

Amantecas: artists from Amantla

Aztec: people of Aztlan; also called Mexica

Aztlan: "place of white herons"

Cacique: Indian chief, local political boss

Calmecac: school for the upper classes

Calpultin: districts or *barrios* (neighborhoods) in Tenochtitlan

Macehualtin: workers, farmers

Mayeques: servants, serfs

Mexicatl Teohuatzin: supreme military priest

Pipiltin: nobleman

Pochtecas or *oztomeca*: merchant or tradesman from Pochtlan or Ŏztoman

Tenochtitlan: "place of Tenoch" or "place of the prickly pear"

Tetecuhtin: governor

Tlamacazqui or *teohua*: "the one who offers the sacrifice to the gods"; "he who takes care of God"

Tlatlacotin: slaves

Tlatoani or *Tlacatecuhtli*: chief of a tribe, commander in chief, king, lord, supreme ruler

VICEROYALTY: DEFINITIONS OF POLICIES AND INSTITUTIONS

Audiencia: A judicial and administrative council named by the king to rule in the Colony. Each viceroyalty was divided into a number of *audiencias*.

Audiencia Gobernadora: Government in power for a short period of time, because of the viceroy's death while in office.

Caudillo: A leader, figurative boss.

Consejo de Indias: Institution in Spain to advise the Crown with a permanent committee of members (royal councils) who "understand things of the colonies."

El Real Patronato Indiano: The right of the Crown of Spain to propose a list of names for ecclesiastical office (e.g., bishops) and to interfere in all religious issues in New Spain, except matters of dogma.

Encomienda: In theory, the right to collect taxes/tribute from a number of Indians within a designated area. *Encomenderos* usually viewed the land as their own and took it illegally.

Gobierno Provisional: Term used to designate provisional government not directly appointed in Spain but in the colony/viceroyalty.

Juez de Residencia: Judge of a judicial inquiry into an official's conduct after his term. Appointed by the Spanish Crown.

La Casa de Contratación: A regulatory body in Seville, Spain, for the Atlantic trade. The *Casa*'s chief task was to ensure that taxes were collected from the subjects of the Spanish Crown in their colonies. It was in charge of civilian and criminal matters and had the faculty to issue permissions for trips and explorations and could give information to sailors. The casa also acted as a trustee of those who died in the West Indies.

Oidor: A member of the *audiencia* board.

Santo Oficio: This was the Inquisition's tribunal. It was charged with punishing heresy and determining which books whose reading was forbidden. The Inquisition did not have jurisdiction over Indians.

Viceroy: A person ruling a country, province, or colony as the deputy of a sovereign. The viceroys of the Spanish Crown in America ruled only in Mexico and Peru.

Visitador: An special envoy from the king of Spain. The *visitador* was a royal inspector.

APPENDICES

Appendix A

PLANS, TREATIES, CONSPIRACIES, AND CONSTITUTIONS SINCE 1799 (IN CHRONOLOGICAL ORDER)

Conspiración de los "Machetes," 1799
The Machetes Conspiracy was headed by Pedro de la Portilla against Viceroy Miguel José de Azanza. It was called "of the *Machetes*" because of the weapons carried by the rebels.

Conspiración de Valladolid, 1809
The Valladolid Conspiracy took place in December 1809. Its purpose was to create in Mexico a congress that would govern New Spain (Mexico) on behalf of Ferdinand VII. Uncovered before it materialized, the conspiracy failed in its goal.

Conspiración de Querétaro, 1810
This conspiracy was put into effect as a result of the Valladolid Conspiracy. It was promoted by Captain Ignacio Allende, Miguel Domínguez, and his wife, Josefa Ortiz de Domínguez. Its purpose was to form a governing board of the viceroyalty that would enable them to achieve political emancipation from the viceroy's command. It also failed.

Constitución de Apatzingán, 1814
This became the first constitutional law drafted in Mexico. It contained the thoughts of José María Morelos y Pavón and called for independence, declared Catholicism as the state religion, and advocated for the unity of Mexico. It was never implemented.

Plan de Iguala, 1821
Proclaimed by Agustín de Iturbide on February 24, 1821, in Iguala, Guerrero. It attempted to end the civil war that was ravaging Mexico. It also attempted to achieve independence. It consisted of two different documents. One was a proclamation of twenty-three articles, and the second was the actual Plan of Iguala. Based

on this plan, Iturbide formed the army of the three guarantees that would eventually win Mexico's independence.

Tratado de Córdoba, 1821

A treaty signed by Agustín de Iturbide and the last viceroy, Juan O'Donojú, on August 24, 1821. The treaty recognized Mexico's independence under a monarchy that had Ferdinand VII in ultimate control of the empire. Mexico's independence, however, was not recognized by Spain until 1836.

Plan de Casa Mata, 1823

With this plan, Antonio López de Santa Anna raised arms against Agustín de Iturbide in an attempt to have Mexico's congress reinstated. It was the first step in a move to install the first republican system of government in Mexico.

Constitución de 1824

Drafted on October 24, 1824, the Constitution attempted to establish a new federal and republican system of government. It was inspired by the constitutions of Cadiz and the United States of America, and by the ideals of the French revolution.

Plan de Montaño, 1826

The plan was drafted in 1826 by General Juan Maule Montaño, and was seconded by Nicolás Bravo in December of 1827. Its intended purpose was to expel the U.S. ambassador to Mexico, Joel R. Poinsett, and to end the power of the secret Masonic political societies that had been formed in Mexico.

Motín de la Acordada, 1828

It took place in the former headquarters of the Acordada, or what was the tribunal and jail of Mexico City. The uprising was a byproduct of the struggle for power between General Vicente Guerrero, a populist candidate, and the minister of war, General Manuel Gómez Pedraza. The motín was headed by General José María Lobato, Colonel Santiago García, and Lorenzo de Zavala, among others.

Plan de Jalapa, 1829

The plan was signed by General Melchor Múzquiz and Colonel Facio on December 4, 1829. Supposedly, its intended purpose was to reestablish the Constitution of 1824. Realistically, it sought to oust Vicente Guerrero and bring General Anastasio Bustamante to the presidency. It was seconded in Mexico City and then in Puebla. It ended Guerrero's rule.

Plan de Veracruz, 1831

The plan was an uprising of the garrison in Veracruz on January 2, 1831, against President Anastasio Bustamante, who was accused of betraying the Constitution of 1824. It occurred shortly before General Vicente Guerrero's assassination, and it helped bring Bustamante's rule to a close.

Plan de Cuernavaca, 1834

This plan was a blueprint for a revolutionary movement that occurred in April 1834 in support of religion, law, and Antonio López de Santa Anna. Santa Anna was installed in the presidency later that same month.

Constitución de "Las Siete Leyes," 1835

It was sworn in by President Justo Corro, who abolished the federalist regime and established a centralist republican government in its place. It created the "Conserving Power," which was the ultimate authority over the president, congress, and the judiciary branch of the Mexican government. It also lengthened the president's term to eight years.

Treaty of Santa María–Calatrava, 1836

The Treaty of Santa María–Calatrava was signed in Madrid, Spain, on December 28, 1836. Miguel Santa María signed for Mexico and José María Calatrava signed for Spain.

Plan de Jalisco o Guadalajara, 1846

Pronounced by the garrison of Guadalajara headed by Colonel José María Yañez on May 20, 1846. This plan was aimed against Mariano Paredes y Arrillaga and favored federalism. It also proclaimed Antonio López de Santa Anna to be the *caudillo*.

"Polkos" Pronunciamiento y Plan, 1847

This was a pronouncement headed by General Matías de la Peña Barragán protesting against a decree promulgated by the radical vice president and the acting president, Valentín Gómez Farías. The decree called for the expropriation of properties of the Catholic Church to raise funds to combat the American invasion. The "Polkos" pronouncement demanded the annulment of the decree and the return of Antonio López de Santa Anna to the presidency.

A generally accepted explanation for the name "Polkos" is that the people involved with the uprising were military officials who belonged to Mexico's richest families and were known for their preference of the dance called the Polka.

Guerra de Castas de Yucatan, 1847

By the middle of 1847, a group of Mayan Indians from the south and west of the Yucatan peninsula rebelled against whites, *mestizos*, and other Indians living in other regions. The causes for the rebellion were many and their root was political, economical, and agrarian. There was also some personal animosity between prominent individuals.

The people of several towns were massacred and there were many illegal apprehensions and killings of people. The war spread into many parts of the peninsula and at one point an attempt was made to involve the United States and Great Britain. At the time Yucatan wanted to split from Mexico, from which it was completely isolated, except by sea.

The fighting ended in 1853, but the final peace treaty, signed between Mexico and Great Britain, was signed in 1893. It included the delimitation of the border between Yucatan and Belize.

Tratado de Guadalupe Hidalgo o de Paz, Amistad y Convivencia, 1848

In February 1848 the Mexican government signed a peace treaty with the United States and relinquished its ownership of New Mexico, Alta California, and its claim to Texas. A total of 1.49 million square miles were exchanged for the amount of $15 million.

Tratado de La Mesilla (or de Gadsden), 1853–54
This treaty sold more Mexican land to the United States. Antonio López de Santa Anna needed money, and the United States offered to buy the lower portion of New Mexico and Arizona, approximately 62,138.81 square miles, for $10 million for a railroad route to California.

Plan de Ayutla, 1854
Proclaimed on March 1st, 1854, by General Florencio Villarreal, representing General Juan Alvarez and other generals, this plan called for the unseating of General Antonio López de Santa Anna from the presidency. It created a more democratic approach to the selection of the president of Mexico by appointing representatives from each state to the election of an interim president, who would later act as counsel to the elected president. The triumph of this plan gave birth to the Constituent Congress of 1856, which elaborated the Constitution of 1857.

Ley Juárez, 1855
Written by Benito Juárez, this set of laws ended the special religious and military privileges, especially the separate courts, dating from the colonial period.

Ley Lerdo (also called Ley de Desamortización de Bienes en Manos Muertas or Ley de Corporaciones Civiles y Eclesiásticas), 1856
This law was written by Sebastián Lerdo de Tejada. It authorized the government to confiscate land from the Catholic Church, charging that the church was neglecting the cultivation of the land. This law, however, exempted the land on which churches were built, and the churches and convents themselves.

Constitución de 1857
Issued by the Constituent Congress on February 5, 1857. It established a republican, representative, and federalist system of government for Mexico. It established individual rights for the people and protection under the law. It instituted secular education, freedom of the press, and was clearly anticlerical.

Plan de Tacubaya, 1857
This plan was proclaimed by General Félix Zuloaga on December 17, 1857. Its goal was to abolish the Constitution of 1857 and to deny recognition to Ignacio Comonfort as president.

Plan de Navidad, 1858
Proclaimed by General Miguel M. Echegaray and Manuel Robles Pezuela on December 20, 1858, this plan called for the removal of President Félix Zuloaga and demanded the installation of General Miguel Miramón as president. Miramón, however, disavowed the plan and supported Zuloaga.

Leyes de Reforma, 1859
On July 1859 the liberals, headed by Benito Juárez, issued the Reform Laws that allowed the government to nationalize the property of the church. These laws also marked a clear and complete separation between church and state. They suppressed religious communities and forbade the establishment of new convents. They strengthened civil law, making marriage a civil matter and initiating a nonreligious national civil registry. They also ordered the secularization of all graveyards, and decreed freedom of religion and a reduction in the number of religious holidays.

Tratado McLane-Ocampo, 1859

The government of Benito Juárez signed this treaty in December 1859. It would have ceded Baja California to the United States, and allowed America perpetual right of free transit in three parts of the Mexican Republic. In exchange, Mexico asked for diplomatic recognition. The treaty, however, failed to gain support in the U.S. Senate and was never ratified. It would have cut Mexico into three parts.

Tratado Mon-Almonte, 1859

During the war of reform, Mexico had two governments. One of them, the Mexican conservative government of Félix Zuloaga, signed this treaty in Paris on September 26, 1859. Juan N. Almonte was the Mexican representative, and Alejandro Mon represented Queen Isabel II of Spain.

In this treaty, the conservatives committed Mexico to giving compensation to the heirs of Spanish nationals killed in the haciendas of Chiconcuac and San Vicente. The treaty also established that the government would arrest and punish those responsible for the killings. The governments of Great Britain and France were to set the amounts for the indemnification. Benito Juárez, the president of the liberal government, did not recognize the treaty and declared Almonte a traitor.

Tratado de Miramar, 1864

Signed by Napoleon III, this treaty committed France to support the empire of Maximilian in Mexico with 25,000 soldiers. It also established that the Mexican conservatives would be responsible for the economic support of the French troops while in Mexico.

Plan de La Noria, 1871

On November 8, 1871, from his hacienda of La Noria, General Porfirio Díaz launched this plan against President Benito Juárez. Díaz accused Juárez of trying to remain in power indefinitely, and declared himself against reelection. It declared support for the reformist principles and for the Constitution of 1857. In spite of the fact that Díaz's insurrection was supported by several important generals, the loyalist army, commanded by General Sóstenes Rocha, defeated the rebels in the Cerro de la Bufa.

Plan de Tuxtepec, 1876

Proclaimed on January 1, 1876, in Tuxtepec, Oaxaca, by a group of military followers of General Porfirio Díaz, the plan was aimed against President Sebastián Lerdo de Tejada. It supported the Constitution of 1857, the Reform Act of 1873, and the Law of December 1874. It rejected the possibility of reelection of the president or governors. It did not recognize the presidency of Lerdo, but did recognize Díaz as the supreme commander of the army, and named him secretary of the treasury and war. The rebels succeeded militarily.

Plan de San Luis Potosí, 1910

Presidential candidate Francisco I. Madero proclaimed this plan, declaring illegal the elections of 1910 and repudiating the government of Porfirio Díaz. It announced November 20, 1910, as the starting date for the revolution, and called the people to join it.

Tratados de Ciudad Juárez, 1911
In May 1911, Pascual Orozco occupied militarily the city of Ciudad Juárez. On May 21, Porfirio Díaz signed the treaties with the rebels, resigning the presidency.

Plan de Ayala, 1911
Proclaimed on November 28, 1911, by the revolutionary armies of Emiliano Zapata, this plan called for "Land and Liberty." It called for the restoration of lands stolen from the Indians.

La Decena Trágica, 1913
This is the name given to a ten-day period of tragic events in Mexico City, during which a fraction of the army rebelled against the legitimate government of Francisco I. Madero. It began on February 9, 1913, and ended on February 18, after hundreds of people died in the indiscriminate shelling.

Victoriano Huerta, who had been appointed by Madero to put down the rebellion, betrayed the president. Huerta ordered the seizure of both Madero and Vice President José María Pino Suárez, and later, on February 22, Huerta ordered their execution.

Plan de Guadalupe, 1913
It was signed by the governor of Coahuila, Venustiano Carranza, in the hacienda of Guadalupe on March 26, 1913. It repudiated the government of Victoriano Huerta and the legislative and judiciary powers of the federation. It made Carranza, the "First Chief of the Constitutionalist Army."

Tratados de Teloyucan, 1914
The federal army surrendered to the Constitutionalist Army through this treaty, on August 14, 1914.

Constitución de 1917
Having restored the constitutional order in Mexico, Venustiano Carranza called for a congress in the city of Querétaro to formulate a new constitution. Based on the Constitution de 1857, the new constitution embodied in its language many of the principles that had guided the revolutionary struggle. It also updated those articles that dealt with education, labor law, and land tenure.

Plan de Agua Prieta, 1920
In this plan, Alvaro Obregón, Adolfo de la Huerta, and Plutarco Elías Calles repudiated the government of Venustiano Carranza.

Acuerdos De la Huerta-Lamont, 1922
In these agreements, the government of Alvaro Obregón, represented by Adolfo de la Huerta, recognized the obligation of Mexico to repay damages to the property of American citizens caused by the revolution.

Acuerdos de Bucareli, 1923
Alvaro Obregón signed these accords, committing Mexico to respect the properties of American companies and individuals and to pay cash for them if emergency circumstances required him to nationalize them.

Guerra Cristera o Cristiada, 1927–1929
This was a rebellion by Catholic peasants protesting the religious persecution they were suffering at this time from the government of Plutarco Elías Calles. Also

underlying this rebellion was a struggle for land tenure. Their battle cry, similar to the "Land and Liberty" of the Zapatistas, was "Land and Religion." It was a political struggle as well.

Plan de Hermosillo, 1929

This was a revolt organized by General José Gonzalo Escobar against Plutarco Elías Calles. It took place in March 1929, and quickly failed.

Tratado de Tlatelolco, 1963

Published in February 29, 1963, during the presidency of Adolfo López Mateos, this treaty advocated the denuclearization of the American continent. In 1967 it was signed in Mexico City, with the approval of the United Nations. In 1977 President Jimmy Carter of the United States also signed the treaty, establishing Latin America as a nuclear-free zone.

La Carta de los Derechos y Deberes Económicos de los Estados, 1972

It was an attempt by President Luis Echeverría to make the superpowers accept and recognize the sovereignty of any individual state over its natural resources and its political and social regime. It also advocated a fair exchange of technologies and trade between countries of different economic size.

Tratado de Libre Comercio, 1994

Signed between Mexico, Canada, and the United States, this was an agreement to gradually eliminate tariffs and nontariff barriers to free trade between the three countries. It was advocated by Presidents Carlos Salinas de Gortari, George Bush, and Brian Mulrooney. It was signed by President Bill Clinton, who also favored it, and his two counterparts.

Tratados de Paz en Chiapas, 1996

The first of a series of Treaties negotiated between the Indians of Chiapas and the federal government was signed in 1996. It recognized the rights and culture of the indigenous people of Mexico. For the first time since the Spanish conquest in 1521, the original people of the land were recognized by their fellow countrymen as full equals and capable of formulating their own human and civil rights. There are five treaties still pending.

Appendix B

NAMES OF MEXICAN POLITICAL PARTIES

FPP	Federación de Partidos del Pueblo	Federation of Parties of the People
PAN	Partido de Acción Nacional	National Action Party
PARM	Partido Auténtico de la Revolución Mexicana	Authentic Party of the Mexican Revolution
PCM	Partido Comunista Mexicano	Mexican Communist Party
PCN	Partido Católico Nacional	National Catholic Party
n/a	Partido Conservador	Conservative Party
n/a	Partido Cooperatista Nacional	National Cooperativist Party
PDM	Partido Demócrata Mexicano	Mexican Democratic Party
PFCRN	Partido del Frente Cardenista de Reconstrucción Nacional	Party of the Cardenist Front of National Reconstruction
PLC	Partido Liberal Constitucionalista	Constitutionalist Liberal Party
PLM	Partido Laborista Mexicano	Mexican Labor Party
PLM	Partido Liberal Mexicano	Mexican Liberal Party
n/a	Partido de la Masonería Yorkinos & Escoceses	Masonry (It became a political party)
PMS	Partido Mexicano Socialista	Socialist Mexican Party
PNA	Partido Nacional Agrarista	Agrarian National Party
PNAR	Partido Nacional Antireeleccionista	Anti-reelectionist National Party

PND	Partido Nacional Democrático	Democratic National Party
n/a	Partido Nacional Porfirista	Porfirist National Party (party of Porfirio Díaz)
PNR	Partido Nacional Revolucionario	Revolutionary National Party; a predecessor of the PRI (from 1938 to 1946)
PP	Partido Popular	Popular Party
PPS	Partido Popular Socialista	Socialist Popular Party
n/a	Partido Reeleccionista	Reelectionist Party
n/a	Partido Reyista	Reyista Party (party of General Bernardo Reyes)
PRD	Partido de la Revolución Democrática	Democratic Revolutionary Party
PRI	Partido Revolucionario Institucional	Institutional Revolutionary Party
PRM	Partido de la Revolución Mexicana	Party of the Mexican Revolution; a predecessor of the PRI (from 1929 to 1938)
PRT	Partido Revolucionario de los Trabajadores	Workers Revolutionary Party
PSDM	Partido Social Demócrata Mexicano	Mexican Social Democratic Party
PST	Partido Socialista de los Trabajadores	Workers' Socialist Party
PSUM	Partido Socialista Unificado Mexicano	Mexican Unified Socialist Party
PVEM	Partido Verde Mexicano	Mexican Green Party
UNO	Partido Nacional de la Oposición Unificada	Unified National Opposition Party

Appendix C

ACRONYMS

CNDH	Comisión Nacional de Derechos Humanos National Commission on Human Rights
CONACYT	Consejo Nacional de Ciencias y Tecnología National Council on Science and Technology
CONASUPO	Compañía Nacional de Subsistencias Populares National Company of Public Commodities
CTM	Confederación de Trabajadores de México Confederation of Mexican Workers
EPR	Ejército Popular Revolucionario Popular Revolutionary Army
EZLN	Ejército Zapatista de Liberación Nacional The Zapatista National Liberation Army
GATT	Acuerdo General sobre Aranceles Aduaneros y Comercio General Agreement on Trade and Tariffs
INEGI	Instituto Nacional de Estadística, Geografía e Informática National Institute of Geography, Statistics, and Information
IMSS	Instituto Mexicano del Seguro Social Mexican Institute of Social Security
IPN	Instituto Politécnico Nacional National Polytechnic Institute

ISSSTE	Instituto de Seguridad y Servicio Social para los Trabajadores del Estado Institute of Insurance and Social Services for Federal Employees
OEA	Organización de los Estados Americanos Organization of American States
PEMEX	Petróleos Mexicanos Mexican Petroleum Company
TLC	Tratado de Libre Comercio North American Free Trade Agreement (NAFTA)
UNAM	Universidad Nacional Autónoma de México National Autonomous University of Mexico
UNESCO	Organización de las Naciones Unidas para la Educación, la Ciencia y la Cultura United Nations Educational, Social, and Cultural Organization
URSS	Unión de Repúblicas Soviético Socialistas Union of Soviet Socialist Republics

Appendix D

CHRONOLOGY

Entries in bold indicate kings of Spain.

THE AZTECS

1325	Tenoch
1377–1389	Acamapichtli
1390–1410	Huitzilihuitl
1416–1428	Chimalpopoca
1428–1440	Itzcoatl
1440–1469	Moctezuma Ilhuicamina
1469–1483	Axayacatl
1483–1486	Tizoc
1486–1502	Ahuizotl
1502–1520	Moctezuma Xocoyotzin
1520	Cuitlahuac
1520–1525	Cuauhtemoc

CONQUEST

1516–1556	**Charles V (Charles I of Spain)**
1521	Cristóbal de Tapia

1522–1524	Hernán Cortés
1524–1527	Provisional Government
1526 (sixteen days)	Luis Ponce de León
1526–1527 (seven months)	Marcos Aguilar
1527–1528	Alonso de Estrada
1528–1530	First *Audiencia*
1530–1535	Second *Audiencia*

VICEROYALTY

1535–1550	Antonio de Mendoza
1550–1564	Luis de Velasco I
1556–1598	**Philip II**
1564–1566	Third *Audiencia*
1566–1567	Gastón de Peralta
1567–1568	*Audiencia Gobernadora*
1568–1580	Martín Enríquez de Almanza
1580–1583	Lorenzo Suárez de Mendoza
1583–1584	Fourth *Audiencia*
1584–1585	Pedro Moya de Contreras
1585–1590	Alvaro Manrique de Zúñiga
1590–1595	Luis de Velasco II
1595–1603	Gaspar de Zúñiga y Acevedo
1598–1621	**Philip III**
1603–1607	Juan de Mendoza y Luna
1607–1611	Luis de Velasco II
1611–1612	Fray García Guerra
1612 (eight months)	Audiencia Gobernadora
1612–1621	Diego Fernández de Córdoba
1621–1665	**Philip IV**
1621 (six months)	Fifth *Audiencia*
1621–1624	Diego Carrillo de Mendoza y Pimentel
1624 (two days)	Audiencia Gobernadora
1624–1635	Rodrigo Pacheco y Osorio
1635–1640	Lope Díez de Armendáriz
1640–1642	Diego López Pacheco de Cabrera y Bobadilla
1642 (five months)	Juan de Palafox y Mendoza

1642–1648	García Sarmiento de Sotomayor
1648–1649	Marcos de Torres y Rueda
1649–1650	Sixth *Audiencia*
1650–1653	Luis Enríquez de Guzmán
1653–1660	Francisco Fernández de la Cueva
1660–1664	Juan de Leyva y de la Cerda
1664 (five months)	Diego Osorio de Escobar y Llamas
1664–1673	Antonio Sebastián de Toledo Molina y Salazar
1665–1675 & 1675–1700	**Charles II**
1673 (twenty-three days)	Pedro Nuño Colón de Portugal y Castro
1673–1680	Fray Payo Enríquez de Rivera
1680–1686	Tomás Antonio de la Cerda y Aragón
1686–1688	Melchor Portocarrero Lasso de la Vega
1688–1696	Gaspar de la Cerda Sandoval Silva y Mendoza
1696 (ten months)	Juan de Ortega Montañés
1696–1701	José Sarmiento Valladares
1700–1746	**Philip V**
1701–1702	Juan de Ortega Montañés
1702–1710	Francisco Fernández de la Cueva Enríquez
1710–1716	Fernando de Alencastre Noroña y Silva
1716–1722	Baltasar de Zúñiga Guzmán Sotomayor y Mendoza
1722–1734	Juan de Acuña
1734–1740	Juan Antonio de Vizarrón y Eguiarreta
1740–1741	Pedro de Castro Figueroa y Salazar
1741–1742	Seventh *Audiencia*
1742–1746	Pedro Cebrián y Agustín
1746–1759	**Ferdinand VI**
1746–1755	Francisco de Güemes y Horcasitas
1755–1760	Agustín Ahumada y Villalón
1759–1788	**Charles III**
1760 (two months)	Eighth *Audiencia*
1760 (six months)	Francisco Cajigal de la Vega
1760–1766	Joaquín de Monserrat

1766–1771	Carlos Francisco de Croix
1771–1779	Antonio María de Bucareli y Ursúa
1779 (four months)	Ninth *Audiencia*
1779–1783	Martín de Mayorga
1783–1784	Matías de Gálvez y Gallardo
1784–1785	Tenth *Audiencia*
1785–1786	Bernardo de Gálvez
1786–1787 (six months)	Eleventh *Audiencia*
1787 (three months)	Alonso Núñez de Haro y Peralta
1787–1789	Manuel Antonio Flores Maldonado Martín de Angulo y Bodquín
1788–1808	**Charles IV**
1789–1794	Juan Vicente de Güemes Pacheco de Padilla Horcasitas y Aguayo
1794–1798	Miguel de la Grúa Talamanca y Branciforte
1798–1800	Miguel José de Azanza
1800–1803	Félix Berenguer de Marquina
1803–1808	José de Iturrigaray
1808	**Ferdinand VII**
1808 (one day)	Twelfth *Audiencia*
1808–1809	Pedro de Garibay
1809–1810	Francisco Javier de Lizana y Beaumont
1810 (four months)	Thirteenth *Audiencia*
1810–1813	Francisco Javier Venegas
1813–1816	Félix María Calleja del Rey
1816–1821	Juan Ruiz de Apodaca
1821 (two months)	Francisco Novella
1821 (one month)	Juan O'Donojú

WAR OF INDEPENDENCE AND FIRST EMPIRE

1810–1811	Miguel Hidalgo y Costilla
1811 (two months)	Ignacio María de Allende y Unzaga
1811	Ignacio López Rayón
1813–1815	José María Morelos y Pavón
1817–1821	Vicente Guerrero
1821	Agustín de Iturbide

1822–1823	Agustín de Iturbide
1823–1824	Supreme Executive Power

INDEPENDENT MEXICO

1824–1829	José Miguel Ramón Audaucto "Guadalupe Victoria" Fernández y Félix
1829 (transition)	Manuel Gómez Pedraza
1829 (eight months)	Vicente Guerrero
1829 (five days)	José María Bocanegra
1829 (eight days)	Provisional Government
1830–1832	Anastasio Bustamante
1832 (three months)	Melchor Múzquiz
1832–1833	Manuel Gómez Pedraza
1833 (one month)	Antonio López de Santa Anna
1833–1834	Valentín Gómez Farías
1834–1835	Antonio López de Santa Anna
1835–1836	Miguel Barragán
1836–1837	José Justo Corro
1837–1839	Anastasio Bustamante
1839 (five months)	Antonio López de Santa Anna
1839 (nine days)	Nicolás Bravo
1839–1841	Anastasio Bustamante
1841 (one month)	Francisco Javier Echeverría
1841–1842	Antonio López de Santa Anna
1842–1843	Nicolás Bravo
1843 (seven months)	Antonio López de Santa Anna
1843–1844	Valentín Canalizo
1844 (three months)	Antonio López de Santa Anna
1844 (twelve days)	José Joaquín Herrera
1844 (three months)	Valentín Canalizo
1844–1845	José Joaquín Herrera
1846 (six months)	Mariano Paredes y Arrillaga
1846 (one month)	Nicolás Bravo
1846 (four months)	José Mariano Salas
1846–1847	Valentín Gómez Farías

1847 (one month)	Antonio López de Santa Anna
1847 (one month)	Pedro María Anaya
1847 (four months)	Antonio López de Santa Anna
1847 (two months)	Manuel de la Peña y Peña
1847–1848	Pedro María Anaya
1848 (four months)	Manuel de la Peña y Peña
1848–1851	José Joaquín Herrera
1851–1853	Mariano Arista
1853 (one month)	Juan Bautista Ceballos
1853 (one month)	Manuel María Lombardini
1853–1855	Antonio López de Santa Anna
1855 (one month)	Martín Carrera
1855 (one month)	Rómulo Díaz de la Vega
1855 (two months)	Juan N. Alvarez
1855–1858	Ignacio Comonfort
1858 (eleven months)	Félix Zuloaga
1858–1859	Manuel Robles Pezuela
1858–1861;	Benito Pablo Juárez García
1861–1865;	
1865–1867	
1859–1860	Miguel Miramón
1860 (two days)	José Ignacio Pavón
1860–1861	Miguel Miramón
1863–1864	*Junta de Regencia*

SECOND EMPIRE

1864–1867	Ferdinand Maximilian de Hapsburg

RESTORATION OF THE REPUBLIC

1867–1872	Benito Pablo Juárez García
1872–1876	Sebastián Lerdo de Tejada
1876–1877	José María Iglesias

DÍAZ DICTATORSHIP

1876 (one month)	Porfirio Díaz
1876–1877	Juan N. Méndez

1877–1880	Porfirio Díaz
1880–1884	Manuel González
1884–1911	Porfirio Díaz

REVOLUTION AND MODERN MEXICO

1908–1919	Emiliano Zapata
1910–1920	Francisco "Pancho" Villa
1911 (six months)	Francisco León de la Barra
1911–1913	Francisco I. Madero
1913 (less than an hour)	Pedro Lascuráin Paredes
1913–1914	Victoriano Huerta
1914 (one month)	Francisco S. Carvajal
1914–1915	Eulalio Gutiérrez Ortiz
1915 (five months)	Roque González Garza
1915 (four months)	Francisco Lagos Cházaro
1917–1920	Venustiano Carranza
1920 (five months)	Adolfo de la Huerta Marcor
1920–1924	Alvaro Obregón
1924–1928	Plutarco Elías Calles
1928–1930	Emilio Portes Gil
1930–1932	Pascual Ortiz Rubio
1932–1934	Abelardo L. Rodríguez
1934–1940	Lázaro Cárdenas
1940–1946	Manuel Avila Camacho
1946–1952	Miguel Alemán Valdés
1952–1958	Adolfo Ruiz Cortines
1958–1964	Adolfo López Mateos
1964–1970	Gustavo Díaz Ordaz
1970–1976	Luis Echeverría Alvarez
1976–1982	José López Portillo Pacheco
1982–1988	Miguel de la Madrid Hurtado
1988–1994	Carlos Salinas de Gortari
1994–	Ernesto Zedillo Ponce de León

Appendix E

ALPHABETICAL INDEX OF RULERS

Entries in bold indicate kings of Spain.

Acamapichtli	1377–1389
Acuña, Juan de	1722–1734
Aguilar, Marcos	1526–1527
Ahuizotl	1486–1502
Ahumada y Villalón, Agustín	1755–1760
Alamán, Lucas	1829
Albornoz, Rodrigo de	1524–1527
Alemán Valdés, Miguel	1946–1952
Alencastre Noroña y Silva, Fernando de	1710–1716
Allende y Unzaga, Ignacio María de	1811
Almonte, Juan N.	1863–1864
Alvarez, Juan N.	1855
Allende, Ignacio	1811
Anaya, Pedro María	1847, 1847–1848
Arista, Mariano	1851–1853
Avila Camacho, Manuel	1940–1946
Axayacatl	1469–1483
Azanza, Miguel José de	1798–1800

Barragán, Miguel	1835–1836
Beleño, Eusebio	1786–1787
Beltrán de Guzmán, Nuño	1528–1530
Berenguer de Marquina, Félix	1800–1803
Bocanegra, José María	1829
Bravo, Nicolás	1823–1824, 1839, 1842–1843, 1846
Bucareli y Ursúa, Antonio María de	1771–1779
Bustamante, Anastasio	1830–1832, 1837–1839, 1839–1841
Cajigal de la Vega, Francisco	1760
Calleja del Rey, Félix María	1813–1816
Calles, Plutarco Elías. *See* Elías Calles, Plutarco	
Canalizo, Valentín	1843–1844, 1844
Cárdenas, Lázaro	1934–1940
Carvajal, Francisco	1914
Carranza, Venustiano	1917–1920
Carrera, Martín	1855
Carrillo de Mendoza y Pimentel, Diego	1621–1624
Carrillo, Luis	1567–1568
Castro Figueroa y Salazar, Pedro de	1740–1741
Catani, Pedro	1810
Ceballos, Juan B.	1853
Cebrián y Agustín, Pedro	1742–1746
Cerda y Aragón, Tomás Antonio de la	1680–1686
Cerda Sandoval Silva y Mendoza, Gaspar de la	1688–1696
Ceynos, Francisco	1530–1535, 1564–1566
Charles V (Charles I of Spain)	**1516–1556**
Charles II	**1665–1675 & 1675–1700**
Charles III	**1759–1788**
Charles IV	**1788–1808**
Chimalpopoca	1416–1428
Colón de Portugal y Castro, Pedro Nuño	1673
Comonfort, Ignacio	1855–1858
Corro, José Justo	1836–1837
Cortés, Hernán	1522–1524

Croix, Carlos Francisco de	1766–1771
Cuauhtemoc	1520–1525
Cuitlahuac	1520
De la Huerta Marcor, Adolfo	1920
De la Madrid Hurtado, Miguel	1982–1988
De la Peña y Peña, Manuel	1847, 1848
Delgadillo, Diego	1528–1530
Díaz de la Vega, Rómulo	1855
Díaz Ordaz, Gustavo	1964–1970
Díaz, Porfirio	1876, 1877–1880, 1884–1911
Díez de Armendáriz, Lope	1635–1640
Domínguez, Miguel	1823–1824
Echaverri, Francisco Antonio de	1760
Echeverría, Francisco Javier	1841
Echeverría Alvarez, Luis	1970–1976
Elías Calles, Plutarco	1924–1928
Enríquez de Almanza, Martín	1568–1580
Enríquez de Guzmán, Luis	1650–1653
Enríquez de Rivera, Fray Payo	1673–1680
Estrada, Alonso de	1524–1527 (as part of Provisional Government), 1527–1528
Farfán, Pedro	1583–1584
Ferdinand VI	**1746–1759**
Ferdinand VII	**1808**
Fernández de Córdoba, Diego	1612–1621
Fernández de la Cueva, Francisco	1653–1660
Fernández de la Cueva Enríquez, Francisco	1702–1710
Fernández y Félix, José Miguel Ramón Audaucto "Guadalupe Victoria"	1823–1824 (as part of Supreme Executive Power), 1824–1829
Flores Maldonado Martín de Angulo y Bodquín, Manuel Antonio	1787–1789
Gálvez, Bernardo de	1785–1786
Gálvez y Gallardo, Matías de	1783–1784

García Galdós, Juan	1621
García Guerra, Fray	1611–1612
García Sarmiento de Sotomayor	1642–1648
Garibay, Pedro de	1808–1809
Gómez Farías, Valentín	1833–1834, 1846–1847
Gómez Pedraza, Manuel	1829, 1832–1833
González Garza, Roque	1915
González, Manuel	1880–1884
Grúa Talamanca y Branciforte, Miguel de la	1794–1798
Güemes Pacheco de Padilla Horcasitas y Aguayo, Juan Vicente de	1789–1794
Güemes y Horcasitas, Francisco de	1746–1755
Guerrero, Vicente	1817–1821, 1829
Gutiérrez Ortiz, Eulalio	1914–1915
Hapsburg, Ferdinand Maximilian of	1864–1867
Herrera, José Joaquín	1844, 1844–1845, 1848–1851
Herrera, Vicente	1784–1785
Hidalgo y Costilla, Miguel	1810–1811
Huerta, Victoriano	1913–1914
Huitzilihuitl	1390–1410
Iglesias, José María	1876–1877
Iturbide, Agustín de	1821, 1822–1823
Iturrigaray, José de	1803–1808
Itzcoatl	1428–1440
Juárez García, Benito Pablo	1858–1867, 1867–1872
Labastida, Pelagio Antonio de	1863–1864
Lagos Cházaro, Francisco	1915
Lascuráin Paredes, Pedro	1913
León de la Barra, Francisco	1911
Lerdo de Tejada, Sebastián	1872–1876
Leyva y de la Cerda, Juan de	1660–1664
Lizana y Beaumont, Francisco Javier de	1809–1810

Lombarini, Manuel María   1853

López de Santa Anna, Antonio   1833, 1834–1835, 1839, 1841–1842,
                                 1843, 1844, 1847, 1853–1855

López Mateos, Adolfo   1958–1964

López Pacheco de Cabrera y Bobadilla,   1640–1642
  Diego

López Portillo, José   1976–1982

López Rayón, Ignacio   1811

Madero, Francisco I.   1911–1913

Maldonado, Alvaro   1530–1535

Maldonado, Francisco   1528–1530

Malo de Villavicencio, Pedro   1741–1742

Manrique de Zúñiga, Alvaro   1585–1590

Maximilian. *See* Hapsburg

Mayorga, Martín de   1779–1783

Méndez, Juan N.   1876–1877

Mendoza, Antonio de   1535–1550

Mendoza y Luna, Juan de   1603–1607

Michelena, Mariano   1823–1824

Miramón, Miguel   1859–1860, 1860

Moctezuma Ilhuicamina   1440–1469

Moctezuma Xocoyotzin   1502–1520

Monserrat, Joaquín de   1760–1766

Morelos y Pavón, José María   1813–1815

Moya de Contreras, Pedro   1584–1585

Muñoz, Alonso de   1567–1568

Múzquiz, Melchor   1832

Negrete, Pedro Celestino   1823–1824

Novella, Francisco   1821

Núñez de Haro y Peralta, Alonso 1787

Obregón, Alvaro   1920–1924

O'Donojú, Juan   1821

Ormachea, Juan B.   1863–1864

Orozco, Jerónimo   1564–1566

Ortega Montañés, Juan de   1696, 1701–1702

Ortiz de Matienzo, Juan	1528–1530
Ortiz Rubio, Pascual	1930–1932
Osorio de Escobar y Llamas, Diego	1664
Otálora, Pedro	1612
Pacheco y Osorio, Rodrigo	1624–1635
Palafox y Mendoza, Juan de	1642
Parada, Alonso de	1528
Paredes y Arrillaga, Mariano	1846
Pavón, José Ignacio	1860
Peralta, Gastón de	1566–1567
Peralta, Matías de	1649–1650
Philip II	**1556–1598**
Philip III	**1598–1621**
Philip IV	**1621–1665**
Philip V	**1700–1746**
Ponce de León, Luis	1526
Portes Gil, Emilio	1928–1930
Portocarrero Lazo de la Vega, Melchor	1686–1688
Puga, Vaso de	1564–1566
Quintanar, Luis	1829
Quiroga, Vasco de	1530–1535
Ramírez de Fuente Leal, Sebastián	1530–1535
Robles, Dr.	1583–1584
Robles Pezuela, Manuel	1858–1859
Rodríguez, Abelardo L.	1932–1934
Roma y Rossell, Francisco	1779
Ruiz Cortines, Adolfo	1952–1958
Ruiz de Apodaca, Juan	1816–1821
Salas, Mariano	1846, 1863–1864 (as part of *Junta de Regencia*)
Salinas de Gortari, Carlos	1988–1994
Salmerón, Juan de	1530–1535
Sánchez, Paredes	1583–1584
Sande, Francisco de	1583–1584

Santa Anna. *See* López de Santa Anna

Sarmiento de Sotomayor, Garcia	1642–1648
Sarmiento Valladares, José	1696–1701
Suárez de Mendoza, Lorenzo	1580–1583
Tapia, Cristóbal de	1521
Tenoch	1325
Tizoc	1483–1486
Toledo Molina y Salazar, Antonio Sebastián de	1664–1673
Torres y Rueda, Marcos de	1648–1649
Valecillo, Paz de	1621
Velasco, Luis de (I)	1550–1564
Velasco, Luis de (II)	1590–1595, 1607–1611
Velez, Pedro	1829
Venegas, Francisco Javier	1810–1813
Victoria, Guadalupe. *See* Fernández y Félix	
Villa, Francisco "Pancho"	1910–1920
Villalobos, Pedro	1564–1566
Villanueva y Zapata, Luis	1583–1584
Vizarrón y Eguiarreta, Juan Antonio de	1734–1740
Zapata, Emiliano	1908–1919
Zedillo Ponce de León, Ernesto	1994–
Zuazo, Alfonso	1524–1527
Zuloaga, Félix	1858
Zúñiga y Acevedo, Gaspar de	1595–1603
Zúñiga Guzmán Sotomayor y Mendoza, Baltazar de	1716–1722

BIBLIOGRAPHY

Aboites, Jaime. *Industrialización y desarrollo agrícola en México*. Mexico: Universidad Autónoma Metropolitana-Xochimilco Editorial Plaza y Valdés, 1989, 203 pp.

Agustín, José. *Tragicomedia Mexicana 2*. Mexico: Editorial Planeta Mexicana, S.A. de C.V., 1992, 293 pp.

Alonso, Jorge et al. *Las Elecciones en México: Evolución y perspectivas*. Mexico: Siglo XXI editores, S.A. de C.V., 1985, 385 pp.

Ayala Anguiana, Armando. *JLP: Secretos de un Sexenio*. 4th ed. Mexico: Editorial Grijalvo, S.A., 1984, 151 pp.

Camp, Roderic A. *Mexican Political Biographies 1935–1982*. 2nd ed. Tucson: University of Arizona Press, 1982, 447 pp.

Cárdenas de la Peña, Enrique. *Gobernantes de México*. Mexico: Celanese Mexicana, San Angel Ediciones, 1977.

Caso, Alfonso. *El Pueblo del Sol*. Mexico: Fondo de Cultura Económica, 1953, 125 pp.

Casasola, Agustín Víctor. *Historia Gráfica de la Revolución*. Vols. I, II, III, IV. Mexico: Archivo Casasola, Mexico, 1900–1940.

Casasola, Gustavo. *Biografía Ilustrada del General Porfirio Díaz 1830–1965*. Mexico: Editorial Gustavo Casasola, S.A., 1970, 158 pp.

———. *Biografía Ilustrada de Don Venustiano Carranza*. Mexico: Editorial Gustavo Casasola, S.A., 1974, 151 pp.

———. *Biografía Ilustrada del General Alvaro Obregón 1880–1970*. Mexico: Editorial Gustavo Casasola, S.A., 1975, 141 pp.

———. *Biografía Ilustrada del General Emiliano Zapata 1879–1970*. Mexico: Editorial Gustavo Casasola, S.A., 1975, 108 pp.

————. *Biografía Ilustrada del General Lázaro Cárdenas 1895–1970*. Mexico: Edit. Gustavo Casasola, S.A., 1975, 121 pp.

————. *Biografía Ilustrada del General Plutarco Elías Calles 1877–1970*. Mexico: Editorial Gustavo Casasola, S.A., 1975, 129 pp.

Caso, Alfonso. *El Pueblo del Sol*. Mexico: Fondo de Cultura Económica, 1953, 125 pp.

Conte Corti, Egon Caesar. *Maximiliano y Carlota*. 2nd ed. Mexico: Fondo de Cultura Económica, 1971, 707 pp.

Cosío Villegas, Daniel et al. *A Compact History of Mexico*. Mexico: El Colegio de Mexico, 1975, 157 pp.

Crónica del Sexenio 1982–1988 del Primero al Sexto Año. *Las Razones y las Obras Gobierno de Miguel de la Madrid*. Mexico: Fondo de Cultura Económica, 1988.

Cue Canovas, Agustín. *Historia Política de México*. Mexico: Libro-Mex. Editorial, 1957, 314 pp.

De la Huerta, Adolfo. *Memorias de Don Adolfo de la Huerta*. Mexico: Editorial Guzmán, 1957, 335 pp.

Díaz del Castillo, Bernal. *Historia de la Conquista de Nueva España*. Mexico: Editorial Porrúa, Colección Sepan Cuántos, 1960, 700 pp.

Diccionario Porrúa. Mexico: Editorial Porrúa, 1964.

Diccionario Porrúa: Historia, Biografía y Geografía de México. Vols. I, II. Mexico: Porrúa, 1976.

Enciclopedia de México. Vol I. 2nd ed., Mexico: Secretaría de Educación Pública, 1987.

Encyclopaedia Britannica. 23 vols. Chicago: University of Chicago, 1971.

Fuentes Mares, José. *Santa Anna: Aurora y Ocaso de un Comediante*. 3rd ed. Mexico: Editorial Jus, 1967, 335 pp.

García Granados, Rafael. *Diccionario Biográfico de Historia Antigua de México*. Mexico: Instituto de Investigaciones Históricas, Universidad Nacional Autónoma de México, 1952.

García Soler, León. *Mito y Método en la Sucesión Presidencial*. Mexico: Editorial Grijalbo, S.A., 1982, 318 pp.

Garrido, Luis Javier. *El Partido de la Revolución Institucionalizada. Medio Siglo del Poder político en México. La Formación del Nuevo Estado (1928–1945)*. Mexico: SEP-Siglo XXI Editores, 1986, 493 pp.

González de la Garza, Mauricio. *Ultima Llamada*. 2nd ed. Mexico: Editores Asociados M., S.A. EDAMEX, 1981, 341 pp.

Grayson, George W. *A Guide to the 1994 Mexican Election*. Washington, D.C.: CSIS, 1994, 52 pp.

Guzmán, Eulalia. *Actas y Dictámenes de la Comisión de Investigaciones sobre Ixcateopan, Guerrero*. Mexico: Instituto de Investigaciones Históricas, Universidad Nacional Autónoma de México, 1952.

Henríquez Ureña, Pedro. *Historia de la Cultura en la América Hispánica*. 9th ed. Mexico: Fondo de Cultura Económica, 1973, 171 pp.

Kandell, Jonathan. *La Capital, the Biography of Mexico City*. New York: Random House, 1988, 640 pp.

Krickeberg, Walter. *Las Antiguas Culturas Mexicanas*. 2nd ed. Mexico: Fondo de Cultura Económica, 1964, 476 pp.

Loret de Mola, Carlos. *El Juicio.* 3rd ed. Mexico: Editorial Grijalbo, S.A., 1984, 156 pp.

Magner, James A. *Men of Mexico.* Freeport, N.Y.: Books for Libraries Press, 1942–1968, 614 pp.

Maret, Robert. *Mexico.* New York: Walker and Company, 1971, 208 pp.

McHenry, J. Patrick. *A Short History of Mexico.* Garden City, N.Y.: Dolphin Books, 1962, 240 pp.

Meyer, Michael C. *Huerta: A Political Portrait.* Lincoln: University of Nebraska Press, 1972, 272 pp.

Monsiváis, Carlos. *La Poesía Mexicana del Siglo XX.* Mexico: Empresas Editoriales, S.A., 1966, 838 pp.

Moreno, Daniel. *Los Partidos Políticos del México Contemporaneo 1916–1985.* 10th ed. Mexico: Editorial PAX-MÉXICO, 1985, 478 pp.

Newlon, Clarke. *The Men Who Made Mexico.* New York: Dodd, Mead & Company, 1973, 273 pp.

Nieto L., J. de Jesús. *Diccionario Histórico del México Contemporáneo (1900–1982).* Mexico: Editorial Alhambra Mexicana, S.A. de C.V., 1986, 214 pp.

Orozco Linares, Fernando. *Fechas Históricas de México.* Mexico: Panorama Editorial, S.A., 1981, 262 pp.

———. *Gobernantes de México. Desde la época Prehispánica hasta nuestros días.* Mexico: Panorama Editorial, S.A., 1985, 475 pp.

Pazos, Luis. *Historia Sinóptica de México de los Olmecas a Salinas.* Mexico: Editorial Diana, 1994, 165 pp.

Portes Gil, Emilio. *Autobiografía de la Revolución Mexicana.* Mexico: Instituto Mexicano de la Cultura, 1964, 865 pp.

Riding, Alan. *Distant Neighbors: A Portrait of the Mexicans.* New York: Alfred A. Knopf, 1985, 385 pp.

Romero Flores, Jesús. *Historia de los Estados de la República Mexicana.* Mexico: Edición Botas, 1964, 496 pp.

Sejourné, Laurette. *América Latina: Antiguas Culturas Precolombinas.* Vol. 21. Spain: Editorial Siglo XXI, 1971, 331 pp.

Silva Herzog, Jesús. *Breve Historia de la Revolución Mexicana.* Vols. I and II. Mexico and Buenos Aires: Fondo de Cultura Económica, 1960.

Suárez, Luis. *Echeverría en el Sexenio de López Portillo.* 2nd ed. Mexico: Editorial Grijalbo, S.A., 1984, 320 pp.

Suplemento Especial de *La Opinión. México Hoy.* Los Angeles: Lunes 3 de diciembre de 1984, 24 pp.

Teja Zabre, Alfonso. *Historia de México.* Mexico: Editorial Botas, 1961, 402 pp.

Thomas, Hugh. *Conquest: Montezuma, Cortés, and the Fall of Old Mexico.* New York: Simon & Schuster, 1993, 812 pp.

Valdiosera Berman, Ramón. "Gobernantes de México." *Artes de Mexico* no. 175, 1960, 98 pp.

Vasconcelos, José. *Breve Historia de México.* Mexico: Compañía Editorial Continental, S.A., 1956, 565 pp.

Vázquez Gómez, Francisco. *Memorias Políticas.* Mexico: Imprenta Mundial, 1933, 599 pp.

Womack, John. *Zapata and the Mexican Revolution.* New York: Alfred A. Knopf, 1969, 435 pp.

Wyman, Donald L. *Mexico's Economic Crisis: Challenges and Opportunities*. San Diego: Center for U.S.–Mexican Studies, University of California, 1983, 126 pp.

XLVI Legislatura de la Cámara de Diputados. *Los Presidentes de México ante la Nación, Informes, Manifiestos y Documentos de 1821 a 1966*. Mexico: Tomo V, 1966, 977 pp.

Yañez, Agustín. *Santa Anna Espectro de una Sociedad*. Mexico: Ediciones Océano, S.A., 1982, 264 pp.

INDEX

Page numbers for main entries are indicated in boldface type.

Abrazo de Acatempan, 60, 61
Academy of Fine Arts, 44
Acamapichtli, **5**, 6
Acercamiento Nacional, 126
Acordada, 37
Acordada uprising, 65, 66, 84
Act of Independence, 53, 54, 56
Acuña, Juan de, **38–39**
Agrarian Code, 123–24
Agrarian Law, 116–17. *See also* Land
Agreement of Velasco, 72
Agriculture: and Acamapichtli, 5; and
 Alencastre Noroña y Silva, 37; and
 Arista, 81; and Cárdenas, 123; and
 Cerda Sandoval Silva y Mendoza, 34;
 and Colón de Portugal y Castro, 32;
 and Cortés, 16; and Díaz, 100, 104,
 105, 107; and independence, 63; and
 Juárez, 91; and Mendoza, 20; and
 Obregón, 119; and Philip II, 21; and
 Ruiz Cortines, 128; and viceregal pe-
 riod, 19; and Zúñiga Guzmán Soto-
 mayor y Mendoza, 38
Aguascalientes, 81

Aguascalientes Convention, 115, 116,
 118
Aguilar, Jerónimo de, 11, 12
Aguilar, Marcos, 16, **17**
Ahuizotl, **8**
Ahumada y Villalón, Agustín, **41**
Alamán, Lucas, 65, **67**
Alameda, 24
Alameda Park, 43
Alamo, 71. *See also* Texas
Albornoz, Rodrigo de, **16**
Albuquerque, New Mexico, 30
Aldama, Juan, 52, 58
Alemán Valdés, Miguel, **126–27**, 128,
 129
Alencastre Noroña y Silva, Fernando
 de, **37**
Alfaro Siqueiros, David, 129
Allende y Unzaga, Ignacio María de,
 52, 57, 58, 63
Almazán, Juan Andrew, 125
Almonte, Juan N., **93–94**
Alta California, 49
Alvarado, Pedro de, **12–13**

Alvarez, Juan N., 66, 82, **84–85**, 86, 91
Amanteca people, 4
Anaya, Pedro Maria, **79**, 80
Anne of Austria, 21, 24
Apache people, 28, 44
Arango, Doroteo. *See* Villa, Francisco "Pancho"
Arbenz, Jacobo, 128
Archives, 41, 47, 67, 122
Arista, Mariano, 69, 77, **81**, 88
Art, architecture, 30, 35, 44
Asúnsulo, Manuel, 109
Audiencia: eighth, 41; eleventh, 45, 50; fifth, 26; first, 17; fourth, 23; ninth, 44; second, 18; seventh, 39; sixth, 30; tenth, 44; third, 21; thirteenth, 51; twelfth, 50
Audiencia gobernadora, 22, 26
Augustinian order, 23. *See also* Catholic Church
Auto de Fe (Act of Faith), 29
Avila Camacho, Manuel, 115, **125–26**, 128
Axayacatl, **7–8**
Axayacatl Palace, 12, 13
Azanza, Miguel José de, **48–49**
Azcapotzalco, 6
Aztec people, 1–10, 12–14

Baena, Francisca de, 21
Baja California, 32, 35, 36, 122
Baja California Norte, 127
Banco de Crédito Agrícola y Ejidal, 119
Banco Hipotecario y de Obras Públicas, 122
Banditry, 39
Banking industry, 134
Bank of Mexico, 119
Barbara of Braganza, 40
Barlovento fleet, 28, 30, 31, 37
Barradas, Isidro, 66, 69
Barragán, Miguel, **71**, 72
Battle of Agua Prieta, 119
Battle of Calpulalpan, 89
Battle of Zacatecas, 114
Bazaine, Francoise, 83, 96

Beleño, Eusebio, **45**
Belize, 42, 63
Beltrán de Guzmán, Nuño, **17**
Berenguer de Marquina, Félix, **49**
Blanquet, Aureliano, 109
Bocanegra, José María, **66–67**, 68
Bonaparte, Joseph, 46–47, 51
Bonilla, Ignacio, 117
Boturini, Lorenzo, 39, 40
Bourbon, House of, 35–36
Bravo, Nicolás, **62**, 63, 64, **73**, 75, 77, 78, 84
Brazil, 135
Bucareli promenade, 43
Bucareli Treaties, 119
Bucareli y Ursúa, Antonio María de, **43–44**
Bullfighting, 49
Bustamante, Anastasio, 66, 67, **68**, 69, **72–74**, 85, 87

Caballito, El, 48
Cabañas, Lucio, 131, 132
Cabrera, Luis, 116
Cacique (supreme priest), 2
Cadereyta, 28
Cajigal de la Vega, Francisco, **42**
Calatrava, José María, 54
Calderón de la Barca, Madame, 74; *Life in Mexico*, 74
Calendar, 7
Calleja del Rey, Félix María, **52**, 59
Calles, Plutarco Elías. *See* Elías Calles, Plutarco
Camacho Solís, Manuel, 138
Campeche, 31
Canalizo, Valentín, **75**, 76
Cárdenas, Cuauhtémoc, 138, 142
Cárdenas, Lázaro, 120, **123–25**, 126, 127, 129
Cardiology Institute, 126
Caribbean, 31
Caro Quintero, Rodolfo, 136
Carranza, Venustiano, 108, **109–10**, 111, 114, 115, **116–17**, 118, 119
Carrera, Martín, **83–84**
Carillo, Fuentes, Amado, 142
Carrillo, Luis, **22**

Carrillo de Mendoza y Pimental, Diego, 27
Carta de Deberes y Derechos Económicos de los Estados, La, 132
Carvajal, Francisco, 111, 117, 118
Casa de Cuna, 43
Casa de la Moneda, 20
Castro, Fidel, 128
Castro Figueroa y Salazar, Pedro de, 39
Catani, Pedro, 51
Cathedral of Guatamala City, 35
Cathedral of Mexico City, 22, 26, 29
Cathedral of Morelia, 35
Cathedral of Puebla, 22
Catholic Church: and Ahumada y Villalón, 41; and Alencastre Noroña y Silva, 37; and Arista, 81; and Croix, 43; and Díaz, 100; and Elías Calles, 120; and Enríquez de Rivera, 33; and Fernández de la Cueva Enríquez, 36, 37; and Gómez Farías, 78; and independence, 60, 61; and Juárez, 91, 97; and New Spain, 19; and Núñez, 46; and Osorio, 31; and Palafox y Mendoza, 29; and politics, 65; and Portes Gil, 120–21; and Portocarrero Lazo de la Vega, 34; and Rodríguez, 122; and Salinas, 138; and Santa Anna, 75; and Sarmiento Valladares, 35; and Tejada's law, 86; and Zuloaga, 88. See also individual orders
Ce Acatl, 2
Ceballos, Juan B., 81–82
Cebrián y Agustín, Pedro, 39–40
Ceinos, Francisco. See Ceynos, Francisco
Celaya, 57, 68
Census, 47
Cerda Sandoval Silva y Mendoza, Gaspar de la, 34
Cerda y Aragón, Tomás Antonio de la, 33
Cerralvo fortress, 27
Cerro de las Campanas, 90, 93, 97
Céspedes, Manuel, 76
Ceynos, Francisco, 18, 21

Chalco, 6
Chamizal, 130
Chapultepec Castle, 78
Chapultepec Hill, 5
Charles II, 32, 35
Charles III, 41–42, 44, 46
Charles IV, 46–47, 48, 50, 51
Charles V (Charles I of Spain), 16, 17, 19–20
Chiapas, 8
Chiapas uprising, 138, 139, 141
Chichimec people, 1, 24
Chile, 132
Chimalpopoca, 6
Cholula, 12
Chontales people, 17
Científicos, Los, 104
Civil rights, 91, 96, 97, 100, 128, 133
Civil service, 120
Clinton, Bill, 140, 141, 142
Coahuila, 86
Codorniu, Manuel, 61
Coinage, 20, 38, 43, 103
College of Tepoztlán, 46
Collegiate Church of Our Lady of Guadalupe, 38
Colombia, 135
Colón de Portugal y Castro, Pedro Nuño, 32
Colosio, Luis Donaldo, 138, 139–40
Columbus, Christopher, 11
Comanche people, 28, 41
Commerce. See Trade
Commerce Tribunal, 22
Communications, 103
Communism, 121, 129. See also Socialism
Comonfort, Ignacio, 82, 84, 85–87, 87–88, 91, 94, 99
Confederación Regional Obrera Mexicana, 119
Confederation of Mexican Workers, 124, 125, 142
Congress, 75, 76, 86
Congresso Constituyente, 67
Conquest, 11–18
Conservative Party, 87, 88, 89, 90, 93–94, 95, 96

Constitutionalist Army, 110, 114, 116, 118, 119
Constitution of 1812, 51, 53
Constitution of 1824, 67, 76, 78
Constitution of 1857, 86, 87, 91, 93, 97, 98, 99
Constitution of 1917, 117, 120, 122
Convention of Aguascalientes, 111
Cornejo, Gómez, 26
Corral, Ramón, 105
Corro, José Justo, 71–72
Cortés, Hernán, 9, 12, 13, 15–16
Cortés, Martín, 21, 22
Creelman, James, 104
Criollo, 15, 28, 51, 55
Cristero movement, 125
Cristero Revolt, 120
Croix, Carlos Francisco de, 43
CROM. See Confederación Regional Obrera Mexicana
CTM. See Confederation of Mexican Workers
Cuauhnahuac, 7
Cuauhtemoc, 9–10
Cuautitlan, 6
Cuba, 31, 43, 130, 132
Cuicuilco, 1
Cuitlahuac, 9, 13
Culhuacan, House of, 5
Custom duty, 71

Decena Trágica, La, 113
Degollado, Santos, 82
De la Cruz, Sor Juana Inés, 33
De la Gándara, Francisca, 52
De la Huerta Marcor, Adolofo, 111, 117, 118–19
De la Madrid Hurtado, Miguel, 134–36, 137
De la Peña y Peña, Manuel, 79–80
Delgadillo, Diego, 17
Democratic Party, 104
Despertador Americano, El, 59
Díaz, Félix, 113
Díaz, Porfirio, 98, 99, 100–102, 104–5, 109, 110, 111, 112, 113, 114, 115
Díaz de la Vega, Rómulo, 84

Díaz de Solis, Juan, 11
Díaz Ordaz, Gustavo, 130–31, 132
Díaz Serrano, Jorge, 135
Dictatorship, 65
Díez de Armendáriz, Lope, 28
Disease, 13, 15, 20, 22, 32, 39, 42, 44
Dolores parish, 57
Domínguez, Belisario, 114
Domínguez, Miguel, 62–63
Dominican order, 23. See also Catholic Church
Drainage, 25, 27, 28, 29, 33, 34. See also Flooding
Drug trade, 136, 138, 139
Durazo, Arturo, 134, 135

Echaverri, Francisco Antonio de, 41
Echegaray, Miguel María de, 88
Echeverría, Francisco Javier, 74
Echeverría Alvarez, Luis, 131–33
Economy: and Alemán, 127; and Avila Camacho, 125; and Cárdenas, 124; and De la Madrid, 135; and Díaz, 104, 107; and Díaz Ordaz, 131; and Echeverría Alvarez, 132; and Juárez, 97; and Lerdo, 98; and López Portillo, 133–34; and Salinas, 136–37; and Zedillo, 140, 141
Education: and Acamapichtli, 5; and Avila Camacho, 125; and Cárdenas, 123; and Díaz, 100; and Elías Calles, 120; and Gómez Farías, 70; and González, 103; and Guadalupe Victoria, 65; and Güemes Pacheco, 47; and Juárez, 91, 98; and Mendoza, 20; and New Spain, 26; and Philip III, 25; and Rodríguez, 122; and Velasco, 20
Eisenhower, Dwight D., 128
Ejército Zapatista de Liberación Nacional, 138
Ejido, 137
Electricity industry, 130, 132
Elías Calles, Plutarco, 108, 117, 118, 119, 121, 122, 123, 126
El Salvador Peace Agreements, 138
England. See Great Britain
Enríquez de Almanza, Martín, 22

Enríquez de Guzmán, Luis, 30
Enríquez de Rivera, Fray Payo, 32–33
EPR. *See* Popular Revolutionary Army
Escobar, José Gonzalo, 121
Escuela Nacional Preparatoria, 98
Estrada, Alonso de, 16
Estrada, José María Gutiérrez de, 16
EZLN. *See* Ejército Zapatista de Liberación Nacional

Farfán, Pedro, 23
Federal Electoral Law, 126
Federal Work Law, 122
Félix Gallardo, Miguel Angel, 136
Ferdinand VI, 40, 42
Ferdinand VII, 46, 49, 50–51, 52, 53, 56
Fernández de Cevallos, Diego, 138
Fernández de Córdoba, Diego, 26
Fernández de la Cueva, Francisco, 30
Fernández de la Cueva Enríquez, Francisco, 36
Fernández y Félix, José Miguel Ramón Audaucto "Guadalupe Victoria," 62, 63, 64–65, 67
First Empire, 61
Flooding, 20, 27, 29, 42. *See also* Drainage
Floral Wars (*Guerra Florida*), 7
Flores Maldonado Martín de Angulo y Bodquín, Manuel Antonio, 46
Florida, 38, 42
Forey, Elias Frederick, 93–94
Forsyth, John, 83
France: and Almonte, 93; and Cerda Sandoval Silva y Mendoza, 34; and debt collection, 92; and De la Cerda, 34; and de Zúñiga, 38; and New Spain, 36; occupation by, 83, 85, 87, 88, 89, 92, 94–95, 96; and Pacheco, 27; and Parián market riot, 72; and Philip V, 35; and Spain, 46, 48, 55; and United States, 95
Franciscan order, 22, 23, 24. *See also* Catholic Church

Gaceta de México, La, 38, 44
Gálvez, Bernardo de, 45

Gálvez, José de, 42, 48
Gálvez y Gallardo, Matías de, 44
Gambling, 123
Garcia Abrego, Juan, 141
García Galdós, Juan, 26
García Guerra, Fray, 25–26
García Sarmiento de Sotomayor, 29
Garibay, Pedro de, 50
General Agreement on Tariffs and Trade (GATT), 135
General Indian Court, 22
Godoy, Manuel, 46, 48, 49
Gómez Farías, Valentin, 70, 73, 74, 78, 91
Gómez Farías, Vicente, 65
Gómez Pedraza, Manuel, 65–66, 68
González, Manuel, 100, 102, 103
González, Pablo, 108, 110, 114, 116, 117
González Garza, Roque, 115
Government, 45, 87, 100, 104. *See also* Politics
Great Britain: and Acuña, 38; and Avila Camacho, 126; and Cárdenas, 125; and Cerda Sandoval Silva y Mendoza, 34; and debt collection, 92, 94, 96; and De la Cerda, 34; and New Spain, 22, 42; threat from, 63
Great Temple of Tenochtitlan, 7, 8, 12
Grijalva, Juan de, 11–12
Grúa Talamanca y Branciforte, Miguel de la, 48
Grupo Contadora, 135–36
Guadalajara, 89
Guadalupe, 33
Guadalupe, Shrine of, 34, 37, 46
Guajardo, Jesús, 110
Guanajuato, 57, 68
Guatemala, 129
Güemes Pacheco de Padilla Horcasitas y Aguayo, Juan Vicente de, 47–48
Güemes y Horcasitas, Francisco de, 40–41
Guerra de los Pasteles (Pastry War), 72
Guerra Florida. See Floral Wars
Guerrero, Gonzalo, 11

Guerrero, Pedro, 60
Guerrero, Vicente, 53, **60–61**, 63, 65, 66, 67, 68, 85
Guerrilla movement, 134
Guevara, Ernesto "Che," 128
Guillén Vicente, Rafael Sebastián, 141
Gutiérrez Ortiz, Eulalio, 111, **114–15**, 116
Gutiérrez Rebollo, José de Jesús, 142
Guzmán, Gaspar de, 26
Guzmán Loera, Joaquín "El Chapo," 136

Hacienda, 109
Hapsburg, Ferdinand Maximilian of, 60, 83, 87, 90, 92, 93, 94, **95–97**
Hawks group, 132
Hernández Galicia, Joaquín "La Quina," 129, 136
Herrera, José Joaquín, 69, **76**, 77, 80–81
Herrera, Vicente, **44**
Heyn, Piet, 27
Hidalgo y Costilla, Miguel, 51–52, 56–58, 59, 61, 63
Holland, 27
Hospice of the Poor People, 43
Hospital Real, 24
Housing, 125, 127
Houston, Sam, 72
Huachichiles, 22
Huaxtec people, 8
Huejotzingan people, 9
Huerta, Victoriano, 109, 110, 112, **113–14**, 116, 118, 119, 121, 123, 126, 128
Huitzilihuitl, **5–6**, 7
Huitzilopochtli (war god), 3, 5, 6, 7
Humboldt, Alexander von, 43, 47

Iglesias, José María, **99**, 100, 102
IMF. *See* International Monetary Fund
Independence, 49, 52, 55–64, 72
Indian peoples. *See* Indigenous people
Indigenous people: and Bucareli, 43; and Cerda Sandoval Silva y Mendoza, 34; conquest of, 15; and Enríquez de Rivera, 33; and First *Audiencia*, 17; and Flores Maldon-

ado, 46; and García Guerra, 25–26; and Herrera, 81; and independentist army, 55; and Leyva, 31; and Moya de Contreras, 23; and Ortega Montañés, 36; and Philip III, 25; and Popé Revolt, 33; and Toledo Molina y Salazar, 31–32; and Velasco, 24; and Zapata, 108; and Zúñiga Guzmán Sotomayor, 38; and Zúñiga y Acevedo, 24. *See also specific peoples*
Industry, 63, 81, 91, 123, 124–25, 127. *See also specific industries*
Inglis, Frances Erskine. *See* Calderón de la Barca, Madame
INPI. *See* National Institute for the Protection of Infants
Inquisition. *See* Tribunal of the Holy Inquisition
Instituto de Seguridad y Servicio Social para los Trabajadores del Estado, 130
Instituto Politécnico Nacional, 128, 129
Instrucción, 37
Inter-American Indigenous Congress, 125
International Monetary Fund, 135, 140
IPN. *See* Instituto Politécnico Nacional
Isabella of Portugal, 19
Isabella of Valois, 21
Isabelle II, Queen of Spain, 51
Isabelle of Bourbon, 27
Isabelle of Parma, 35, 40, 41
Island of Sacrificios, 22
ISSSTE. *See* Instituto de Seguridad y Servicio Social para los Trabajadores del Estado
Isthmus of Tehuantepec, 8
Iturbide, Agustín de, 53, 54, 56, 59, 60, **61**, 62, 68, 69, 71, 75, 77, 79–80, 81, 84, 85
Iturrigaray, José de, **49–50**
Itzcoatl, **6–7**
Ixtlixochitl, 6

Jaramillo, Rubén, 129
Jesuit order, 22, 24, 36, 42. *See also* Catholic Church
Jiménez, Mariano, 52, 58

Juárez García, Benito Pablo, 83, 85, 86, 87, 88, 90–93, 96, 97–98, 101, 103
Juárez Law, 91
Junta de Notables, 74, 95
Junta de Regencia, 87, 93–94
Junta Superior de Gobierno, 92, 94

Kearny, Stephen, 77
Kennedy, John F., 130

Labastida, Pelagio Antonio de, 94
Labor: and Cárdenas, 123; and Díaz, 104, 107; and López Mateos, 129; and Obregón, 119; and Ortiz Rubio, 122; and Rodríguez, 123; and Ruiz Cortines, 128; and Velázquez, 125; and Zapata, 109
Labor union, 123, 124, 129, 137
Lagos Cházaro, Francisco, 115–16
Laguna community, 124
Laguna de Términos, 37, 38
Laja River, 49
Land, 116–17, 123, 129. *See also* Agriculture
Landowner class, 65
Language, 14–15, 34
Lascuráin Paredes, Pedro, 113, 114
Law, 22, 23, 26, 27, 38, 39, 44, 47
Legorreta Chauvet, Eduardo, 136
León de la Barra, Francisco, 110, 111–12
Leonhardy, Terence, 132
Lerdo de Tejada, Sebastián, 86, 98–99, 101
Lerma, 26
Leyes de Reforma, 81
Ley Tejada, 86
Leyva y de la Cerda, Juan de, 30–31
Liberal Party, 65, 87, 88, 90, 95
Limantour José Ives, 104, 105
Linares, 37
Lizana y Beaumont, Francisco Javier de, 51
Lombardini, Manuel María, 82
López de Santa Anna, Antonio, 61, 62, 64, 65–66, 69–71, 72, 73, 74–75, 76, 77–78, 78–79, 82–83, 84, 85, 86, 87, 88, 91

López Mateos, Adolfo, 115, 127, 128, 129–30, 131
López Pacheco de Cabrera y Bobadilla, Diego, 28, 29
López Portillo Pacheco, José, 131, 133–34, 135
López Rayón, Ignacio, 58–59, 68
Lorencillo, 33
Louisiana, 48
Louis XIV, 26, 32, 35
Lozano García, Antonio, 140

Macehualtin (common people), 2, 4
Machete Conspiracy, 49, 55
Madero, Francisco I., 104, 105, 108, 109, 110, 111, 112–13, 114, 115, 116, 118, 128
Madrazo, Carlos A., 131
Madrazo Cuellar, Jorge, 140
Magdalena Bay, 104
Maldonado, Alvaro, 18
Maldonado, Francisco, 17
Malinche, La, 12, 14
Malo de Villavicencio, Pedro, 39
Manila Galleon, 21
Manrique de Zúñiga, Alvaro, 23–24
Marguerite of Austria, 24, 26
Maria Anna of Austria, 27, 32
Marie Amalia of Saxony, 42, 46
Marie Anne of Bavaria, 35
Marie Anne of Neuberg, 32
Marie Antoinette of the Two Sicilies, 51
Marie Christine of Naples, 51
Marie Isabelle of Portugal, 51
Marie Josefa Amalia of the Two Sicilies, 51
Marie Louise d'Orléans, 32
Marie Louise of Parma, 46, 50
Marie Louise of Savoy, 35, 40
Marina, Doña, 12, 14
Márquez, Leonardo, 81
Martínez, Arnoldo, 129
Mary of Portugal, 21
Mary Tudor, 21
Masonic order, 61, 63, 65
Mata, Filomeno, 129
Matlazinca people, 7

Maximillian. *See* Hapsburg, Ferdinand
  Maximilian of
Maxtla, 6
Maya Indians, 8, 11, 113
Mayeque (serf), 2, 4
Mayorga, Martín de, **44**
McLane-Ocampo Treaty, 92
Medicine, 18, 21, 39, 49
Mejía, J. Antonio, 73
Mejía, Tomás, 86, 93, 97
Méndez, Juan N., 100, **102–3**
Mendocino Codex, 20
Mendoza, Antonio de, **20**
Mendoza y Luna, Juan de, **25**
Mérida, 45
Mesilla Treaty, 82
Mestizo, 15, 19, 31–32, 35, 36, 43, 55
Mexica people. *See* Aztec people
Mexicatl Teohuatzin (priest), 3
Mexico City: and Bucareli y Ursúa, 43;
  and Díez de Armendáriz, 28; and
  disease, 39, 42; and 1985 earth-
  quake, 135; and Enríquez de Rivera,
  33; and fire, 39; and flooding, 27,
  29; and Gálvez y Gallardo, 44; and
  Güemes Pacheco, 47; occupation of,
  92; and social unrest, 32. *See also*
  Tenochtitlan
Michelena, José Mariano, 51, **62**
Michoacán, 7, 80
Mier y Terán, Luis, 102
Mijes people, 17
Military: and Arista, 81; and Cárdenas, 123; and Castro Figueroa y Salazar, 39; and Cortés, 16; and Flores
  Maldonado, 46; and Gómez Farías,
  70, 78; and González, 103; and Juárez, 97; and Moctezuma Ilhuicamina, 7; and Ruiz Cortines, 128;
  and Santa Anna, 74–75, 82
Mina, Francisco Javier, 53
Minimum wage, 123, 128
Mining: and Acuña, 38; and Arista, 81;
  and Bucareli y Ursúa, 43; and Díaz,
  104, 107; and Enríquez de Guzmán,
  30; and Güemes Pacheco, 47; and
  Güemes y Horcasitas, 41; and independence, 63; and Philip II, 21; and

Velasco, 20, 24; and viceregal pe-
  riod, 19; and Zúñiga y Acevedo, 24
Mining College, 47
Mining Tribunal, 43
Miramón, Miguel, 86, 87, **88–90**, 93,
  97
Mixquic, 5
Moctezuma, Maria Andrea, 35
Moctezuma II. *See* Moctezuma Xocoy-
  otzin
Moctezuma Ilhuicamina, **7**
Moctezuma Xocoyotzin, **8–9**, 12, 13,
  14
Moderate Party, 65
Monserrat, Joaquín de, **42**
Moñtano, Otilio, 109
Montepío, 43
Mora y Del Río, José, 120
Morelos y Pavón, José María, 52, **59–
  60**, 61, 64, 65, 85
Moya de Contreras, Pedro, 22, **23**
Mulatto people, 43
Muñoz, Alonso de, **22**
Museum of Natural History, 67
Múzquiz, Melchor, **68–69**

NAFTA. *See* North American Free
  Trade Agreement
Nao of China, 21, 40
Napoleon I, 46–47, 51, 55
Napoleon III, 92, 93, 94, 95, 96
Narváez, Pánfilo de, 12
National Anti-Reelection Party, 104
National Banking Commission, 119
National Board of Tourism, 122
National Commission for Free Text-
  books, 130
National Commission of Human
  Rights, 138
National Finance Bank, 123
National Institute for the Protection of
  Infants, 121
National Museum, 65
National Revolutionary Party, 120,
  121–22
National Solidarity Program, 137–38
National University of Mexico, 121
Nayarit, 38

Negrete, Pedro Celestino, **62**
Netzahualcoyotl, 6, 7
New Galicia, 17
New Mexico, 30, 33, 42
New Santadar, 41
News media, 20, 38, 44, 59, 68, 70, 82, 91, 133
Nicaragua, 134
Niños Héroes, 78
Noche Triste, La (The Sad Night), 9, 13
North American Free Trade Agreement, 137
Novella, Francisco, **53**
Nuestra Señora de Covadonga, 40
Nuevo León, 86
Núñez de Haro y Peralta, Alonso, **45–46**

Obregón, Alvaro, 108, 110, 111, 114, 115, 116, **117–19**, 121, 123
Ocampo, Melchor, 82, 85, 91, 92
O'Donojú, Juan, **53–54**, 56
Oil industry, 124–25, 126, 129, 132, 133, 136
Olympics, 130
Oregón, Alvaro, 120
Orihuela, Francisco, 86
Ormachea, Juan B., **94**
Orozco, Jerónimo, **21**
Orozco, Pascual, 108, 109, 110, 113, 118, 119
Ortega, Jesús Gonzáles, 92
Ortega Montañés, Juan de, **34–35**, 36
Ortiz De Letona, Pascacio, 57
Ortiz de Matienzo, Juan, **17**
Ortiz Rubio, Pascual, **121–22**, 126, 129
Osollo, Luis G., 86
Osorio de Escobar y Llamas, Diego, **31**
Otálora, Pedro, **26**
Oxtoman, 4
Oztomeca (merchant), 4

Pacheco y Osorio, Rodrigo, **27**
Padilla, Ezequiel, 126
Palafox y Mendoza, Juan de, 28, **29**

Palma, Héctor Luis "Güero," 141
PAN. *See Partido de Acción Nacional*
Panama, 135
Parada, Alonso de, **17**
Paredes y Arrillaga, Mariano, 74, 76, 77, 81, 86
Parián market riot, 72
Partido de Acción Nacional, 137, 138, 139, 140, 142
Partido de la Revolución Democrática, 138, 142
Partido Revolucionario Institucional, 120, 121, 127, 128, 129, 131, 132, 133, 135, 137, 138, 139, 141–42
Partido de la Revolución Mexicana, 124, 125, 126, 127, 142
Pastry War, 72
Patiño, José, 36
Pavón, José Ignacio, 87, **89**
Peasantry, 85, 105, 107, 131, 137
Pensacola, 42
Peralta, Gastón de, **21–22**
Peralta, Matías de, **30**
Pérez de la Serna, Juan, 27
Pershing, John, 111
Peru, 135
Petén, 8
Petroleum. *See* Oil industry
Philip II, 19, 21, 24
Philip III, **24–25**, 26
Philip IV, **26–27**, 31, 32
Philip V, **35–36**, 40, 41
Philip of Anjou, 32
Picaluga, Francisco, 66
Pima people, 36–37, 42, 44
Pino Súarez, José María, 109, 113, 114, 115, 117
Pipiltin (nobleman), 2
Piracy: and Alencastre Noroña y Silva, 37; and Azanza, 49; and Cebrián, 40; and Charles II, 32; and de Zúñiga, 38; and Díez de Armendáriz, 28; and Enríquez de Almanza, 22; and Fernández de la Cueva, 30; and Osorio de Escobar y Llamas, 31; and Pacheco y Osorio, 27; and Philip V, 36; and Portocarrero Lazo

de la Vega, 33–34; and Zúñiga Guzmán Sotomayor, 38

Plan de Agua Prieta, 117, 118, 119, 121, 122, 123

Plan de Ayala, 109, 112

Plan de Ayutla, 82, 84, 85, 86, 87, 88, 91, 101, 102

Plan de Casa Mata, 61, 62, 68, 69, 75

Plan de Cuernavaca, 70, 81

Plan de Guadalupe, 111, 116

Plan de Iguala, 64, 67, 68, 69, 76, 77, 84, 85

Plan de Jalapa, 66, 68

Plan de Jalisco-Guadalajara, 77

Plan de la Noria, 101, 103

Plan de Montaño, 70

Plan de Navidad, 88

Plan de San Luis, 105, 109, 112

Plan de Tacubaya, 74, 77, 86, 87, 91

Plan of Tuxtepec, 98, 99, 103

Plan of Veracruz, 68

PNR. *See* National Revolutionary Party

Pochteca (merchant), 4

Pochtlan, 4

Poinsett, Joel B., 65, 71

Police, 47, 82

Politics: and Avila Camacho, 126; and Cárdenas, 124, 125; and Díaz, 100; and election of 1828, 65; and Elías Calles, 120; and independence, 63–64; and Rodríguez, 123; and Salinas, 137; and Zedillo, 141–42. *See also specific parties*

Polk, James, 77

Ponce de Léon, Luis, **16–17**

Pope Pius XI, 122

Popé Revolt, 33

Popular Revolutionary Army, 141

Portes Gil, Emilio, **120–21**, 126

Portilla, Pedro de la, 49

Portocarrero Lazo de la Vega, Melchor, **33–34**

Posadas Ocampo, Juan Jesús, 139, 140

Poverty, 37, 45, 70, 100, 107, 108, 138

PRD. *See Partido de la Revolución Democrática*

Press. *See* News media

PRI. *See Partido Revolucionario Institucional*

Prieto, Guillermo, 85

Printing. *See* News media

PRM. *See Partido de la Revolución Mexicana*

Prosecutor's tribune, 26

Public works: and Ahumada y Villalón, 41; and Alemán, 127; and Alencastre Noroña y Silva, 37; and Bucareli y Ursúa, 43; and Chimalpopoca, 6; and Cortés, 16; and Croix, 43; and Díaz, 100; and Díaz Ordaz, 131; and Echeverría Alvarez, 132; and Elías Calles, 119; and Enríquez de Rivera, 33; and Fernández de Córdoba, 26; and Gálvez, 45; and Gálvez y Gallardo, 44; and González, 103; and Güemes Pacheco, 47; and Juárez, 97, 98; and Lerdo, 98; and Mendoza y Luna, 25; and Moctezuma Ilhuicamina, 7; and Monserrat, 42; and New Spain, 26–27; and Portocarrero Lazo de la Vega, 34; and Ruiz Cortines, 128; and Sarmiento Valladares, 35; and Tizoc, 8; and Vizarrón y Eguiarreta, 39

Puebla, 41, 42, 69, 86

Puente de Calderón, 52, 58

Puga, Vasco de, **21**

Purepecha Indians, 7

Querétaro, 28, 86, 90

Querétaro Conspiracy, 55, 57

Quetzalcoatl, 1, 2, 3, 9, 14

Quetzalcoatl *Tlaloc* Tlamacazqui (priest), 3

Quetzalcoatl *Totec* Tlacamazqui (priest), 3

Quintanar, Luis, 66, **67–68**

Quiroga, Vasco de, **18**

Race, 15, 60, 61

Railroad, 103, 104, 125, 127

Ramírez, Margarito, 109

Ramírez de Fuenleal, Sebastián, **18**

Reagan, Ronald, 135, 136

Real Cofradía de Guadalupe, 36
Rebelíon de los Cañoneros, 102
Reform Laws, 91, 95, 96, 98, 99
Religion, 3, 15, 16, 30, 60, 61, 70, 91.
 See also Catholic Church
Republic, 97–99
Revolutionary period, 107–11
Reyes, Bernardo, 109, 113
Robles Domínguez, Alfredo, 128
Robles Pezuela, Manuel, 87, **88**
Rodríguez, Abelardo L., **122–23**, 126
Roma y Rossell, Francisco, **44**
Royal and Pontifical University of
 Mexico, 20
Royal Treasury, 47
Rueda, Petronila, 29
Rueda, Torres, 29
Ruffo, Ernesto, 137
Ruiz Cortines, Adolfo, **127–28**, 129
Ruiz de Apodaca, Juan, 53, 60
Ruiz Massieu, José Francisco, 138, 140–
 41

Sad Night, The (*La Noche Triste*), 9,
 13
Salanueva, Antonio, 90
Salas, Eugenio, 85
Salas, José Mariano, **77–78**, **94**
Salas-Bravo agreement, 78
Salazar, Juan de, 29
Salazar, Othón, 129
Salic Law, 51
Salinas de Gortari, Carlos, **136–39**,
 140
Salinas de Gortari, Raúl, 139, 140
Salmerón, Juan de, **18**
Salto del Agua, 34
Salvatierra, Juan Mariá, 35
San Carlos Bank, 44
Sánchez Paredes, **23**
Sandanista Revolution, 134
Sande, Francisco de, **23**
San Diego Fortress, 26
Sandoval, Francisco Rojas, 25
San Juan de Letrán, 20
San Juan de Ulúa, 72, 73
San Luis de Potosí, 24
San Luis Potosí, 86, 92

San Miguel, 57
Santa Anna. *See* López de Santa Anna,
 Antonio
Santa Cruz de la Tlaltelolco, 20
Santa Fe, New Mexico, 24
Santa María, Miguel, 54
Santanista, 81, 82
Sante Fe of Mexico (hospital), 18
Sante Fe of the Lagoon of Uayámeo
 (hospital), 18
Sarmiento Valladares, José, **35**
Second Empire, 94–97
Secular clergy, 22, 23, 36. *See also*
 Catholic Church
Seminario Concilar, 34
Seri people, **44**
Seven Laws Constitution, 74
Shroud Letter, 44
Silao, 89
Siqueiros, David Alfaro. *See* Alfaro Si-
 queiros, David
Slavery, 2, 4, 20, 23, 36, 57, 65
Smallpox. *See* Disease
Socialism, 125. *See also* Communism
Social Security, 126
Social unrest, 32, 34, 64. *See also* spe-
 cific figures and movements
Society, 4, 15, 19, 22
Sol, El, 61
Spain: and Bustamante, 68; and Cárde-
 nas, 124; and Conquest, 11–15; and
 debt collection, 92, 94, 96; and Fer-
 dinand VII, 53; and France, 46, 48,
 55; and López Portillo, 134; and
 Mexico, 66; and Moctezuma Xocoy-
 otzin, 9; and Ortiz Rubio, 122
"Strip of the Wanderings of the Aztec
 People," 40
Student activism, 128, 131, 132
Suárez de Mendoza, Lorenzo, **22**

Tabasco, 45, 74
Tacuba, 2, 6
Tapia, Cristóbal de, **15**
Tarahumara Indians, 30
Tarascan people, 8
Taxation, 30, 36, 75, 82
Tayautzin, 6

Taylor, Zachary, 77
Tehuantepec, 31
Tejada's law, 86
Tenoch, 5
Tenochtitlan, 1, 2, 4, 5, 12, 14. *See also* Mexico City
Teohua (priest), 3
Teotihuacan, 1
Tepanec people, 6
Tepehuanes people, 26
Tepepa, Emiliano, 109
Tetecuhtin (governor), 2
Texas, 37–38, 71, 72, 74, 76
Texcoco, 2, 6, 7
Textiles, 47, 48–49
Tezozomoc, 5–6
Thirty-minute earthquake, 37
Ticoman, 1
Tizoc, 8
Tizoc Stone, 8
Tlacaeletl, 6
Tlacatecatl (warrior chief), 4
Tlacatecuhtli (army chief), 2
Tlacochcalcatl (spear chief), 4
Tlahuac, 5
Tlaloc (rain god), 3, 7
Tlamacazqui (priest), 3
Tlatelolco, 7
Tlatelolco Treaty, 130
Tlatlacotin (slaves), 2, 4
Tlatoani (supreme ruler), 2, 4
Tlaxcala, 12, 13, 24
Tlaxcaltecan people, 9
Tobacco, 38
Toledo Molina y Salazar, Antonio Sebastián de, 31–32
Tolsa, Manuel, 48
Toltec people, 1, 2, 5
Torres Burgos, Pablo, 109
Torres y Rueda, Marcos de, **29**, 30
Totonac people, 8
Trade, 21, 30, 41, 47, 71, 104. *See also* Economy
Tragic Ten Days (*La Decena Trágica*), 113
Tratados de Teoloyucan, 110
Treasury, 52, 75, 81
Treaties of Cordoba, 54

Treaty of Guadalupe, 81
Treaty of Miramar, 96
Treaty of Santa María-Calatrava, 54
Tresguerras, Francisco Eduardo, 49
Tribunal of the Holy Inquisition, 22, 29, 43, 51, 52
Triple Alliance, 2, 3, 6, 7
Trotsky, Leon, 124, 126
Truman, Harry S., 127
Tuxpan, 8
Tyler, John, 76

UNAM. *See* Universidad Nacional Autónoma de México
Union. *See* Labor union
Union of Soviet Socialist Republics, 121, 126
United States: and Alemán, 127; and Avila Camacho, 126; and Cárdenas, 125; and Charles III, 42; and De la Madrid, 135, 136; and France, 95; and Hidalgo, 57; and Huerta, 114; and Juárez, 92, 93; and López Mateos, 130; and López Portillo, 134; and Magdalena Bay, 104; and Mesilla Treaty, 82; and Miramón, 89; and Obregón, 119; and Texas, 72, 76; and Villa, 111; war with, 77, 78, 79, 84, 86; and Zedillo, 140
Universidad Nacional Autónoma de México, 129
University City, 127
Urrea, Blas, 72, 74
Uruguay, 135
U.S.S. Dolphin, 114

Valecillo, Paz de, **26**
Valladolid Conspiracy, 51, 55, 56, 61, 62
Vasconcelos, José, 121, 122
Vázquez, Genaro, 131, 132
Vázquez Gómez, Emilio, 109, 110
Vázquez Gómez, Francisco, 105, 109
Velasco, Luis de (I), **20**
Velasco, Luis de (II), **24**, **25**
Velázquez, Diego, 12
Velázquez, Fidel, 125, 142
Velez, Pedro, 66, **67**

Venegas, Francisco Javier, **51–52**
Venezuela, 135
Veracruz, 24, 33, 34, 38, 68, 72, 76, 81
Verdad y Ramos, Francisco Primo de, 50
Viceregal period, 18–54
Victoria, Guadalupe. *See* Fernández y Félix, José Miguel Ramón Audaucto "Guadalupe Victoria"
Vidaurri, Santiago, 86
Villa, Francisco "Pancho," 108, 109, **110–11**, 113, 114, 115, 116, 118, 119, 123
Villa de Ayala, 109
Villalobos, Pedro, **21**
Villanueva y Zapata, Luis, **23**
Villa Rica de la Vera Cruz, 12
Virgin of Guadalupe, 39, 40
Vizarrón y Eguiarreta, Juan Antonio de, **39**

War of *Castas*, 84
War of Reform, 85, 89, 94, 96
War of Spanish Succession, 35, 36
Wilson, Henry Lane, 113
Woman suffrage, 128
Worker. *See* Labor
World Bank, 135, 140

World Cup, 136
World War II, 125–26

Xaltocan, 6
Xochimilco, 5

Yáñez Pinzón, Vicente, 11
Yanhuitlán, 8
Yaqui Indians, 123
Yermo, Gabriel, 50
Yucatan, 73, 74, 80, 84, 124

Zacapoaxtla Revolution, 86, 94
Zacatecas, 24, 70–71, 114
Zapata, Emiliano, **108–10**, 111, 112, 113, 115, 116, 117, 123
Zapata, Eufemio, 109
Zapotec people, 17, 90
Zaragoza, Ignacio, 88, 92
Zavala, Lorenzo de, 65, 66
Zedillo Ponce de Leon, Ernesto, 138, **139–42**
Zorilla, José Antonio, 136
Zuazo, Alfonso, **16**
Zuloaga, Félix, 86, **87–88**, 91
Zúñiga Guzmán Sotomayor y Mendoza, Baltazar de, **37–38**
Zúñiga y Acevedo, Gaspar de, **24**

About the Author

JUANA VÁZQUEZ-GÓMEZ is a freelance writer for publications such as the *Los Angeles Times* and *LATINA* and *Moderna* magazines and runs a translation service. She won the 6th annual Silver Feather Award for best travel story written in the Spanish language, published in the United States in 1981. She is the author of *Prontuario de Gobernantes de México, 1325–1989* (1989).

ISBN 0-313-30049-6

EAN

9 780313 300493

90000>

HARDCOVER BAR CODE